30 YEARS OF THE IRONMAN TRIATHLON WORLD CHAMPIONSHIP

30 Years of the Ironman Triathlon World Championship

By Bob Babbitt
Foreword by Jim Lampley

Meyer & Meyer Sport

CONTENTS

British Library Cataloguing in Publication Data
A catalogue record for this book is available from the British Library

Bob Babbitt:
Maidenhead: Meyer & Meyer Sport (UK) Ltd., 2008
ISBN 978-1-84126-114-0

© 2008 by Meyer & Meyer Sport (UK) Ltd.
Adelaide, Auckland, Budapest, Cape Town, Graz, Indianapolis,
Maidenhead, New York, Olten (CH), Singapore, Toronto
Member of the World
Sport Publishers' Association (WSPA)
www.w-s-p-a.org
Printed and bound by: FINIDR, s. r. o., Český Těšín
ISBN 978-1-84126-114-0
E-Mail: verlag@m-m-sports.com
www.m-m-sports.com

IRONMAN is a registered trademark of World Triathlon Corporation

I've sacrificed.
I've suffered.
I'm ready.

Photo by Rich Cruse

SWIM 2.4 MILES

FOREWORD

BY JIM LAMPLEY

"You're going to be going back to Hawaii. It's a new event, something where they swim, they bike, then they run a marathon, back to back to back. They call it a triathlon."

The caller was Dennis Lewin, Coordinating Producer of ABC's *Wide World of Sports* and my boss for the eight months of the year I wasn't spending in the studio in New York hosting college football telecasts. The year was 1980, and I wasn't sure I had heard Denny right.

"They run a full marathon, 26 miles?"
"That's right."
"They run a full marathon after they swim and they bike?"
"Correct."
"How far do they swim and bike?"
"The swim is about two and a half miles — in the ocean. And the bike ride is 112 miles."
"One hundred and twelve miles? That's crazy!! How did they come up with these distances?"
"It's what's available. They do the swim right in front of the Outrigger Canoe Club, out and back. Then they ride all around the perimeter of the island. Then they run the route of the Honolulu Marathon."
"Are they sure someone can actually do this?"
It seemed like a logical question.
"Believe it or not, it's already been done. I'm sending you an article from Sports Illustrated. We're just going to do a report of some kind, because the event takes the whole day."

I thought I had seen a lot. I thought I may have seen most everything competitive sports had to offer. Six years into an on-air network career that had begun by accident when I was chosen from a talent hunt to perform a newly-minted gimmick role on the sidelines of college football games, I was still pretty much the junior member of an announcing staff that included Jim McKay, Howard Cosell, Keith Jackson, Chris Schenkel, Frank Gifford, Bill Flemming and Curt Gowdy. All of them were Hall of Fame broadcasters who had more than paid their dues searching out the thrill of victory in the farther reaches of the Wide World culture. So now I had inherited the wrist wrestling, the log rolling, the barrel jumping, the New York State Fireman's competition, the motorcycles on ice, the Oriental World of Self Defense — an endless stream of eccentric events, the very things I had chuckled at when watching them in my teen and college years. But the triathlon, I could tell, was something different. It might be a circus, or it might be a legitimate harbinger of something big coming down the track. I knew our approach to televising it would play a role in determining which of those two identities it would achieve.

Of course, you had to be there. In the world of ultra-endurance sports, the producers and crewmembers who went to Oahu that first time are a bit like the gaggle of souls who stood on the sand dune at Kitty Hawk and watched the Wright brothers lift a strange contraption into the onrushing wind. The toughest part was going back to the world of Brooks Brothers suits and Gucci shoes in New York and trying to communicate the majesty of what we'd seen. What was originally planned as a brief report became a full hour-and-a-half Wide World episode. A year later the number of competitors multiplied so dramatically the event had to be moved to the roomier Big Island. And another year later our cameras settled, in the gathering twilight of an impossibly beautiful South Pacific afternoon, on the dwindling energy of an angular woman named Julie Moss.

We had seen images like this before, mostly in newsreels of old Olympic marathons. But never had an athlete struggled so graphically, so desperately, for such a long period of time in front of the camera as did Julie Moss. Conditioned by years of "as though live" fakery in the voiceover narrations of taped and filmed Wide World events, ABC Sports producers and executives wanted me to conduct a "plausibly live" commentary of the show's last segment to hype the drama of Julie's plight. Having already twice previously won the battle to voice the event in past tense, documentary style — in my view the only dignified way to treat an obviously pre-recorded event of this stature — I flatly refused to play this game. We fought and fought. The ultimate compromise was to simply do it as sparsely as possible so that most of the drama played out with no commentary whatsoever. The pictures told the story. Every word on the history tape of the show is a word I fought not to put there.

At the end of all that, Julie Moss catapulted the Ironman Triathlon from an obscure cult event to its present status as the flagship of a fully-developed sport. It is critical to the sport's identity that she accomplished that unintentionally. The heart of any ultra endurance event's appeal is that anyone can try it and to participate is an honor at least equal to winning. Even in the current atmosphere of advanced professionalism, with prize money and sponsorships equal to those of many older, more established sports, triathletes understand that their bond to the anonymous strivers of their culture is central to the charm of their experience. Without that bond, they might not exist.

As the '80s progressed, the ultra-endurance culture spawned even more extreme, even more painful tests of human willpower — 100-mile footraces in altitude and extreme heat, sleep-deprivation bike races from one coast to the other, winter triathlons in sub-zero blizzards — and Wide World explored them all. But the Ironman became a staple of the sports landscape, something which no longer needed explanation and validation to brook the incredulity of the uninitiated. But none of us who took that first trip to Oahu, or were there in the streets of Kona for the last mile of Julie Moss' ordeal, would ever forget triathlon's beginnings — and the drama of watching something lift off and take flight right before our very eyes.

BIKE 112 MILES

Photo by Robert Oliver

Photo by Rich Cruse

INTRODUCTION

BY JUDY AND COMMANDER JOHN COLLINS

The history of triathlon is a short one, but Ironman has been an important part of that history from near the beginning. Fewer than four years elapsed between the first modern triathlon in San Diego and the first Ironman in Hawaii in 1978. In only two more years, Ironman was featured on national television, spawning events across the United States and the rest of the world in rapid succession. Our family has been privileged to be observers to the entire process, having been participants in that first triathlon in 1974 and in various Ironman events over the years.

John Collins takes a long look into the future of Ironman.

Ironman started as a casual event among running and swimming friends in Hawaii. In fact, if we had not been required to obtain permits for the swim, there probably would have been no formal organization at all, just a few of us out for a long day of fun. We were always arguing about whether runners or swimmers were more fit. The only existing combined event was a joint effort between the Mid-Pacific Road Runners and the Waikiki Swim Club and was much too short to test endurance. The announcement of the first Ironman took place at an awards ceremony for a long-distance running event and was the culmination of that argument. The course was simply a combination of the three major endurance events on the island, the Waikiki Rough Water Swim, the annual bicycle race around Oahu and the Honolulu Marathon. Luckily the geography allowed the three events to be strung together. It is the unvarnished truth that no one there had any idea of the worldwide movement that triathlon and Ironman would become.

After the running of the first event, we thought that the Ironman had the potential to become a local success and might even attract some competitors from the mainland. About 200 competitors was the upper limit. Support for the event was difficult to come by. A few good running and swimming friends, mostly from the military, carried the load in the first years, but much more support was needed. We thought that we might be able to get help if we included a relay category.

Of course, the power of publicity changed all that. The *Sports Illustrated* article in 1979, followed by the ABC television coverage in 1980, changed our little local "'70s happening" into a worldwide phenomenon. When I received Navy orders to Washington, the event was taken over by the local Nautilus Fitness club, and eventually fell into the capable hands of Valerie Silk. She shepherded Ironman through all the turbulent times to come, dealing with the major media players, the emerging professional triathlete movement, the introduction of prize money and the booming numbers that required limitation of the number of competitors on the course.

The thousands of enthusiastic Ironman triathletes and many sold-out events worldwide indicate that our casual little event was actually the birth of a movement whose time had come. It is a good feeling to have played a part in that movement. We can still be found on some of the courses, marveling at the endurance of the human body and spirit.

14

RUN 26.2 MILES

WHAT ARE YOU... NUTS?

I have been lucky enough to have been at every Ironman Triathlon World Championship either as a participant or as a reporter since my first race on Oahu way back in February of 1980. The Ironman is an event that has changed my life. No question about it. There is something special that comes along with attempting the impossible. Impossible? Yep. Back in the early days, no one knew if someone could actually swim 2.4 miles, ride 112 and run 26.2 back to back to back. When I first raced, I thought that you swam 2.4 miles and rode 56 on day one, camped out, then rode the other 56 and ran the marathon on the second day. I even had saddlebags with a tent and sleeping bag that I was planning on carrying with me on race day. Do it all in one day? What are you... nuts?

Obviously, a lot of people are nuts. Since the first group of 15 plunged into the surf off Waikiki on Oahu in 1978, a total of 34,764 have crossed the finish line in Hawaii. Crossing that finish line makes you a member of a very exclusive club. It's a club where the dues are perseverance, dedication and a will to finish that is tougher to crack than a five-year-old walnut.

The Ironman Triathlon World Championship is about much more than the course. It's about the wind and the heat and the unpredictability of both. It's about the mythology surrounding Madame Pele and the history and nuances of the Big Island, its people and the endless lava fields.

The Ironman to me is unique in so many ways. Commander John Collins created the Ironman to find out who is indeed the world's fittest athlete by combining the Waikiki Rough Water Swim, the Around Oahu Bike Ride and the Honolulu Marathon.

Julie Moss pulled on America's heartstrings when she collapsed just meters from the finish in 1982 while leading the race. A national television audience sat wide-eyed as this amazing young woman collapsed again and again before crawling the last few feet. Her finish proved once and for all that the Ironman might be a race, but in the end the struggle was strictly personal and that eventually it would come down to you against you. How bad do you want it? That is the Ironman's bottom line.

When I first flew to Oahu after reading an article about the 1979 Ironman in *Sports Illustrated*, my goal was to get one of the infamous hole-in-the-head trophies awarded to each finisher. It was the ultimate keepsake from the ultimate event.

When you finish, you carry something deep inside yourself from that day forward that you call on whenever you need to. When things get tough in life, you know you can handle whatever has been dished out because you have completed the toughest day in sport. It's a calling card that you will carry with you forever.

I wanted to bring you, the reader, the amazing images that make the event....well...*the Ironman*. Words and video can help paint the picture, but the shots you will see in this book from Lois Schwartz, Robert Oliver, Rich Cruse, Peter Read Miller, Tracy Frankel, Dave Epperson and Carol Hogan freeze frame the action and let you feel the heat and the wind and the excitement of the lava fields as well as Alii Drive.

If you have finished the Ironman Triathlon World Championship, this book is for you. If you have tried to get to Kona for the Big Dance this book will help enhance that commitment.

If you are looking for a goal or looking to take your life to a level you have never seen before, the Ironman has your name on it.

Dave Scott, Mark Allen, Scott Tinley, Paula Newby-Fraser, Natascha Badmann and 34,000 others have learned their life lessons on the Kona Coast on an island that can be beautiful, mysterious and brutal all at the same time.

The stories you will read are past accounts I've written over the past two decades of covering the Ironman. Hopefully, you will see and feel my passion for the Ironman and its warriors through my words: Mark Allen and Dave Scott going at it year after year after year. Cool Hand Luc Van Lierde of Belgium breaking the course record in his first time out. Paula Newby-Fraser dominating eight times and collapsing just once. An amputee named Jim MacLaren changing the perceptions of what someone with a prosthetic can do. Julie Moss taking the word courage to another level. Jim Howley proving his doctors wrong when he attempted the Ironman with AIDS and a T-cell count of four.

The Ironman from the very beginning has sought to change perceptions of what can and cannot be accomplished. Any goal you set is within reach, including the Ironman.

I hope you enjoy this trip down memory lane.

Commander Collins' famous words have moved 26,000 people to the most famous finish line in sports:

"Swim 2.4, ride 112, run 26.2. Then brag for the rest of your life."

Getting there is up to you.

See you on the starting line!
Bob Babbitt
January 2008

1978-1980: THE OAHU YEARS

Imagine: It's February 1978 and you are one 15 brave souls standing on Sans Souci Beach in Waikiki. It is exactly 2.4 miles from where you are to where your bike is sitting with your support crew. The waves are rolling in and your stomach is rolling over. After hopefully completing the swim, you will mount up and ride 112 miles around a big chunk of the island of Oahu. If you somehow come through that unscathed, then all that is left to do is the Honolulu Marathon, a mere 26.2 miles, this time on foot. If you finish? You're an Ironman.

Lewis and Clark and Captain Cook are called explorers. The Fanatic 15 could relate. This eclectic collection of military men and regular folks was seriously going where no man had ever gone before. Lyn Lemaire, the first woman, wouldn't join the party until the following year, 1979.

People ask all the time: How much has the Ironman changed in 25 years?

The answer is simple: A lot.... and not much. Yes, the bikes are better, people now know how to train and what to eat, and some actually have an idea as to their approximate finish times for each of the three disciplines.

But the forces behind the Ironman still make the day a crapshoot at best. In shorter races, the professionals have their race and their times down to a science. Not in Hawaii, not in the Ironman. The best in the world have at one time or another been relegated to the brink of collapse, to walking the marathon — light stick bouncing on their chest, chicken soup at the ready.

That's why the finish line is so important, so special. Whether you're shooting for the $120,000 first-place check like Chris McCormack in 2007, hoping to be presented with the first ever hole-in-the-head trophy like taxi driver Gordon Haller in 1978, or hoping to be the first 81 year old to cross the finish line under 17 hours like Robert McKeague, the Ironman to this day is a beacon for that adventure gene in all of us.

This page, top: After a one-day postponement in 1979, the weather was still ominous on race day. The 15 entrants listen to final instructions.
Center: The entire field lines up for the swim start on Sans Souci Beach.
Bottom: Lyn Lemaire, the first woman to attempt the Ironman, comes out of the water. She would finish fifth overall. Among her fellow top five finishers, her 6:30 bike split was second only to Tom Warren's 6:19.
Opposite page, left: The 1979 pre-race favorites, defending champion Gordon Haller (left) and Superman John Dunbar.
Top: Hank Grundman, 1980 Race Director.
Bottom: John Dunbar before the 1979 race.
Photos by Peter Read Miller

In 1978 and 1979, the Ironman featured two athletes with one goal. Both Navy SEAL John Dunbar and taxi driver and fitness fanatic Gordon Haller were there to win the Ironman. Gordon Haller won in 1978, coming from behind to pass a staggering Dunbar in the run. Dunbar's support crew ran out of water and hydrated their athlete with beer as a last resort.

Big mistake.

Haller won the race. Dunbar, after mixing alcohol with about 11 hours of depletion and effort, bounced off of cars on his way to second place. The first of many Iron Rivalries was born. Ironically, Commander John Collins finished that first race in 17 hours, the time that a few years later would become the cutoff time. He also stopped for a bowl of chili during the bike ride.

Haller and Dunbar came back in 1979 and all the pre-event hype surrounding the, again, 15 participants was the rematch between the two. No one thought much of the tavern keeper from San Diego named Tom Warren. Dunbar showed up wearing a Superman outfit and his crew was dressed just like their leader. Haller and Dunbar posed for photos. Warren waited patiently for his turn. He knew a simple truth that would become the menu for success at the Ironman: Résumés don't win races, people do.

What they didn't know was that Warren had swam at USC and could ride, run and swim all day. He had a motorhome by the ocean in his hometown of Pacific Beach that had a bike hung on the back, assorted paddleboards mounted on the roof and a gaggle of running shoes swinging from the side-view mirror. He ran the five-mile loop along the beach so often that he actually had created a black line around the light pole that served as his turnaround point. As he made the turn he'd put his sweaty palm on the pole. Fifteen years and thousands of miles later, the lightpole had a stripe to call its own. He prepared for Hawaii by riding his bike for hours on end in the sauna and running endless miles along the San Diego coast. He took the lead early in the bike ride and left Dunbar 48 minutes behind. Journalist Barry McDermott and photographer Peter Read Miller from *Sports Illustrated* covered the Ironman that year, making Warren a star, and creating a buzz for this new event. Warren ended up showing off his Ironman hole-in-the-head trophy on the *Johnny Carson Show* and Commander Collins was bombarded with folks wanting to come to Oahu to do this crazy event.

"Tom," Carson said as he turned the trophy over, "Did you notice there's a screw missing?"

The Ironman was on its way.

Opposite page, top left: Tom Warren, the surprise of the day, getting ready for the run. Center: Two-time second place finisher John Dunbar gets on his bike while his Superman support crew looks on. Bottom: Dunbar sporting long pants and duct tape. Top right: A pair of cyclists on the narrow back roads of Oahu. Bottom right: They called this Three Hanky Hill. This page, top and bottom: Warren trained in his sauna to acclimatize to the heat. It obviously worked. Photos by Peter Read Miller

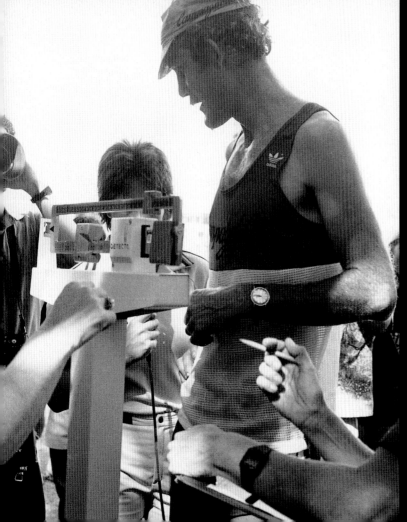

Okay, I admit it. I had absolutely no idea we were supposed to finish the whole damn thing in one day. I remember thinking when I found out that these people were absolutely, positively out of their skulls.

The year was 1980, there were only 108 of us in Oahu for the start of the third annual Ironman Triathlon, and who would have figured that EVERYONE would try to swim 2.4 miles, ride 112 and run 26.2 one right after the other? My plan was to, hopefully, dogpaddle my way through the swim, ride to the other side of Oahu, maybe 60 miles or so, then camp out. I'd get up in the morning, ride the rest of the way back to Aloha Tower and then run the marathon. Now, doesn't that sound more sensible? It sure did to me.

Before I left San Diego, I had racks put on my $60 police-auction Centurion with the charred rear triangle (hey, why do you think it was only $60?) so I could hang my newly acquired panniers on them. Inside would be my sleeping bag and provisions. I was totally set up for the road. A red Radio Shack radio mounted on the handlebars and held in place with a bungie cord, solid rubber tires to prevent those annoying flats (you had to wax the rims to get those babies on) and a little black electrical tape to cover up the charred stuff. I was ready to roll!

But when I got to the starting line that morning and met my support crew (everyone had to have one), they suggested that they carry the sleeping bag and the rest of my goodies in their Fiat convertible. Since they were going to be close by, I thought why not?

The day before the race, my roommate Ned

Overend (who since then has won the World Mountain Bike Championships and was the first inductee into the Mountain Bike Hall of Fame) and I were standing on the balcony of a hotel overlooking the stormy Pacific in downtown Waikiki. The race organizers had called us together for a pre-race briefing. As Ned and I watched wave after wave hammer by, we both suddenly realized that the chances of us getting through the surf of the Waikiki rough water swim course in storm conditions were somewhere between slim and none. So when the race director announced that the Ironman swim was being moved to Ala Moana Channel, Ned and I were ecstatic.

The deal was this: ABC was over in the islands to film cliff diving on Sunday. If this Ironman thing went off on schedule on Saturday, ABC could film it. If the weather forced a delay to Sunday, there was no way. So they moved the swim to Ala Moana Channel, which was protected from the surf.

While Ned and I were excited to be given a chance to get out of the water alive, the hardcore swimmers weren't happy at all.

"What a wussy event," they grumbled. Obviously, those dudes hadn't done all their swim training in a 120-lengths-to-the-mile condo pool like Ned and I had. The biggest wave we ever had to deal with was when Mr. and Mrs. Curran jumped into the pool at the same time one day and almost propelled us out onto the deck. But that's another story.

When I finally came out of the water on Ironman Day, I was just slightly ahead of Olympic cyclist John Howard, who spent half

Above: Post 2.4-mile swim, Author Bob Babbitt, sporting number three, poses with his police-auction bike equipped with solid rubber tires and radio. The tube socks, long-sleeved shirt and shorts with a belt completed the ensemble.

Opposite page:
Top left: Because of the huge surf and storm warnings, the swim was moved from the ocean in Waikiki to the Ala Moana Channel.

Top right: Dave Scott's parents had followed Scott with a spare bike mounted on the roof of their station wagon, just in case.

Bottom left: Athletes were weighed throughout the day. If they lost five percent of their body weight, they would be pulled from the event. John Howard is the man on the scale.

Bottom right: A brass band at the finish? A huge finish line structure? Not quite. In 1980, a string was about it for Dave Scott.

Photos by Carol Hogan

continued...

EDITOR'S NOTE: Now there were 108 entrants looking to become an Ironman. I was one of them. In 1979, it was Sports Illustrated. In 1980, another huge leap for the Ironman: ABC's Wide World of Sports. Commander Collins had taken their initial call, but he wasn't sure if the event and television were a match made in heaven.

"I told them they could come if they'd like," remembers Collins. "But that I couldn't see how the thing would make good television. During the swim you're basically underwater, the bike ride takes you out into the middle of nowhere and the run is in the dark. I told them that watching grass grow would be more exciting. I couldn't figure out how they'd make it compelling, but they did."

It was compelling because Dave Scott, a swim coach and water polo star at University of California, Davis, beat John Howard, the first big star to come to the Ironman. Howard was America's Cyclist of the 70s and a Pan American Games Gold Medalist. He thought he could fake it in the swim, destroy everyone on the bike ride and hang on in the run. Howard lost an hour to Scott in the swim, took 35 minutes back during the ride and lost 43 minutes in the run.

There was a theory that triathletes were simply good at three different sports. After Dave Scott beat John Howard the theory was scrapped. The best triathletes are great at all three.

an hour washed up on the coral. I ran to the shower and, after waiting my turn behind a father and his son (who just happened to be in the park at the time), put on a long-sleeved shirt, my tennis shoes, jammed enough Hawaiian sweet bread into the pocket of my shirt to feed Guatemala, mounted up and took off.

On the second of two laps of the Channel, I'd seen one of my all-time favorite Ironman characters walking his way through the swim. Yep, John Huckaby, known to himself and a few others as "The Incredible Huck," was actually strolling his way through the 2.4-mile bay swim. He's probably the only Ironman competitor in history to be treated for blisters on his feet after the swim.

Incredible was in his late 50s at the time, and had an impressive running resumé. The guy knew long distance running. But unfortunately, he was allergic to swimming. So there he was, right at the shoreline, in waist-deep water, walking along and actually stroking with his arms as he walked. After getting out of the water and working his way through the bike, Incredible set out on the run course. During the middle of the night, he disappeared. His crew searched for him frantically, not knowing that the nickname Incredible also described his appetite. About 2:30 a.m. the mystery ended when Huck came strolling out of a Waikiki diner, napkin in hand. When it's time for breakfast, it's time for breakfast, ya know?

I, on the other hand, was actually starting to get into this long-distance cycling routine when a member of my support crew set up on the side of the road for a food hand-off. I'd seen this sort of thing in the Tour de France. I readied myself, reached out with my right hand and, before I knew what hit me, became the proud owner of a white bag with golden arches on it. How did I know that a Big Mac, fries and a Coke weren't on the Ironman diet? It sure tasted good to me. At mile 80 my crew followed up with a root beer snow cone.

By this point, I'd given up the notion of making this a two-day adventure. My crew was so into it I couldn't imagine pulling over and setting up camp just yet. And anyhow, I was enjoying the heck out of myself.

When I pulled into the transition area at Aloha Tower, my crew had a major surprise waiting for me: A full-on oriental massage, complete with soothing music and massage oils. They laid me down on a bamboo cot and proceeded to give me the best massage I've ever had. Twenty minutes later, I started out on the run.

I trotted through Waikiki and out onto the Honolulu Marathon course. I ate Hawaiian sweet bread, drank water and simply ran and walked my way through the first 20 miles. All of a sudden, though, just past 20, I felt this urgency to pick up the pace. I ran through the Hawaiian darkness silhouetted in the lights of my support crew's car. Those last six miles just seemed to fly by. Suddenly, I came upon a white chalk line drawn across the street. I slowed and looked to my right. In the park, underneath a light bulb strung from a telephone pole, sat an official-looking guy with a pad of paper in his hand.

"Hey, are you in the race?" he yelled. "Yeah!" I replied. "Well you're done. Good job," he said.

I walked towards the voice and sat on the grass for a minute to catch my breath. There were four other finishers lying there chatting with their support crews. No one was moving or saying much except one guy who, for some unknown reason, was doing handstand push-ups. After the official wrote my name down, my crew poured me into the back of the Fiat and took me back to the hotel.

I trudged up the stairs to my room. I vividly remember the moon coming through the window and illuminating the red-as-a-lobster scorched outline of Ned's back. I asked him how his race had gone.

"Well, Pam [his girlfriend, now wife, and support person] had a hard time getting through the traffic in Waikiki. She didn't catch me for awhile," Ned said.

"When did she catch up to you?" I asked. "At mile 80," he laughed. "And then she lost me again in the marathon!"

I can't believe it's been 28 years. It seems like only yesterday.

Oahu
1978, 1979 and 1980
138 total entrants
Your own support crew
No cut-off times
Weigh stations
Spectacular views.

A limited venue
But no limit
to the spirit of adventure
In the original Ironmen.

THE BIG ISLAND

Photo by Tracy Frankel

1981: KONA BOUND

Race Director Valerie Silk had little choice. For three years the Ironman had been a quaint event: Bring your own support crew. Enjoy the experience with your family and friends. Hang out all night if you'd like to.

One problem: With 100 people you can almost do that. With upwards of 300? Forget it. There was no way there would be roads blocked off on the island of Oahu for the Ironman and Silk was smart enough to see the handwriting on the proverbial wall.

If the event was to stay in Hawaii, there was only one place to go: The Big Island. Tons of lava-coated landscape.

So on February 14, 1981, the Ironman opened up its new home to a ton of new Ironhopefuls, including 1980's third-place finisher 34-year-old John Howard and 22-year-old Linda Sweeney of San Diego.

Howard was a three-time Olympic cyclist. Sweeney was a good runner and swimmer who couldn't shift gears, rode a bike with a side-view mirror, a pack on the front with her water bottle, a tape player, a towel and cassettes of *The Who* and *The Tubes* inside.

"I distinctly remember flying through mile 90 blasting *White Punks on Dope*," she recalls.

Howard was a man on a mission totally committed to this new sport. After losing to Dave Scott in 1980, he returned home to Austin, Texas and worked with a swim and running coach planning his revenge.

It showed. Although Scott wasn't there, Howard raced as if he was. He swam 40 minutes faster than in 1980, ran a 3:23:48 marathon and went 9:38:27 to win by about 25 minutes.

Sweeney, on the other hand, never expected to be in the lead on the bike or to win. She did both.

In the process she even changed gears a few times.

Clockwise: Scott Molina weighing in after the bike.
Even in 1981, the Ironman was a formal affair.
A photographer takes an extreme angle on John Howard.
Fuzzy seat cover, padded handlebars and slippers.
Yep...I'm all set for the Ironman.
Linda Sweeney looking great after her surprising win.
Sweeney on her high-tech bike with the side-view mirror
and the pack on the handlebars. (Inside the pack she
had her tape player, tapes and towel.)
Photos by Carol Hogan

Top left and right: Race Director Valerie Silk and her assistant Earl Yamaguchi

Bottom: John Howard mounting up.

Opposite page, clockwise: John Howard was not happy with his third-place finish in 1980. He came back in 1981 as much more than just a cyclist. After getting out of the ocean he rode and ran his way to the title.

The youngest and the oldest Ironmen were 14-year-old Robin Tain (left) and 73-year-old Walt Stack (right).

Howard takes first place.

Stack making his way to the finish line Sunday morning, over 26 hours and 20 minutes after the start of the Ironman.

Photos by Carol Hogan

The race for the overall win

ends in the daylight.

The race for the elusive

Ironman finish line on Alii Drive

goes on deep into the night.

Photo by Dave Epperson

FEBRUARY 1982: MOSS & McCARTNEY

BY DON NORCROSS

To etch a place in the public's psyche, a sport needs a defining moment — a play, a game, or a statement that captures national attention. In baseball, you can argue that it was Jackie Robinson breaking the color barrier. Or Bobby Thomson's "Shot Heard 'Round the World." In football, the Jets' stunning victory over the Baltimore Colts, guaranteed days earlier by Joe Namath, comes to mind.

In triathlon, there is no debate. The sport struck a chord in the public's conscience on February 6, 1982 when Julie Moss, a 23-year-old college student working on a senior thesis, stumbled, fell and crawled to the finish at Ironman Hawaii. Television caught it all, a few moments that changed the fledgling sport forever.

We watched her huge lead evaporate, watched as Kathleen McCartney stole her glory, passing Moss 15 feet shy of the finish line to win the grueling event. But Moss did not quit. While her body gave out, her will did not. She crawled through the darkness, then lunged with her left hand, touching far more than the finish line.

"That is our moment," says Bob Babbitt, co-publisher of *Competitor* magazine. "It told viewers Ironman wasn't just about winning. It was about getting to the line."

Twenty-one years later, much about the sport has changed. While Kona is still the sport's Mecca, today there are Ironman races in Malaysia, Japan, South Korea, Australia, France, Germany, Austria, Switzerland, Brazil, the Canary Islands, Canada, New York, Florida and California.

In 1982, 326 people made their way to Kona to compete. Today, USA Triathlon, the sport's national governing body, estimates more than 200,000 people annually compete in U.S. triathlons. For winning that memorable race, McCartney had a medal draped around her neck. Today, Kona winners cash $100,000 checks.

The Moss-McCartney showdown is hardly the sole reason for triathlon's growth. That would be turning your head and ignoring Dave Scott, Paula Newby-Fraser and Mark Allen. But the snowball started that evening 21 years ago.

"It was a courageous thing," says two-time Hawaii winner Scott Tinley, the men's winner that day. "Julie was young. She didn't know. She was a college coed. She was innocent, and therein lies the heroic deed."

Moss and McCartney. Like Mantle and Maris, Abbott and Costello, Sonny and Cher, they will forever be linked. But coming into that '82 race, they didn't even know each other. Both were college students, Moss at Cal Poly San Luis Obispo, McCartney at University of California, Irvine. They learned about Ironman in different ways: Moss watched ABC's *Wide World of Sports* coverage of Ironman Hawaii in 1981 and was "mesmerized by it." McCartney had been to Kona before, watching her boyfriend and future husband, Dennis Hearst, compete. Moss showed up just wanting to finish.

Buoyed by two half-Ironman victories, McCartney showed up intending to win.

Off the bike, the novice Moss' lead was nearly 18 minutes — by today's standards, an eternity. With eight miles remaining in the marathon, McCartney had cut that down to eight minutes. Still, the lead was sizeable.

But again, Moss was a rookie. She couldn't translate the lead to something tangible.

"I had no idea what it meant to be eight minutes ahead," she says. "It could have been eight seconds. I just kept thinking I had to get there as quickly as I could."

And that's where Moss may have lost the race. Exerting too much too soon.

With four miles remaining, McCartney realized the helicopters hovering over the two women were growing closer.

"I kept my pace as fast as I could," says McCartney. With half a mile remaining, dusk settling and Moss still nowhere to be seen, McCartney adopted a realistic attitude: "I'm coming in second," she thought.

Meanwhile, a drama was unfolding up ahead. About a quarter of a mile from the finish, Moss collapsed and sat there, staring at the street, unable to walk, much less run, for three minutes. McCartney sensed something eerie was happening.

"The crowd was different," she says. "There are thousands along Alii, and usually they're making noise. But they were subdued. Then somebody yelled, 'You can catch her!' I got an adrenaline rush and picked up my pace."

Moss fell again 100 yards shy of the finish.

Clockwise:
*Kathleen McCartney enjoys a
surprise win.
Julie Moss walked, crawled, and
collapsed at the finish line.
It was courageous, dramatic and
unbelievable. It is also the moment
that changed the Ironman forever.*

Photos by Carol Hogan

She got up, then stumbled again 50 yards short of the finish. She fell again, 15 yards from the end.

McCartney had no clue about Moss' struggles. The final stretch was winding, dark and crowded with people. She didn't see Moss on the ground, didn't know when she passed the vanquished heroine.

"I couldn't even see the finish line," says McCartney. "Suddenly there was this ABC truck an arm's distance away. They had bright lights up in the trees to illuminate the area. I asked where the finish line was. The ABC truck rolled forward, they put up the [finish-line] tape and said I'd won. I jumped up and down. I was excited, ecstatic, dazed and confused. I just didn't realize the contrast to what Julie had gone through."

Behind the bedlam of McCartney's victory, Moss crawled toward the finish line. McCartney finished in 11 hours, 9 minutes, 40 seconds. Twenty-nine seconds later, Moss lunged forward to touch the finish line.

Weeks later, having seen the pictures of her dramatic finish, Moss told the *San Diego Union-Tribune*: "Have your ever seen pictures of dead people? When I saw the picture of the finish line, I thought, 'That's what dead people look like.' But you know what? My eyes were closed, but I was smiling. I knew, finally, it was all over."

Note: Neither woman fared particularly well at Kona after their historic race. Hearst did place fourth twice. Moss never finished in the top 10 again. She failed to finish three times. Hearst has not raced at Kona since 1988.

Editor's Note:

Julie Moss' dramatic finish in February 1982 on ABC's Wide World of Sports propelled the Ironman onto the national stage and changed the event forever. Twenty years after that race, in 2002, Julie Moss and Kathleen McCartney (who now uses her husband's surname, Hearst) were asked to look back at that day and reflect on it's impact. Both women speak passionately about how much their experiences at Kona have affected them.

"In 20 years, yes, you do a lot of living," says the red-headed Moss, still vivacious and outgoing, triathlon's Lucille Ball. "There's the very real side of life. Some things work out well. Some things don't."

"I think once you've raced and achieved and enjoyed the fitness, the camaraderie, the training, the setting of goals, the achieving of goals, it's something that stays with you your whole life," says Hearst.

"For me, having won the Ironman, for the rest of my life I am going to feel like a champion," she adds. "I was the champion of the world on that given day. When you have that accomplishment under your belt, it affects your whole attitude. It adds a rosier glow to your whole life. You want to be the best at absolutely everything you can. I don't want to do anything second rate."

But more than Hearst, the winner, the 1982 race is remembered for Moss. The little red-headed college girl who fell, stumbled, stumbled some more, couldn't get up, but somehow, some way, reached the finish line.

"We've grown old together," Moss says of her relationship with Kona. "But it took me a long time to own my image in that race. I represent something to people. Twenty years later, I'm not about being an amazing athlete. It's about having the personal qualities to not give up when things get really hard."

Moss pauses, loading her mental bank for another verbal withdrawal. "The underlying theme for me is that this triathlon community is real. It's familiar, and it's familial. And always a nice source to tap into."

This page:
Top: Bike leader Kim Bushong getting a little bit of help from the ABC van.
Bottom: Dave Scott on the Queen Kaahumanu Highway.

Opposite page:
Far left: Scott Tinley wins his first Ironman title.
Top right: Tinley charges out of the transition area at the Kona Surf Hotel.
Center right: Mark Montgomery at the bike turnaround.
Bottom right: Tom Warren, 1979 champion, finishes 10th.

Photos by Carol Hogan

OCTOBER 1982: IRONHEAD

Editor's Note:
Because of the amazing growth of the event and the increasing demand from all over the world, in 1982 a second Ironman was added in October to give athletes from colder climates an opportunity to participate.
From 1982 on, the Ironman would be held in October on the Saturday closest to the full moon.

BY MIKE PLANT

Mark Allen was a raw rookie, a first timer, wet behind the ears. Dave Scott had already won the Ironman once and finished second once.

Scott was in his usual position on the way to Hawi. He was leading. Allen, cycling smoothly, pulled up next to Scott and proceeded to try and make small talk.

"Hey, what do you say we go for a run after this?" jokes Allen.

Scott was not amused.

"Dave clicked into another gear and took off," remembers Allen. "I tried to do the same but something wasn't right. My derailleur broke and I was left on the side of the road as Dave rode away from me."

It was the first encounter between the two and it set a tone. Scott dominated the day, outsplitting second-place finisher Scott Tinley in the swim, bike and the run and winning by over 20 minutes. Twenty minutes ahead of second place, 10 minutes ahead of the course record, Scott swam, rode and ran every mile as if he had some terrible beast panting at his heels.

Allen would be back to race another day.

Unfortunately for him, so would Scott.

During the marathon, young Julie Leach was leading, but wrestling with her inner demons. She could hear the helicopter overhead. She had just passed defending champion Kathleen McCartney going in opposite directions less than a mile from the turnaround and felt her lead slipping away.

"I thought she'd catch me at 18, 19 or 20 miles," says Leach. "But I told myself if it wasn't until 24 miles, I was going to go for it." She did and ended up with a four-minute cushion at the end. But it was never easy.

"It was miserable," Leach says. "You count every mile and every aid station. You think 'When is this going to end?'" she admits. "Four hours of running. Can you believe that? Six hours of biking and four hours of running. That's stupid. Insane. Ironhead."

But her green eyes were sparkling and her strong, angled face was grinning. What she meant was Iron Heart and there was one of those beating in the chests of all 776 finishers. You don't get to be an Ironman without one.

Clockwise from top left: Julie Leach could feel herself fading. She knew she had to cool herself down as quickly as possible.

Twenty minutes ahead of second place, 10 minutes ahead of the course record, Dave Scott swam, rode and ran every mile as if he had some terrible beast panting at his heels.

The two women, defending champion Kathleen McCartney (left) and Julie Leach (right), passed each other less than a mile from the turnaround. No words were exchanged.

Scott Tinley in second place.

Dave Scott hammering on the Queen Kaahumanu Highway.

Photos by Mike Plant

ALII DRIVE

*The crowds on Alii Drive
close in to watch Dave Scott win his
third — and toughest — Ironman title.*

Photo by Dave Epperson

41

1983: 33 SECONDS

When he went by Scott Tinley there was no doubt. I'm gone, don't even think about coming after me. That was the soon-to-be trademarked Dave Scott pass that Tinley, Mark Allen and many others would become accustomed to on the Kona Coast.

The hard part about going hard early is that you tend to pay for it later. Dave Scott did. Parts of the Dave Scott Express were scattered all over the Queen K Highway during the latter parts of the marathon. Tinley learned a valuable lesson that day: Never, ever give up. The heat and the winds of the Kona Coast accumulate and, at some point, the body adapts or shuts down. Scott's eyes were rolling in the back of his head and Tinley was eating up ground in huge chunks.

But it was too little, too late. Tinley could see Scott go limp at the finish line a mere 33 seconds up the road.

Thirty-three seconds. Think about it. A total of 140.6 miles had come down to a mere 33 ticks of the clock — the closest finish in Ironman history. If only Tinley had gone harder sooner.

If only Tinley had not conceded the race so early.

If only Tinley realized that the Ironman was a different animal, that anything or everything can happen out there in the lava fields.

If only...

Clockwise from top: Scott Tinley (left) wondering what might have been if he went harder earlier. On the right is Tinley's brother Jeff who finished third at the Ironman in both February 1982 and October 1982.

Tinley looking strong in the marathon.

How tough was it? Take a look at Dave Scott's eyes. At the end he was hanging on by a thread.

Sylviane Puntous of Canada winning the first of her two titles. Her sister Patricia was five and a half minutes back.

Let's see...I've got my nose coat and my banana. I'm ready to go!

Photos by Dave Epperson

1984: THE PASS

BY MIKE PLANT

It was hot. Somewhere along Hawaii's Kona Coast a cool breeze was blowing, but there wasn't a hint of it in the parking lot of the Kona Surf Hotel. Overhead, a clear, cloudless sky. The bright mid-day sun blazed, beating down on the head and necks and backs of the large crowd of volunteers and photographers. Video cameramen and reporters who had gathered to watch over 1,000 athletes trade the ridiculous for the simply impossible; trade a pair of cycling shoes, limp and damp and sweaty after 112 miles of hard riding, for a pair of soon-to-be damp and sweaty running shoes. For most onlookers, damp themselves in the steamy humidity, the mere thought of walking to a nearby Pepsi Cola vendor was torture. The idea of running a mid-afternoon marathon was insane.

There were those who were willing, however. Paid for the priviledge even. This was, after all, the Ironman Triathlon World Championship. Eight thousand fools from 31 countries had applied for entrance into the event and only 1,300 had received letters of acceptance. One thousand athletes started the race. Since the heat destroyed so many, some who got in would live to regret their "good fortune." Some who had done the race before were stunned at how tough the event had become in just one year. Other first-timers were shocked to find that the Ironman was not only as nasty as everyone had said, it was much, much worse.

By quarter after one in the afternoon, the lead men had already arrived and departed. Mark Allen had been first, rolling in at approximately 10 minutes before the hour, wearing a face of almost dreamlike concentration. Dave Scott, in second place, was still several miles down the road. He wouldn't arrive for nearly 12 minutes. In the smug words of one knowledgeable but grossly mistaken reporter, "Allen looked as if he could fall down and crawl half the marathon and still win."

Allen, 26, a former lifeguard, had been the triathlete of the year in 1984, winning every time he raced and beating Scott on numerous occasions. But when Scott finally did arrive at the Kona Surf transition area, there wasn't even a hint of resignation in his clean-cut face. He flew in and out of the parking lot, like Allen were a mere 30 seconds up the road. "Go Dave!" the crowd shouted collectively, but Scott was already tuned in to the strange inner cheerleader who seems to surface and pump iron into his veins each October. Scott was one of the lucky ones, unfazed it seemed, by the oppressive heat.

The feeling was summed up nicely by the first Hawaiian resident to finish the bike ride, Mike Anderson, 26, from Honolulu. Anderson arrived at the Kona Surf about 1:45 looking as if he'd been in a war, his white tri suit soaked and stained by an odd mixture of water, sweat and Gatorade. He painfully dismounted his bicycle and then hobbled toward the changing room with his soggy socks half off his feet.

"During the first 10K through town I was high fiving my friends in the crowd. I was going to be the Ironman champion. At the bottom of Pay and Save Hill I was the Ironman champion. By the time I reached the top, I was completely out of gas."

Mark Allen

Clockwise from top:
The Puntous sisters came off the bike in tandem and ended up first and second for the second year in a row.

Mark Allen on the Queen Highway building a huge lead during the bike ride.

After the bike, everyone conceded the race to Allen but Dave Scott. It was the first of many confrontations between Scott (left) and a walking Allen. It would become a pattern. Allen with the lead... Scott with the win.

Photos by Tracy Frankel

"Oh God, " he moans, "what have I gotten myself into?" The crowd laughs, but Anderson didn't. His long, hot day was still five hours away from being over.

Having a sense of humor, even a black one, is important at the Ironman. It was especially so in 1984. The dreadful winds along the bike course were never as ferocious as many had anticipated, but the record heat and a cloudless sky teamed up to become a more insidious enemy. Wind you can fight, and its presence is undeniable. Few competitors, however, were really aware of what the heat was doing to them until it was too late to recover. For almost everyone except the Kona Kid — the amazing Dave Scott — the Ironman marathon became a death march, much grimmer than ever before.

"Last year was fun," says Sylviane Puntous, the women's winner for the second year in a row. "This year was no fun. It was just hard."

Allen was lean and very fit, well rested and very confident after his win over Scott in Nice, France just four weeks earlier. Allen pedaled in the lead quickly, then proceeded to put minutes and miles between himself and second place. Lost in concentration as he spun his way through the bleak, lonely black lava desert, Allen had only the ABC camera van and a bike marshal or two on motor scooters for occasional company. Behind him, Scott seemed to be struggling. Almost everyone conceded the race to the skinny guy from Southern California.

"The run is my strength," says Allen. "In my mind, with the lead I had off the bike, there was absolutely no way Dave Scott was going to beat me."

Allen started celebrating early in the marathon. "During the first 10K through town I was high fiving my friends in the crowd," he continues. "I was going to be the Ironman champion. At the bottom of Pay and Save Hill I was still the Ironman champion. When I reached the top and started into the lava fields, I was completely out of gas. It's hard to win the Ironman when you're walking the marathon."

In just minutes, he went from a sure winner of the most prestigious triathlon in the world to just another endurance freak trying to finish.

Scott insists that he thought the race was over as well. That assertion is hard to believe considering the way Scott flew into and out of the Kona Surf parking lot with his singlet on backwards.

"This is my island," Scott seemed to be saying. "This is my race."

When the lead finally did change hands, a couple of miles before the turnaround at the 17 mile point, it happened very quickly. So quickly, in fact, that the ABC camera crew following the leaders got caught setting up for a static shot on the road, tearing things down and hopping back in their van.

"We have a new leader in Dave Scott," came the message crackling over the walkie talkie. "Dave Scott?" came the question. "What happened to Mark Allen?"

"Ahhh, we'll check on that," replies an embarrassed voice from the camera van.

What happened was very simple. Scott was running a sub-seven minute pace on his way to an Ironman marathon record. Allen was walking, jogging, talking himself into merely staying in the race.

"I've never seen Dave look so strong in a race," says Allen, who was walking when Scott flew by him on the way to the turnaround.

Scott's marathon time confirmed Allen's appraisal. Never before had a runner broken three hours in the marathon, but Scott did it in 1984 by a full seven minutes. Never before had someone broken nine hours for the entire race. Scott did that, too, by more than 10 minutes. For the fourth time, he'd made Ironman his own, this time by nearly half an hour.

There are courses that are hillier, longer or tougher in one way or another. But that long black strip of nastiness through the lava fields of the Kona Coast stands firm as a supreme challenge. Dumb? Probably. Grueling? Hopelessly. Irresistible? Wait until next year. The race committee will be swamped by another record number of people hoping to get in.

Race all you want, but until you look the Ironman in the eye and come to terms with it at least once, you haven't really raced at all.

"The first time I enjoyed it. When I ran, I looked at everybody, I recognized other people. People talked to me, smiled. But it was not like that this year. Nobody talked to me. It was pain, and pain all the time."

1984 Champion
Sylviane Puntous of Canada

Clockwise from left: Dave Scott wins his fourth Ironman title and his third in a row.

Joanne Ernst established herself as someone to watch with a fourth place finish.

Scott is the first Ironman to go under three hours in the marathon.

1985: HIGH-TECH TINLEY

Above: Scott Tinley's bike all ready to go.

*Opposite page, clockwise:
Fortunately for Tinley, his
aerodynamic handlebars worked perfectly
on race day. But when he went to pick up his
bike the morning after his big win, they fell off.*

*Two legends of the Ironman:
Cowman Ken Shirk on the bike and soon-to-be
two-time Ironman champion Tinley.*

Tinley wins his second title.

*Joanne Ernst moved up from
fourth in 1984 to the win in 1985.*

Photos by Lois Schwartz

Scott Tinley had to be concerned. The race he was pointing for, the one he really wanted, was quickly slipping away. He came out of the ocean in 18th place, four minutes behind leader Chris Hinshaw. But he figured on being about five minutes behind at that point, so that was okay. What he hadn't planned on was Hinshaw pulling away from him on the bike. And Hinshaw was definitely pulling away — his four minute lead had expanded to a full nine minutes by the time he hit the turnaround at the tiny tropical village of Hawi.

"The only way I could beat Tinley was to break him down mentally," says Hinshaw "Otherwise, he's just too tough. On a good day here I might run a 3:15 marathon. But on a bad day Tinley will run 3:03. I had to have a big enough lead after the bike so it didn't matter what I ran. After the turnaround life looked good."

Same for Julie Moss who had four minutes on Joanne Ernst at Hawi. But for both Moss and Hinshaw the clock started going the other way on the trip back to Kailua Kona. Tinley, decked out to the gills in aerodynamic duds, moved to within two minutes of Hinshaw by the time he reached the Kona Surf and had the lead — and the race — wrapped up by the two-mile mark of the run.

1986: KLAUS BARTH

Editor's Note:

In 1985, as a 36-year-old school teacher and father of three from Long Beach, California, Klaus Barth surprised everyone by finishing eighth overall. It was a fluke, something that the experts thought would not happen again. In 1986, at 37, he finished an amazing fourth overall behind only Dave Scott, Mark Allen and Scott Tinley. Fifteen years later, while in training to come back to Kona one more time, a brain tumor derailed the Klaus Barth Express. This story is from 2001 and reflects back on Ironman 1986 and on Barth's struggle to beat the odds. He passed away on October 22, 2006. He was 57 years old.

The moment is frozen forever. The head is tilted back as his eyes search the heavens. With his fists clenched and his mouth wide open, the expression is one of pure, unadulterated joy. I squint through the photographer's loop to check out the overhead clock in the photo from the 1986 Ironman. The time is 9:03:42. The place is fourth.

At the time, Klaus Barth was knee deep in applause and adrenaline. His wife, Sherri, and the three kids were sprinting out from behind the barriers to greet him. The Long Beach Wilson High School swim coach had paid his Irondues in full. He collapsed nine miles into the run in 1984 while in ninth place. In 1995, he had finished eighth. When he showed up the following year, he expected to be wearing number eight when he went to the line. That was the rule. Finish first, wear number one the next year. Finish second, wear number two. Not this time, bucko. He was told that they looked upon the 36-year-old's finish from the year before as a fluke, a combination of a lucky day and a weak field.

"I said, 'What the hell, I finished eighth,'" he remembers. "They said 'Hey, nobody raced last year. We've set number eight aside for the right guy. That guy unfortunately is not you."

His race number come race day was 48. Not bad...but certainly not eight. He knew he was ready to go after a full summer of 150-mile rides from his home in Long Beach to Solana Beach and back followed immediately by a 10-mile run on the Long Beach Marathon course. His three kids knew that daddy was getting ready for the race of his life.

That's why Barth was so damn happy at the finish. Eighth place? Fergetaboutit! Barth proved that eighth was indeed a fluke. He was a year older, 37, and he finished fourth. The only guys in front of him? Dave Scott, Mark Allen and Scott Tinley.

Barth is looking to prove people wrong once again. He was hoping to do the Ironman this past October at the age of 50. But that dream was trashed when he had both hernia and knee surgery on July 3. It was the old tag team approach. Knock out the hyperactive Barth, have the hernia guy come in and take care of business, tag off to the knee specialist, and then have him do his thing.

Then something even more brutal came up. While Barth was in a meeting with his tax accountant one day, he suddenly collapsed to the floor with a grand mal seizure. He was about two minutes away from getting in his car and driving off to swim practice. If he had had the seizure in his car, there would be a good chance that Barth would not be alive today.

But he is, and the fight is not over. The cause of the seizure? The doctors eventually found that, besides having the heart of a 20 year old, he had a brain tumor the size of a gumball called a *gliosclastoma multiforme*, the beast of all tumors. It is a grade four out of four, the worst you can get. The surgery on October 5 took over 6 hours and the tumor was malignant. He finished 33 radiation treatments at an experimental program at UCLA in mid-December and started chemotherapy in early January. For radiation, doctors strap a mask to his face and have him lie perfectly still.

"They lock you in this room," he says. "First they close an eight-inch thick door behind you. Then they close another 10-inch thick door." He laughs. "It doesn't make you feel very good about what they are pumping into your body." An injection of gatalinin is followed by a new product called texaphyrin.

Whatever they pump in can't be any tougher than the guy they are pumping it into. To get Barth into the very tight UCLA Program, his wife, Sherri, sent a copy of the poster that Sparkletts Water had created of Barth back when he finished fourth in Hawaii. She mailed it off to the doctors with a note that said: "My husband will make your study look good."

Barth was accepted the next week.

"I told the doctor that I'm going to be a great subject and a great guinea pig," he recalls. "I'm going to prove everyone wrong."

He has coached swimming for 18 years plus soccer and water polo. He knows what hard work, pain and commitment are all about. They put a line into his arm that has to stay there for almost seven weeks.

"All I want to do is ride my bike," he says from his home. "I can't swim or lift or run. Right now I can't lift five pounds." In order to maintain his brain functions, he is taking speech and memory classes and counting out loud every day.

One athlete he coached was a high school kid named Tom Gallagher who eventually became a professional triathlete.

"Gallagher told me that he was scared of me the first time we met," laughs Barth. Now they are the best of friends. They have pulled and pushed and prodded each other through any number of workouts and races. In 1987, they finished Ironman side by side.

"We kept looking for the lead helicopter," says Barth. "We were hoping we'd finish in front of the first woman."

Keep hoping, boys. Erin Baker came steaming by them a half mile before the finish.

"She was flying," recalls Barth. "There was no way we could go with her."

On Halloween, Gallagher came by the Barth home. He rang the bell like any other trick or treater. His costume was one part trick and three parts treat.

"The left side of his head was shaved just like mine," he remembers. "And he had a scar drawn on the side of his head right where mine is." Gallagher can't share the pain, put he can sure share the hope. The fight could be a long one. Sherri, the kids, Gallagher plus Barth's legion of friends know that all too well.

"When I was out on the Ironman bike course, when things got tough, what got me through was thinking about you and the kids," Barth told Sherri more than once.

Times are tough again and the winds are howling. This time, in order to help Barth get through the hardest ride of his life, he needs the triathlon world to think about him.

My gut tells me that Barth will prove the experts wrong, that he will come out the other side and live to race again. You can bet on it.

Top right: A confused Paula Newby-ser was sure she had finished second Puntous. So why was the finish ban-er up for her to break? Because, with Puntous disqualified, Newby-Fraser m South Africa was now the Ironman Triathlon World Champion.

Bottom right: In 1986, Dave Scott ame the first person to go under 8:30 8:28:37) to win his fifth Ironman title.

Bottom middle: They ran side by side, st like always. But eventually Patricia tous pulled away from sister Sylviane vin her first Ironman title. Or did she? After her finish Patricia was told that e had been marked down for drafting n the bike and had been disqualified.

Bottom left: Defending champion Scott Tinley is second once again.

Photos by Lois Schwartz

51

The Iron Dynasty

The greatest of them all.

This photo was taken in 1993, before the

15th anniversary of the Ironman.

IRONically, at that time Mark Allen (four),

Dave Scott (six) and Paula Newby-Fraser (five)

had won an amazing 15 Ironman Triathlon World

Championship titles. With Newby-Fraser's additional three

and Allen's two, they are now at an even 20.

Photo by Melanie Carr

1987: LORD OF THE LAVA

Ironman Commandment Number One: Thou shalt never take thine eyes off the road.

It was mere seconds since the end of the swim. Dave Scott was looking down, trying to get the bike shoe on his right foot to stay on the pedal. Mark Allen, his main competition at the 1987 Ironman, was immediately to his right, and he was trying to do the same thing. Suddenly the two of them inched towards each other in a slow motion bicycle ballet. They smashed shoulders, Allen careening wildly towards the snow fencing and almost going down. He looked up quickly after the sudden collision with a what-the-heck-are-you-doing look on his face. Scott never looked up. He simply kept tugging at his shoe until it was locked down tight, then he was gone. The 112-mile bike race was all of 10 seconds old.

Obviously, Allen was keying on Scott. He stayed inches from the heels of the five-time Ironman Champ throughout the 2.4-mile swim. After their first but not last arm bumping of the day, Allen hurriedly joined the lead pack hammering out on the Queen Kaahumanu Highway. After 40 miles of riding, the pack consisted of Keith Anderson from South Africa followed by Scott, Allen, Mike Pigg and Kenny Glah. Scott Tinley and Tom Gallagher were back a good two minutes.

Ironman Commandment Number Two: *Thou shalt never overlook a guy who rides fast and wears clothes with his own name on them.*

Right at the turnaround, just past the seven-mile the-wind-is-always-in-your-face uphill to Hawi, Tinley magically appeared with Allen, Scott and the rest of the boys. Momentarily he was in the lead.

"Tinley caught us and the pace really picked up," remembers Kenny Glah. "Mike Pigg and I were jamming stuff in our jerseys when I realized 'Oh my god…the press truck is in our lane!' Suddenly they had 150 yards on us out of nowhere. It didn't hit me until that point that the truck would have to stay in our lane."

But two-time winner Tinley knows the importance of the lead vehicle. If the leaders reached the turnaround before him, he was history. They would have a downhill, a tailwind — plus they would be riding in the draft created by the press truck. And because of cyclists now going in both directions, the truck would be forced to stay directly in front of them.

"When I caught them and went into the lead," Tinley recalls, "I was sitting right there next to Dave, six feet off the rear bumper of the press truck. I didn't even have to pedal! I thought 'This is unreal!' Then I got a bad cramp and had to fall back to stretch it out. They were gone."

And so was Tinley — off the back and into what is called the Ironman Twilight Zone. No one in front, no one behind. Just you, the wind, the heat and the black nothingness of the lava fields.

"When Tinley caught us at Hawi," says Scott, "My first thought was 'We're in for it now.' We were going at an incredible pace

after the turnaround."

"We're screwing around putting stuff in our jerseys and they're hammering away," says Glah. "I just dropped it into my 12 [his toughest gear] and took off. I caught up to them and just kept going. The ABC guy goes 'You've got 500 meters on them…is this planned?' I said 'No, but I'll take it'."

Ironman Commandment Number Three: *If thou burns thy legs on the bike, thou will be running on briquettes in the marathon.*

Glah, the young man from Pennsylvania, took it and ran for the next 20 miles or so. The surprise was that Pigg or Allen didn't try to get away.

"I thought Pigg and I would pull away from him [Scott]," says Allen. "But I didn't want to push it. In the back of my mind I kept thinking 'marathon…marathon… marathon'."

Scott wanted to make sure that by the time he got to the marathon a major withdrawal had been made from everyone's legs.

"I wanted to make sure that people were fatigued on the bike," says the man they call Mr. October, in a bit of an understatement. "At 80 miles I went by Kenny aggressively."

Scott likes to race from the front, to race "aggressively". He enjoys himself a little bit more when he is in position to dictate the pace, when no one can see how he looks. But when he went by Glah at 80 miles, when he took the lead, he had company. It was

Allen, the man who sat on his heels in the swim, the guy who showed up in Kona in '86 just two weeks after winning his fifth Nice Triathlon Championship and gave Scott a run for his money. Allen was hanging in the shadows, sticking to Scott like a pushy Girl Scout with 12 extra boxes of Thin Mints to sell.

The two finished the bike ride the way they started it 112 miles earlier — in tandem. Allen was the first to run up the Kona Surf hill, but Scott soon joined him. The two ran side by side down Alii Drive to the cheers of thousands.

"I felt weary getting off the bike," says Scott. "It was the worst I ever felt getting off the bike. The last thing I wanted to do was to go side by side with Mark Allen. We bumped together a couple of times coming down Alii Drive."

But if Scott felt "weary", Allen was feeling positively worn. He had been having stomach problems all week. He didn't know if it stemmed from some raw fish he ate early in the trip or not, but on race morning it felt like his stomach was sucked up into his diaphragm. Allen eventually threw up twice during the last 10 miles of the bike ride.

Surprisingly, Allen felt better shortly after the bike-to-run transition.

"I felt real good coming off the bike," says Allen. "My plan was to pick it up at the turnaround. I decided to just run my pace."

"My pace" was enough to leave Scott 30 seconds behind as they left downtown

Kona and four and a half minutes back by the turnaround at 16 miles. But was he going too hard? Was this shaping up to be a repeat of 1984 when Allen had 13 minutes on Scott off the bike and fell completely apart halfway through the run? Allen didn't think so.

"I know my body well enough not to go too hard," he says adamantly after the race.

But Mark, since you swam behind him and rode behind him...why not run behind him too? Maybe take it easy and then cruise by at 25 miles or so. Let the big guy do all the work.

"You can't put energy in the bank," Allen answers. "If you don't use it now it doesn't mean it's going to be there later. I wasn't going to slow down to run with him. Who knows? He might be tight early and get loose later on. I felt smooth and relaxed during the first part of the run. I never felt I went too hard."

Ironman Commandment Number Four: *Thou shalt never count thy chickens, or thy first-place check, until Dave Scott is seen camped out at an aid station neck deep in chocolate chip cookies.*

With about nine miles to go, Allen could feel something happening to his body. All of a sudden, whenever he put food or drink in at an aid station, he wasn't getting any energy out in return. It was sort of like having a hole in the gas tank. The fuel was getting in there, but the needle still registered 'E'. He felt terrible again.

"It felt like someone was hitting me in the stomach," recalls Allen.

Scott, off in the distance, didn't think that Allen would repeat his 1984 collapse. But he's not the type of guy to just sit back and concede the race either.

"About mile nine or 10, my pace picked up a bit," says Scott. "At 16 miles Mark had four and a half minutes on me, but when I looked at him on the way back to town, he looked glossed over. I thought, 'Let's keep him honest...maybe he'll falter a bit.' Then I made up 40 seconds in one mile, and people going the other way told me that Mark had walked through an aid station."

Bob Bright, race director for the Chicago Marathon, is the elite athlete coordinator for the Ironman.

"When I saw Mark Allen take two steps," says Bright, "I looked back real quick. I knew Dave smelled it. I wanted to go up alongside him and say 'Dave, we've got a little money here...slow down! Wait until you get to Alii Drive to pass him!'"

But Scott wasn't waiting for anything. He has a very distinct way of passing people. Allen calls it the no-remorse-forget-me-I'm-gone pass. He has seen it up close and personal at the 1984 Ironman and in 1983 in Panama City, Florida. Unfortunately for him, he was about to see it again. At 22 miles, Scott flew by, on his way to his record sixth Ironman victory.

"This was the hardest one I've ever done," says a worn out Scott at the finish. Allen would readily agree. He ended up in the hospital, eventually needing three units of blood and seven bottles of IV fluids. He had been bleeding internally throughout the run. Allen had gone as hard and as long as humanly possible. Unfortunately, he came up four miles short. But what do you expect? Scott is the King, the main dude, the Lord of the Lava. And you know what his last commandment is don't you?

Thou shalt never beat Dave Scott on the Kona Coast.

This page:
Left: Third-place finisher Paula Newby-Fraser is welcomed by her boyfriend, Paul Huddle, who took 15th.
Top right: Two-time champion Sylviane Puntous (#101) came up a little bit short, finishing just one minute and 30 seconds behind Baker.
Center right: Kenny Glah finished in the top 10 for the second straight year, this time taking fifth.
Bottom right: Short-course specialist Jan Ripple (#1061) faded on the run to finish 14th.

Photos by Lois Schwartz

Cap secure

Goggles in place

Only 140.6 miles to go.

Photo by Lois Schwartz

1988: WHACK A MOLE

You are standing in a typical I-wish-I-had-200-quarters arcade, one of those fun centers that bombards the senses with an assortment of blips, bleeps screetches and thousands of decibels of sound. The games surrounding you are classics, like Laser Karate and Nuke the Nerds from Neptune. Win often enough and you get to choose from any number of wonderful prizes — maybe a purple rabbit's foot, a plastic ring with polyester tassels on it or a whistle in the shape of a rabid mongoose.

A very fit young woman is in the arcade holding what appears to be a large mallet in both hands. She avoids all of the electronic mumbo jumbo and stands instead in front of the most basic of games. When a mechanical mole pokes its furry little head out of its hole, her job — her duty — is to whack that mole. The more moles you whack, the higher the score. The higher the score, the more rabid mongoose whistles you get to take home with you.

During the week prior to the 1988 Ironman, no one whacked more moles in Kona than 26-year-old Paula Newby-Fraser of Encinitas, California by way of Zimbabwe. Then on race day, Newby-Fraser whacked defending champion Erin Baker and the rest of the women's field with a stunning performance.

"It was one of those days you dream about," says Newby-Fraser. "The perfect race."

Newby-Fraser finished exactly 30 minutes behind the overall winner, Scott Molina, broke the women's course record and finished 11th overall.

Perfect? It was beyond perfect.

She whacked everyone.

The Queen K is ramrod straight,
But the Ironman
Will throw you curves
All day long.

Photo by Robert Oliver

One had six titles, the other none. For 138 miles and eight hours they were never separated by more than a second. The greatest Ironman race of all time, Ironwar, pitted Dave Scott (left) against his arch rival Mark Allen (right). It was a race for the ages.

Photos by Lois Schwartz

1989: IRONWAR

*"If I'm feeling reasonably good,
I'm not going to go as slow as 8:28
[his Ironman course record]. That time is soft.
Last year they had some great cycling times,
but no running times. They sucked.
Scott Molina won with a 3:02.
I haven't run 3:02 in six years!
It'll take a 2:42 or 2:43 to win it this year.
Only two people can run that fast ...
only two people can go under 2:50.
If someone runs over three hours this year ...
they can forget about it.
They'll be two miles down the road."*

Dave Scott, September 1989

With the black nothingness of the Big Island's lava fields as a backdrop and an entourage of spectators on mopeds and bicycles hovering behind, Mark Allen and Dave Scott moved swiftly through the third act of the three-part Ironman play. Their swim times for 2.4 miles were 51:17 and 51:16 respectively. Bike splits? 4:37:52 and 4:37:53.

They began the 26.2 mile marathon in tandem, under a muggy haze — ideal conditions when compared to the usual blast-furnace-from-hell marathon heat the Hawaiian Triathlon Gods are famous for. The two made their bike-to-run transition at the Kona Surf Hotel, headed up the "what-joker-decided-to-put-this-sucker-here?" hill and settled into a little more one-on-one as they strung together sub-six-minute miles down Alii Drive.

"Dave set a really good pace through town," recalls Mark Allen. "I remember thinking, 'I don't know, 26 miles at this pace is going to be pretty tough.'"

The scene was familiar. It had been played out many times before. To many triathlon fans, it must seem like Scott and Allen have been doing reruns for as long as Lucy and Ricky.

Their first meeting in Kona was in 1982, when Allen had mechanical problems on the bike after the runaround in Hawi and was forced to drop out. Allen broke away early in the bike ride in the 1984 Ironman only to be run down by Scott. In 1987, Allen tried a different tactic and waited until the run to break away. Again, Scott ran him down. Scott had six Iron notches on his belt going into 1989. Allen? A pair of pants baggy with expectations in desperate need of something with a notch in it to hold them up.

Throughout the bike ride, Allen's focus was totally on Scott. He ignored Wolfgang Dittrich of West Germany, who put two minutes between himself and the chase pack during the swim. Dittrich then rode off the front for 112 miles, his lead hovering around three minutes early, but dwindling down to less than two by the time he reached the Kona Surf and the bike-to-run transition. Behind him was a pack of riders that included Kenny Glah, Mike Pigg, Rob Mackle, Scott and Allen. Allen was in a zone of his own, lurking in the shadows, monitoring every move Scott would make.

"I never saw his face during the bike," says Scott. There was no need for Allen to show his face. Scott KNEW he was there. After blowing up every time he'd tried to pull away from Scott in previous years, Allen was taking absolutely no chances.

"It was really difficult for me at first reconciling myself to the fact that I was going to have to run with him for 18-26 miles," says Allen. But he knew there was no other way.

On race morning, Ironman's elite athlete liaison Bob Bright was asked what Allen had to do to beat Scott. He said: "Dave is the most consistent guy in every venue. You know he'll be there in the swim and in the bike. And everyone is scared of him when it comes to the run. Allen will have to run a very solid, very mature marathon to win this race. He's got to do what's been most difficult for him. He's got to get off the bike alongside Scott and then run with him all the way. Breathe on him, bump him, maybe spit on him. But stay off the front. He can't do anything flamboyant."

Allen was resigned to the reality of the Ironman. To win the race, you have to stay with The Man.

"I've tried everything else," he says, shaking his head. "There's no reason to out-bike Dave, because he'll just run you down."

The two ran wordlessly along, the mobile spectators sensing the enormity of the performances they were witnessing. The best marathon ever at the Ironman was Scott's 2:49. Allen had a best of 2:55. Both were running well under that pace as they reached the 17-mile turnaround at the inflatable Bud Light beer can. Nine miles to go, both athletes still in synch, only the sound of their breathing and of their shoes skidding ever faster across the pavement breaking the silence.

The fans that followed the leaders did so like they were watching a horror film or awaiting a storm. Something was going to happen, but what would it be, and when? Who would make the first move?

"It was like we were all in the eye of a hur-

ricane," recalls Dan Empfield, the owner of The Quintana Roo Wetsuit and Bicycle Company. "There's this huge thing going on around you. You know something is going to happen. These guys had been going at it for more than seven hours and hadn't been separated by more than a body length."

Dittrich was an early victim of the juggernaut. He was ground up and spit out many miles back, as Scott and Allen moved into the lead in the early part of the run.

"Kenny Glah passed me at mile 12," remembers Dittrich. "But he went by slowly. These two guys? I was running seven minutes per mile and they were gaining more than a minute a mile on me. They went by so fast it was unbelievable!"

Unbelievable was the lady racing just a few minutes behind Dittrich. Her name: Paula Newby-Fraser. And everyone was wondering how she could match her performance of 1988 when she broke the women's course record by half an hour, finished in 9:01:01 and came in 11th overall.

Early in this year's bike ride, Newby-Fraser was challenged by Lisa Laiti, Kristin Hanssen and Jan Ripple. In 1988, Hanssen finished third, racing with a broken wrist in her first Ironman attempt. She went into this year's Ironman a question mark because of an injury-plagued season. After a stress-fractured hip, she'd only begun to run again eight weeks before race day.

Laiti and Ripple dropped back before the bike turnaround, and suddenly Newby-Fraser had only Hanssen to contend with. Sylviane Puntous, a two-time Ironman winner and one of the best runners in the sport, was over seven minutes off the pace. With Erin Baker off racing the Chicago Marathon, Hanssen appeared to be Newby-Fraser's only real competition.

"I was changing the lead with Paula for about 80 miles," remembers Hanssen.

But Newby-Fraser isn't the type to panic. "She was there," Newby-Fraser admits, but she wasn't concerned. "I never give any energy to anyone else out there," she says emphatically. "I was going at my own pace."

08:09:14

TIMEX TIMEX TIMEX

BUD LIGHT

IRONMAN

Her own pace was good for a three-minute lead off the bike over Hanssen and an almost 10-minute lead over Puntous. At the top of Pay and Save Hill that leads out of town, Newby-Fraser had over four minutes on Hanssen.

"I was very patient," says Newby-Fraser. "My times were very similar to last year. Finishing is winning at this race."

Finishing fast doesn't hurt, either. With over a 20-minute lead on Sylviane Puntous, who moved past Hanssen into second place during the run, Newby-Fraser hurtled down the last stretch to the finish on Alii Drive. She knew that she was going to win her third Ironman title and that she was close to breaking her course record . . . and picking up the $5,000 that went with it. A final sprint to the tape put her in at 9:00:56, exactly five seconds under her old record. $1,000 a second? Not a bad reason to sprint, eh?

As Allen and Scott moved closer and closer to downtown Kona, the thought of a sprint to the tape must have been going through their heads, too. Their gap over the fast-closing Aussie Greg Welch was an insurmountable 20 minutes. The only game in town was the one they were playing. But who would make the first move? And when?

"Mark had the inside track at the aid stations," remembers Scott. "Mark would get aid and I'd have to slow down to get it. At mile 23 it happened again and Mark picked up the pace and opened up 20 feet on me. He looked over his shoulder and could see he had a gap. I told myself that I had to come back. But it hurt to come back. Once I got up to him again I thought, 'Okay, I'm back in the race.' Psychologically, I did that to say, 'Okay, Mark, it's not yours yet, you've got to earn it.'"

Just at the base of the long hill into town, 24 miles into the run, Allen decided to earn it.

"When Mark saw that sign, he took off," remembers Scott. "He looked back and in about 15 seconds he had about 20 yards. His fiancé, Julie Moss, was on the press truck pumping her fist. I know what happens when Anna [his wife] does that to me. I thought, 'Oh don't do that, Julie!' He had about 50 yards on me. My legs were pretty

empty, but I kept thinking, 'I've got to stay with him, I've got to stay with him.' I've been in the other position before and I know what a confidence builder it is. You get a gap and you think … 'It's mine!'"

That's exactly what was going through Allen's mind. He had decided beforehand that if the race was tight, if he was still with Scott at mile 24, the last grade would be his spot to make a move.

"He'd always be a little behind me on the uphills, so I thought, 'All right, where's the best uphill?' I thought the best one was the last one into town. I started to push a little bit before the hill to see how he was feeling," says Allen. "Right at the mile 99 highway marker I thought, 'Okay, this is it, man!' I felt good. I felt that I could go hard for two miles."

Hard enough to put 58 seconds between himself and the Lord of the Lava in the last two miles. And fast enough to erase a lot of past Ironman disappointment. He hammered down Pay and Save Hill, turned left and headed for home.

"After 100 yards on the flat, all of a sudden I felt like…YES!" Allen clenched his fists and shook them as he shouted at the top of his lungs. "Every cell in my body was tired of being the almost-guy-there. I was tired of 'You almost won, Mark.'"

There's no almost anymore. Allen needed an incredible 2:40:04 marathon to hold off Dave "Never-Say-Die" Scott, who turned in a 2:41:03 — 18 minutes off his own course record — and, somehow, someway came up short.

Scott gave a what-can-you-do shrug and summed up the race over a post-marathon cup of Exceed.

"I think both of us were testing each other early," he says. "Mark was more confident than ever before in the marathon. Obviously, his strategy paid off. He waited on the run until he got to a point where he thought he could break me. I think it was a picture-perfect race for him. I knew it would come down to the run and that the only other guy who could run with me was Mark Allen. The race was exactly how I predicted it would go," he says with a smile. "Except the finish was wrong."

Opposite page: It was a course record (9:00:56) and her third Ironman Triathlon World Championship title. Waiting for Paula Newby-Fraser at the finish was her boyfriend and future fiancé Paul Huddle. Photo by Lois Schwartz

Above: Fernanda Keller of Brazil put together the second fastest run of the day (3:15:42) to take fourth. Since her first top-five finish in 1989, she has finished in the top 13, 13 years in a row. During that span, she took third place an amazing six times and only once, her 13th place in 1991, did she finish worse than ninth. Photo by Lois Schwartz

Below: Jim MacLaren, a lower leg amputee, went 12:13:50 in 1989. A few years later, in 1992, he went 10:42:50, an amputee course record that still stands. Photo by Tracy Frankel

You vow
You curse
And you chant.
I'm done.
No way.
Never again.
Then the crowds
The lights
The Medal.
The pain is all forgotten.
And you hope you'll get the chance
To do it all over again.

Photo by Robert Oliver

THE CURSE OF PELE

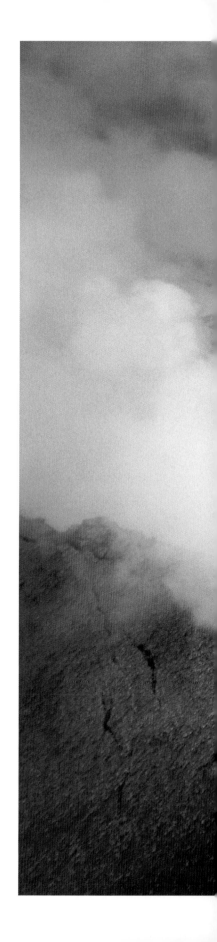

"Forgive me for taking the lava home from the island,"
says one letter. "I didn't realize the danger. Please apologize to
Madame Pele for me and tell her that I'm returning this lava to her.
Since I took it I have had awful luck."

Above: Mark Allen...
meet Madame Pele.
Photo by Tracy Frankel

Mark Allen was the best triathlete in the world for over 15 years. During that time, he won better than 90 percent of the races he entered. Yet, early in his career in the Hawaii Ironman, the guy was snakebit.

In October of 1982, Allen was with Dave Scott halfway through the bike ride when he had a mechanical problem and was forced to drop out. In 1984, his 12-minute gap over Scott disappeared faster than Jimmy Hoffa and the Nehru jacket.

Honey, I Shrunk the Lead Part II, starring Scott, hit Allen again in 1987 — only this time, after Scott passed him during the marathon, Allen ended up in the hospital with internal bleeding.

Scott didn't even race in 1988. Allen flatted twice and was never a factor for the win.

Going into 1989, Allen was the Evel Knievel of the Kona Coast. "Crash-and-Burn" was his middle name. He was 0 for Hawaii and Homer Simpson was given better odds to win the Ironman. Allen's luck came in two categories: hard or bad.

*Pele's awesome presence in
Volcano National Park, Hawaii.
Photo by Catherine Grawin*

Lisa Magno can relate. She's the lava lady.

Every day the administrative interpreter at the Volcano National Park on the Big Island of Hawaii empties cardboard boxes filled with lava rocks of various shapes and sizes onto the floor of her office.

Big lava, small lava…if it's a black rock, she's seen it. All these rocks have been sent back to the Big Island for the same reason: The Curse of Pele. Each box, each rock has its own tale to tell.

"You wouldn't believe some of the stories," says Magno. "I get letters every day telling of financial problems and bad health that they say is directly related to taking lava home from Hawaii. I'm amazed at the number of packages that come in here every week."

"Forgive me for taking the lava home from the island," says one such letter. "I didn't realize the danger. Please apologize to Madame Pele for me and tell her that I'm returning this lava to her. Since I took it I have had awful luck."

Pele is the fire goddess and, according to Haole (pronounced How-lee and meaning non-Hawaiian) legend, it is very risky to take lava from the island. Bad luck always follows.

Most people send their packages back to Pele by certified mail. And they are wrapped very, very carefully, immaculately protected against the barbarians of the mail room.

"A lot of them wrap these rocks like they're packing a fragile piece of art," laughs Magno. "And some of these rocks are so big I don't know how they got them off the island in the first place!"

Enclosed in each package is a letter of explanation identifying precisely where the rock in question was taken from.

"They tell me in their letters that the rocks were taken from some particular location four miles north of the airport," says Magno. " They want us to drive out and return the lava to where they picked it up."

Lisa, do you take the lava back to their original home?

"Nope," Magno responds. "I dump 'em out the back door."

Accompanying the lava rocks is usually a

bottle of gin.

"Pele's favorite beverage," insists Magno. She hesitates, anticipating the next question.

"We take the gin home."

Before the 1989 Ironman, Allen's stepmother told him that she had a premonition about the race.

"She said, 'I have a good feeling about this year,'" Allen remembers.

What he didn't know was that, years earlier, his stepmother had taken a lava rock souvenir from the island, and that she had obviously incurred the wrath of Madame Pele. Before the 1989 race, she brought the rock back to the Big Island.

"She didn't tell me until after the race," says Allen.

Mechanical problems, internal bleeding, flat tires, Dave Scott and the curse of Pele. Allen had enough demons to take home a 12-pack. Hawaii had become his Waterloo, yet it was the one win he needed to complete an amazing career.

In 1989, the lava was returned. In 1989, Allen won his first Ironman title on his seventh try. He won five more Ironman titles after that. A coincidence? Lisa Magno doesn't think so.

"Something's going on," she insists while staring at a pile of some of the nearly 1,000 packages of returned lava she'd received this year alone. "Me? I personally wouldn't take lava home."

Neither would Mark Allen.

1990: THE EQUALIZER

It started early. If you looked to the east, the sun was rising unimpeded over the mountain tops, the fluffy clouds of the past three years only a faint memory. As it reached slowly over the edge, there was a brief respite, a catching of the breath, a final I-know-this-won't-last moment of life giving shade before Old Sol's Big Island Sauna burst into view to hang out his "Open for Business" sign.

As the 1,300 triathletes warming up in Kailua Bay and on the banks of Dig Me Beach scanned the sky, they could almost see the outline of a menacing frown. It was payback time.

The Equalizer was back after several years of cool and calm Ironman weather, and he was none too happy. A lot of people had been talkin' trash in his absence. "The Ironman ain't that tough," they said. He was about to show the Iron Wannabees treading water in the Bay on October 6, 1990 that they could take their aerodynamic stuff and stuff it where he normally don't shine. Bo may know football, baseball, basketball and nuclear physics, but the Equalizer knows wind and heat better than anyone on the planet.

After the cannon set loose the hordes of swimmers on their 2.4-mile journey, spectators, loved ones and journalists alike searched the horizon for a hint of cloud cover — some-where...anywhere. But there was absolutely none.

On the Queen K Highway
Rob Mackle (left),
Mark Allen (center)
and Wolfgang Dittrich (right)
pull away from everyone.
Photo by Lois Schwartz

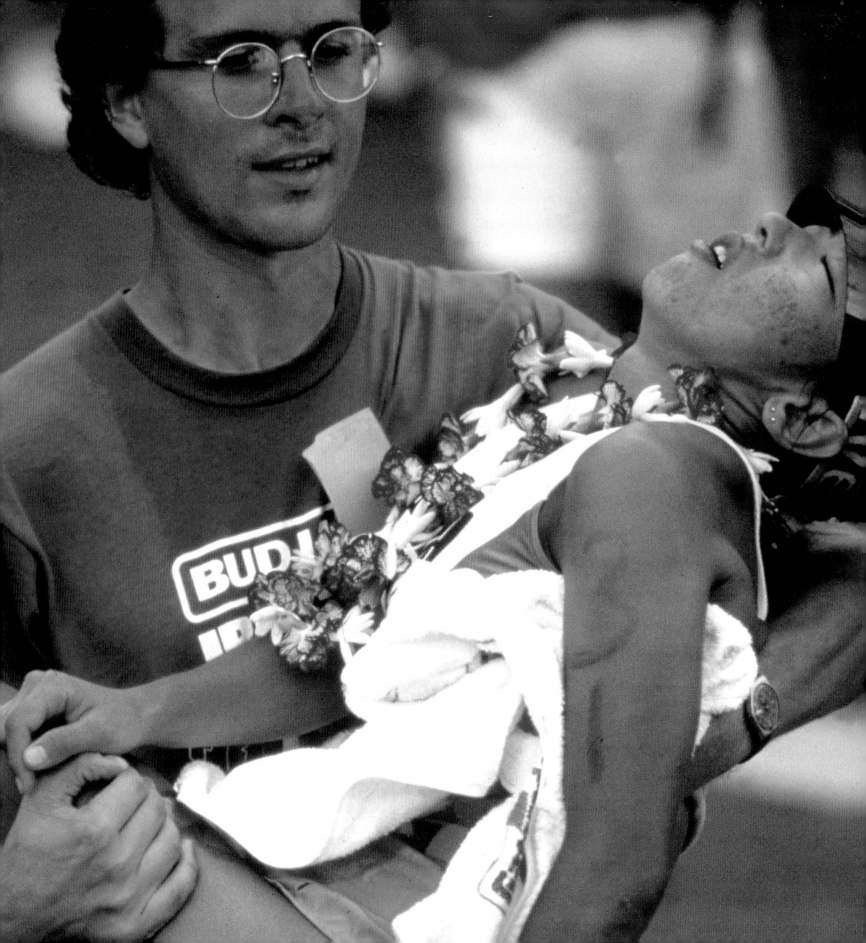

Opposite page:
How tough was the heat of 1990?
Ask Junko Murakami (#31) of Japan.

This page:
Top left: Erin Baker dominated all day long, outsplitting Paula Newby-Fraser in the swim, the bike and the marathon.
Top right: Two-time champion Sylviane Puntous (#20) was one of the victims of the oppressive heat.
Bottom left: Scott Tinley ran his way through the field to second place, his highest finish since his win in 1985.
Bottom Right: Unknown Greg Welch took third in 1989. In 1990, he dropped back a couple of notches to fifth.

Photos by Lois Schwartz

Life is about making the very best of every opportunity. Each year, on one October Saturday morning in Kona, Hawaii, 1,800 excited athletes get the rare opportunity to see if they have what it takes to become an Ironman.

Photo by Rich Cruse

1991: CHECKMATE

The two are locked together in mortal combat. Sweat beads up on both foreheads as they survey the board and scan the memory banks. They search endlessly, desperately for the back breaker, the killer, the pièce de résistance... the mother of all moves.

Pawns, rooks, and castles are all willingly sacrificed for the win, the only goal that matters. When you are on the other side of the table, the pause, that calm before the storm, can seem like forever. A deep breath is taken and "The Move" is finally made. A smile plays at the corner of the lips of the mover and the word that always follows the mother of all moves is spoken loudly and clearly, ending the game, ending the speculation, ending any what ifs. So goes the game of chess. And so goes the yearly game known as the Gatorade Ironman.

Greg Welch surprised everyone but himself by making up 45 seconds on Mark Allen and catching him early in the bike. They were two minutes back of Wolfgang Dittrich of Germany, the leader out of the water.

The message is clear. Welch had to be feeling that Allen was beatable, that he could be had.

"I've done all the groundwork," says Welch at the pre-race press conference. "Mark's been beaten four times this year, twice by me, twice by Mike Pigg."

Last year, Paula Newby-Fraser had trouble in the swim and came out of the water behind Erin Baker. Then she tried to go by Baker on the bike. Wrong.

"She was attached," Newby-Fraser says. "It was like, 'That's it. There's no way she was going to let me ride away.'" Eventually it was Baker who got away on the bike, and the race was over.

"I said to myself, 'This is okay,' says Newby-Fraser. "'Second is okay.' I just wasn't willing to hurt that much."

Known for his intense focus, Mark Allen contemplates his moves on the Ironman chessboard. Photo by Tony DiZinno

Baker is considered the better overall runner of the two. She's run a 2:36 marathon. At the 1990 Canadian Ironman, Baker put together a 2:49 marathon, destroying Newby-Fraser's lead — and her psyche — in the process.

"When Erin caught me by the turn-around, I thought she had cut the course," remembers Newby-Fraser. "I just fell apart after that."

Newby-Fraser was asked if she felt she needed a lead off the bike on Baker. She thought not.

"Not necessarily," she says. "If I can keep myself together mentally, if I can push through on the bike, I should be strong in the run."

Newby-Fraser was feeling extremely confident on the bike. She rode with Allen one day and he had trained with Baker.

"Mark was very encouraging," remembers Newby-Fraser. "We did a ride together and I tried to hang on his wheel for as long as I could. He said I was staying on his wheel a lot longer than Erin could."

Defending champion Baker's strategy was exactly the same as Newby-Fraser's.

"I planned to hammer the first 30 miles of the bike," says Baker. "I got her lead down to 40 seconds at one point. But the next split was two and a half minutes. From that time on to Hawi [the turnaround], I didn't feel good. I couldn't drink at all and threw up all my water. It wasn't a good day. Either I trained wrong or I was psyched out when I heard how good Paula was doing."

For whatever reason, Baker was flat on race day. She had trained in the heat of Palm Springs with her husband, Scott Molina, and Scott Tinley a few weeks before Hawaii. Molina dropped out, Tinley finished sixth and Baker had, by her high standards, a very average day. Had the three done too much heat training too close to race day?

For Newby-Fraser, 1991 was redemption.

"Last year I wasn't prepared for this race," she says. "I was capable of beating Erin, but I was burned out. My personal life wasn't in order and it bothered me that I didn't give her the race that I thought I should have given her." A long pause. "I just didn't have what it took."

But Greg Welch did, and Mark Allen was concerned.

"A couple of years ago, I said that he's the guy coming up who's going to dominate this sport," says Allen. "He began last year by winning the World's. This year he beat me a couple of times pretty handily."

Allen was surprised when Welch caught him so quickly on the bike.

"I thought I was going pretty hard during the early part of the ride, and then Welch was right there next to me," says Allen. "I thought I was going pretty good." At the time Allen was concentrating on cutting into Dittrich's lead. When Welch caught him, catching Wolfgang became secondary. The Dittrich chase group included Jürgen Zäck, Pauli Kiurui, Allen, Welch...and Jeff Devlin.

Devlin, 10th place at the 1990 Ironman, is one of those athletes whose race day performances are just starting to catch up to a limitless potential. Four minutes back of Allen out of the water, he outsplit Allen on the bike by nearly three minutes.

"When I caught those guys, they seemed to be going so slow," says Devlin. "I thought, 'What am I going to do here?' No one wanted to push the pace. Do I try to go by them? If I do, they're just going to sit on me, which they did. I decided to screw this, I'm not going to give them a free ride. I decided to back off and let them go."

The ride turned tactical — Allen content to keep Welch where he could see him.

Welch wanted to let Allen know early that he was planning to be there all day long.

"My plan was to catch him and stay with him," says Welch.

Welch had to dip into his fuel tank to catch Allen on the bike. Then he dipped deeper when he took off at the beginning of the run. Then a calf cramp about 12 miles into the run put Welch in deep something. He was forced to stop, stretch and fall back behind Devlin. But he was revived after diving into his special needs bag.

"I threw down some Aussie rubbish," laughs Welch. "Some dinosaurs from Ralph's. I had 10 strawberry and cream candies and was raring to go." A pause. "I'd love to get a split on that last 10K."

In the game of Ironman chess, sometimes the moves are so subtle no one seems to notice. But they're there. Letting Welch dictate the pace on the bike took that responsibility off Allen's shoulders. It also put his most dangerous competitor right where he wanted him most: smack dab in his sights. No worries like "Where is that guy?" of "How far back is he?"

Allen played the Ironman chess game to perfection for the third time in a row. But he also knows that only three people have ever run a sub-2:50 in Hawaii: Allen, Dave Scott... and Welch. Even though he had to stop and stretch for who knows how long this year, Welch still ran 2:48:10.

So don't count the young Aussie out, Ironman fans. He's learned a few lessons from the Ironmaster. Both Allen and Welch know that this year is history, that the next time around they'll start from scratch, that they'll be playing the-guy-who-makes-the-King-to-Queen's-Highway-move-first-wins game all over again.

it won't take Welch many moves to turn Checkmate into Check... Mate.

It starts slowly but can quickly — and totally — consume. One minute you're powerful and confident, all-knowing and in control. The next minute history is not only your major but your middle name. You're suddenly, without warning, a quivering shell.

Powerful? Not any more. In control? Sorry. He's been traded for an emotion to be named later. Confident? Connie left on the early bus. All-knowing? Replaced by his friend All Over.

When doubt creeps into the subconscious, fatigue and failure are usually waiting at the door, bags nearby, planning to stay for the night. And after six hours of hand-to-hand combat in the lava fields, three-time defending Gatorade Ironman Champion Mark Allen was about to succumb.

After arriving in Kona, Hawaii a week before the October 10 multisport championship of the world, Allen set aside part of each evening to visualize, to play out the upcoming race in his head. After all, no one likes surprises.

"I really try to go over the race in my mind," says Allen. "I go through every scenario. I saw myself racing Greg Welch [second in 1991] and I saw myself with Pauli Kiuru [fourth in 1991]. But I couldn't get this fear out of my mind that there was going to be somebody on the run who I considered stronger than me. At first I thought it would be Jeff Devlin [third in 1991], but it was never clear. I'd convince myself that I'd be all right, but I hadn't resolved that fear." Allen paused momentarily, thinking back. "It was interesting. The night before the race, all of a sudden Cristian Bustos' name came into my mind."

Allen had reason to fear Bustos, who won his first-ever marathon in Santiago, Chile in 2:19. That win got him a ticket to Frankfurt, Germany, where he ran a 2:16. At the Pucon Triathlon in Chile last January, Bustos came off the bike with Allen and put three-and-a-half minutes into him during the 10-mile run.

"In Chile, we came off the bike together," Allen remembers. "All I saw of him was his back disappearing in the distance."

October 10 dawned Ironman cool. Temperatures in the mid to high 80s, partly cloudy, no 50-mile-per-hour gusts anywhere. As the triathletes plunged into Kailua Bay, Allen stopped thinking about Bustos. He wasn't even sure if Bustos, last year's ninth-place finisher, had entered the race.

When the top swimmers emerged a little over 48 minutes later, the German, Wolfgang Dittrich, was the first out of the water and the first to leave the transition area on his bike. Right behind him was Australian Greg Welch, the guy Allen went head-to-head with for nine miles on the run the last time they met in Kona. Allen, swimming better than he has since college, was two minutes behind Welch.

So Mark, in all the scenarios you played out in your mind, did Greg Welch ever come out of the water two minutes ahead of you? Allen laughs. "There was no way in a million years that could happen. His swimming hasn't been as good as mine the last couple of races. I was stunned."

Right off the bat Allen had to play catch-up on the bike. He didn't bridge the gap until mile 20. At that point the group was led by Kiuru of Finland and included Welch, Allen, Dittrich and every press person in Hawaii with access to a motorcycle and a camera.

The entourage hammered north along the Queen Kaahumanu Highway, past Waikoloa and Kawaihae to the bike turnaround at the quaint island village of Hawi. It's a given in the triathlon world that on the way to or on the way back from Hawi the wind will swirl and the cyclists will whine, curse and slow to a crawl. It's one of the few certainties of life, like bears hanging out in the woods or Ross Perot wearing over-sized ear muffs. But for the first time in living memory, the wind in Hawi took the day off.

So did Erin Baker. And without the two-time Gatorade Ironman champion around, her long time rival Paula Newby-Fraser was left to fend for herself. Still, she didn't seem to have a problem finding her way without Baker around.

Opposite page: Mark Allen waited for second-place finisher Cristian Bustos at the finish line.

Above: Allen felt that someone strong and powerful would be with him at some point in the run, but he wasn't quite sure who it would be. It turned out to be Bustos, the pride of Chile.

Photos by Lois Schwartz

Newby-Fraser won her fifth Gatorade Ironman title by over 25 minutes, taking the lead in the bike with a blistering 4:56:34 split and then running a 3:05:24 marathon to put the race away.

"We haven't had weather like this since 1989," says Newby-Fraser. "And we may never see weather like this again. Before I retire, I wanted to go under nine hours. I just had a perfect day."

A perfect $31,000 day. Twenty-third overall, with the fastest swim (53:30), bike and run splits among the top 15 female finishers and a new course record (8:55:28) by over five minutes.

The men took advantage of the we-may-never-see-weather-like-this-again day, too. Out of the water not quite five minutes behind Wolfgang Dittrich, Bustos started the climb to Hawi two-and-a-half minutes down to the fab four of Kiuru, Allen, Welch and Dittrich.

The pace on the bike was intense, with Kiuru doing most of the pushing.

"Pauli hammered the bike," remembers Welch.

"Pauli seemed very confident," says Allen. "He looked like he could grind out that gear all day long. It seemed like he wanted to take something out of us on the bike." He did.

"In previous years it was too slow a ride," insists Kiuru. "I decided to push the pace."

Behind the lead pack, Bustos was making up ground in big chunks.

"I feel good on the hills," says Bustos in his broken English. "I was getting more close... more close."

"When I glanced at the leader board, I saw Cristian's name was there," says Allen. "The next thing I knew he was with us."

Cristian, were you surprised to catch the lead pack on the bike? "No," Bustos says solemnly. A pause, brown eyes sparkling. A big grin. "Not surprised... VERY surprised!"

Fifteen minutes later Jürgen Zäck of Germany joined the Ironman Express as it flew back down the headwindless Queen K Highway.

Along Alii Drive Zäck rode off of the front and put a minute on the chase group by the end of the ride. He was already out on the run by the time the others arrived. Bustos was quickly in and out of transition, followed by Kiuru, Allen, Welch and Dittrich.

Of that group, Allen was only worried about one person.

"Welchy didn't look himself," Allen admits. "He was spinning easily on the bike, but it didn't seem like he had any strength. I didn't think over the long haul that any of the other guys could put it together on the run like Cristian could. He was the one guy I was concerned about."

Allen ran off after Bustos, not feeling particularly good.

"It took me two miles to make up 15 seconds on Cristian," he says. "That's when I realized that he wasn't very tired from the bike ride."

"When you come up on most people from behind you're moving much faster," explains Allen. "If they try to match your pace when you catch up, usually they can't hold it very long. When I caught up to Cristian, he just looked at me out of the corner of his eye and decided that we must have been going way too slow, because he picked it up."

Put yourself in Bustos' racing flats. He'd never led a race as prestigious as the Gatorade Ironman before. Basically, he was waiting for his tour guide to show up.

"I tell myself I have 26 miles to go so be careful," says Bustos. "I wait for Allen...wait for Greg... nobody...nobody...what happened? I wait... wait... wait. Then Allen catch up. I listen to Allen. He not sound very good."

And Allen wasn't feeling much better. He'd spent his entire Ironday reacting to other people. Not exactly the way he envisioned things beforehand. First Welch packed up two minutes during the swim, forcing him to play catch-up. Then Kiuru continually hammered the bike, forcing Allen to ride maybe a little harder than he would have liked.

And now? Bustos was driving him right to the brink.

"For 10 miles I was holding on by the skin of my teeth," remembers Allen. "I was just wondering how soon I could drop out of the race and still save face. Maybe I could break an ankle or something. Anything to take the pain away. Cristian doesn't get intimidated… he doesn't give it up or crater like some of the other guys. He just goes. I wasn't sure if I could even finish the race. I was really starting to have my doubts."

Doubt is the vermin of the endurance athletes. It creeps around the edge of the subconscious before making its full frontal assault. Allen could feel the heat building up in his body. He knows what it's like to blow up at the Ironman. And now he was running shoulder-to-shoulder in the midday heat against a 2:16 marathoner who looked like he could go all day long.

"I tried a few little surges," Allen says, shaking his head. "But we were running way too fast. The pace was really uncomfortable. I thought to myself, 'This is too fast. I'm going to blow up.' Inside my body I felt the same sensation I had in the years when I've blown up. I thought, 'He's going to pull away and then I'll walk and catch a van back to town.'"

Bustos could sense that Allen was struggling.

"I'm thinking… wow… maybe win," he says. A long look skyward. A short pause. "I don't think so."

One-on-one racing evolves over time in a long race like the Ironman. One move, then another. Allen likes to test his opponent's resolve on Pay & Save Hill about nine miles in. With the wind at the runners' backs, the heat can be stifling.

Bustos didn't budge.

The stark nothingness of the lava fields awaits the runners after a left turn at the hill's summit. The crowds diminish and self-doubt flourishes. The cheering of the spectators along Alii Drive is a distant memory. That was miles ago. Now there are only telephone poles that go forever, aid stations that are too far apart, endless empty black lava and the sound of your feet hitting the scorched pavement. If

your inner resolve isn't rock solid, the lava fields will crack you like a peanut.

Ask Allen. He's been the crackee more times than he cares to remember. He knows the feeling. After years of crumbling to Dave Scott in these same lava fields, Allen has learned to use them to his advantage, to make them his friend. In a matter of a few miles, he went from potential crackee to cracker-in-waiting.

"I kept having to draw inside myself," confides Allen. "I had to find my own strength. Then, around 11 or 12 miles, I could feel the momentum shift."

If you sense that your opponent is starting to fall apart a little, the tendency is to move quickly and try to finish him off. Allen has learned not to rush things, to stay on pace and to let the other guy fall apart a little bit more.

Scott taught him well. Never go too early. Remain patient.

"If you surge and they stay with it, there goes your surge," says Allen. "You've wasted it. But if you wait, they're not only further down on their energy level… you've been resting."

Allen could sense that after 14 miles of hard running, Bustos could be had. On an upgrade between miles 14 and 15, Allen picked up the pace and Bustos fell off.

"People kept yelling at me 'You've got to make a move!'" remembers Allen. "But you really have to wait until the time is right. And then when you make the move you have to stay on it until the finish line."

Bustos tried to respond, but there was no way.

"I stayed a long time with Mark," he says proudly. "When feel bad, feel very, very bad. More slow, feel more comfortable." He stops and gestures with his hand. "Mark going… going… going. I thought 'Maybe catch Mark later.'"

Right. Like maybe next year. Allen's 2:42:18 marathon gave him a seven-minute cushion over Bustos at the end and a record-breaking overall time of 8:09:08.

"When I was running with Cristian I told myself, 'Look, why do you do well in races? Not by looking at anyone else. You

do well when you draw energy inside yourself,'" says Allen.

And have the self-confidence to put that energy to use.

"It's funny," he says. "But in a race of eight hours it usually comes down to one moment, to a few footsteps. It's a matter of knowing when to make those footsteps count."

1993: THE KILLING FIELDS

*"I was definitely worried.
No one knows how
to push my buttons
like Erin Baker."*

Paula Newby-Fraser

He lies on a cot, an IV replenishing a vein in his left arm. His breathing is slow and methodical. Chest in... chest out. The left eye is closed, the right at half mast. His quadriceps spasm sporadically, first the right, then the left. The white remnants of salty sweat surround his singlet and the top of each running shoe is coated with blood.

Mark Allen looks like he was just beaten up in an alley.

A prize fight leaves visible wounds. A lump under the eye, a swollen cheekbone, legs that wobble and cease to function, a gash on the forehead. The purpose of the game is to seek and destroy, and the one who inflicts the most damage wins.

The Gatorade Ironman is more subtle: 2.4 miles of swimming, 112 miles of cycling and 26.2 miles of running in the heat and wind of the Kona Coast. It seems like civilized torture, just a case of yuppie excess. But if you look close you can see beyond the veneer. The pain is there, and the blows are real.

Don't kid yourself. Up front where the rewards are huge, the demands and the pressure are immense. The purpose is to debilitate, to intimidate... to annihilate.

As the four-time defending champion, Allen was a moving target all day long. A moving target who dug so deep into his reserves, into his soul, that he had absolutely nothing left.

This page:
*Top: Paula Newby-Fraser running
toward her sixth title.*
*Bottom: Erin Baker took second to
Newby-Fraser for the third time.*

Opposite page:
*Top left: Wendy Ingraham, the top
female swimmer, finished fifth.*
*Middle left: Wolfgang Dittrich
of Germany on the bike.*
*Bottom left: Pauli Kiuru held the lead
over Mark Allen until they were on their
way out of the Natural Energy Lab.*
*Far right: Allen on his way to winning his fifth
Ironman title in a row.*

Photos by Lois Schwartz

THE JOKER'S WILD: GREG WELCH

BY KEN McALPINE

Opposite page: Greg Welch AKA Joker.
Photo by Melanie Carr

Above: Welch first burst onto the scene when he finished third behind Mark Allen and Dave Scott in 1989.
Photo by Rich Cruse

The paw is big and hairy and it's coming across the counter, demanding money. This presents two problems: One, this fuzzy mitt is attached to a beefy and increasingly strident Greek shopkeeper with a knife in his other hand, an attention-getting implement he was using moments ago to disembowel rolls. Two, Greg Welch and his two mates don't have any money. Spent it all at the pub.

Welch reckons this clearly explains how he and his mates ended up in a Sydney hamburger shop ordering food, oblivious to the basics of a cash-and-carry society.

"We forgot we left the pub because we were out of money," he says. "We would have stayed at the pub otherwise."

Faced with a single sensible option, they take it. Running down the street, shopkeeper and knife in hot pursuit, Welch drops his hamburger. Faced with a single sensible option, Welch stops and turns back. Once in the game, Welch is dogged.

"There was no way I was going to miss out on eating my hamburger," he says. Fortunately, at 5' 6", Welch is also short. He bends and scoops up the soggy patty just under the shopkeeper's swipe.

Eventually the cries of the shopkeeper die away in the distance. Welch and his companions hop a train home. The clacking and swaying after the excitement of the chase are too much. Welch spits up the hamburger and a goodly portion of beer in the middle of the train.

In the end, even the most sorely won prizes are temporary. The train clacks on. Welch's head, swinging loose, measures its beat.

It's October 1989, and an odd time for barfing. The Hawaii Ironman is a week away. Around the globe the world's best triathletes are chanting their mantras, spooning down strained cottage cheese and beating most pre-schoolers to bed, putting the final delicate touches on a season's worth of training.

Here in Australia, Welch is eyeballing his evening's excesses. Welch did train today — a hot, hilly beach run is what drove him and his mates to the pub in the first place. That speedwork with the shopkeeper was just icing on the cake.

A full-time construction worker, Welch will touch down in Hawaii and spend much of his time before the race oogling triathlon's elite — awe with sound basis given the fact that Welch hasn't swam more than two miles and rarely runs more than 15 miles in a day in preparation for this race.

He will place third behind Dave Scott and Mark Allen and put himself on the Ironman map.

1994: FANTASY ISLAND

Greg Welch pulled the Timex rep over and proudly showed him the messages he had typed into his new 100-lap watch. Two things he never, ever wanted to forget. One was for the love of his life: I love Sian. The other? It was for the fantasy of a lifetime: Win Ironman.

The gap went from 20 seconds to 12 in the blink of an eye. Welch didn't even need to look. He could hear the breathing, the applause, the "You da man!" shouts and that oh, so familiar duck-like foot strike.

It's hard to hide when you're sauntering through the lava fields wearing a matching peach-colored singlet and swimsuit. Dave Scott was so close Welch could damn near smell the guy. Look back? No way. Remember the first commandment from Racing 101? Thou shalt never look back. A definite sign of weakness, a message to the chaser that yes, there is a major concern.

No, the best response is to be oblivious, to ignore impending doom. "Who am I?" Welch scolded himself again and again, with Scott looming full frame in the rear-view mirror. "Who the hell am I?"

Paula Newby-Fraser would eventually have a similar discussion. Without her nemesis Erin Baker in the field, it appeared that her main competition would be herself. Karen Smyers, last year's fourth-place finisher, was pummeled at the start of the swim, lost her goggles and a precious four minutes to Newby-Fraser at the same time. Sue Latshaw, third in 1993, dropped out. So did last year's sixth-place finisher Heather Fuhr.

Smyers figured to be out of the water ahead of Newby-Fraser and then hoped to stay in front on the bike for as long as she could.

"I lost my goggles in the first 100 meters," remembers Smyers. "It was pretty brutal. That shot my game plan all to hell."

Sensing an early kill, Newby-Fraser passed Wendy Ingraham and Ute Meuckel of Germany early in the bike ride and jetted into the lead.

"I went too hard on the bike," insists Newby-Fraser. "The fluid wasn't settling in my stomach and I had to battle with myself psychologically all day long."

Could she will herself through the lava fields just one more time? This would be her 10th Gatorade Ironman. Wouldn't a seventh win be a great way to bow out?

Newby-Fraser knows better than anyone that lava fields don't offer even one ounce of forgiveness. Go too hard in one event and you pay in the next. Go easy on the bike and try to save energy for the run... and the sun, wind and humidity drain it all away.

"I don't know why it was such a tough day," continues Newby-Fraser. "I worked hard on the swim, and I had a terrific swim and bike ride. But I paid for it in the run."

With interest. She felt awful running up the hill from the Kona Surf, horrible as she dropped down into the pit and even worse as she moved down Alii Drive past the crowds of downtown Kailua-Kona.

"I felt like there was too much energy on Alii Drive," she recalls. "When I got out of town, I stopped at an aid station on the highway and had a talk with myself. 'Come on, get it together,' I said. 'I'm having a hard day... everyone has had a hard day.'" When she started running again, she never stopped.

"It's not fun to have someone like Karen Smyers coming up from behind," she says.

Smyers has good come-from-behind credentials: A 2:42 PR in the marathon and the type of tenacity that will eventually put her in

Above, top: Dave Scott hadn't raced the Ironman in five years. At the age of 40, he finished second to Greg Welch.
Above, bottom: Paula Newby-Fraser zeroes in on win number seven.
Photos by Lois Schwartz

the Gatorade Ironman winner's circle. The tough part is that, if she had had her normal swim, the 12-minute deficit she faced off the bike might have been eight minutes. Then, when she cut off four in the early miles of the run, she could have been in the hunt.

The big word is *if*.

"With about four miles to go, I was seven minutes back," remembers Smyers. "I passed both Scott Tinley and Pauli Kiuru during the run, and that made me realize that you never put this race in the bag. It keeps you humble. You always have to dig so deep."

Last year, Newby-Fraser came into the race undertrained in the run because of injuries and dug into her soul to get her sixth win. This year, Newby-Fraser had to reach inside herself once again to get win number seven.

"I kept talking to myself," she says. "Karen was catching me, but I didn't think she was capable of making up that much time."

She wasn't. Newby-Fraser held onto her almost-eight-minute cushion, talking to herself the whole way in. Asked about coming back in 1995 for win number eight, Newby-Fraser shook her head.

"Mentally, I don't know if I can make those kinds of sacrifices. I have to put so much of my life on hold for this race. I'd like to come back and do the race again, but I don't know if I'll make the same kind of commitment."

Welch's commitment to Ironman this year has been six solid months of race-specific training. And, after 2.4 miles of swimming in a blender, 112 miles of cycling in a wind tunnel and 16 miles of running in a sauna, he discovered all that was only a precursor, an appetizer, a cocktail weenie, a lowly warm-up for the gut-check main course. Now, with 10 miles to go, in 95-degree heat, with the six-time winner of the Gatorade Ironman practically flatting the backs of his racing shoes, Welch was being asked to ante up, to dig down to a place he had never been before.

"I could feel him drawing in on me," he says. "I thought, 'I've got to get rid of this guy.' Dave knows how to race this race. Forget that Dave Scott is 40. It doesn't mat-

ter if he is 40 or 50. He looked awesome."

Dave Scott? What is this, Triassic Park? The last time Scott won in Kona, Ronald Reagan was still President and O.J. Simpson was a happily married man. Scott had been away from the Big Island for five full years, and people were giving better odds on Sister Madonna Buder racing in a Fernanda Keller G-string than on The Man ending up in the same zip code as the leaders.

But there he was. Everyone had their tricked-out rides in the rack with heart monitors and in-your-palm shifters, and when Scott rolled his 26" Carbonframe into the bike corral on Friday afternoon, many in attendance had to stifle a laugh. The shifters were on the downtube. Heart monitor? The guy didn't even have a bike computer. The minimalist in action.

At the pre-race press conference, Pauli Kiuru, last year's second-place finisher, predicted victory and a 2:45 marathon. Scott mentioned that when he last raced Welch in Orange County earlier that summer, he was worried about getting lapped. He was doing this race for himself and his family.

"My kids know I have a racing bike, but they've never seen me use it," Scott explains at the press conference.

They have now. He came out of the water in 51:48, two minutes down on Rip Esselstyn, Nick Croft and Alec Rukosuev and 1:30 down on Welch. The only way he has ever raced this race is from the front. Early on, he went by Mike Pigg like he was anchored in cement.

"Contrary to what people have said, Mark [Allen] and I always had the fastest bike splits here," insists Scott. "I never felt like I was a terrible slouch on the bike."

He was proving to be a terrific slouch. "As I moved up in the field, I visualized that I was leading the race with Greg and Kenny [Glah], " he says.

"I rode up the first hill with Dave," remembers Chuckie V. "Then he took off."

"I don't know how far I can go," says Scott at the pre-race press conference. "But I know I'm as fit as I've ever been."

How did he get that fit? His wife, Anna, booted him from his Boulder home and insisted that he move to Steamboat Springs for about a month to train.

"I felt guilty for about 48 hours," he grins. "It was the first time since the mid-1980s that I could focus totally on my training. I knew after that month that I was more fit on the bike climbing-wise than I had been in my entire career."

Obviously. He caught the leaders past Kawaihae, and he was in a group with just Glah and Welch.

"When I caught Greg and Kenny, I said to myself, 'I'm here, I'm on... Now let's be patient.' My confidence soared."

As usual, Jürgen Zäck led the chase pack. But the bike course record holder found it more difficult to ride his way through the field than in years past.

"I had to use a lot more energy to get away," he recalls. "The conditions were much harder."

Swirling winds buffeted the cyclists coming and going. With the press vehicle escort a thing of the past, bike times were five to 10 minutes slower for many of the leaders. Zäck knew that the only way for him to win was to punish the good runners on the bike and take their running legs away. He also knew that he would pay the piper when he got off the bike.

Zäck caught Glah, Scott, and Welch before the turnaround at Hawi and then, after the turn, he and Glah scorched the downhill back to Kawaihae.

"Ken said to me, 'Let's go, Jürgen,'" remembers Zäck. "I said, 'Okay, Ken.'"

In years past, Welch might have chased. But last year he was injured a week before leaving for Kona and was forced to watch the race from the sidelines.

"I thought about what I learned from watching last year," says Welch. "Jürgen likes to do his thing off the front. 'I'm not going to be suckered into that,' I said to myself. 'I want to have a good run.' The idea is to win the race... not the bike ride. Mark Allen told me to relax and to go with my instincts. 'Go when you want to go,' he told me. 'Be patient.'"

Back on the Queen K Highway the two twosomes, Zäck and Glah and Scott and Welch, started one minute apart and ended up about two minutes apart with 10 miles to go.

Off the bike first, Glah quickly added to his lead, hammered the first few miles and led through the Timex Prime at the Hot Corner seven miles into the run.

Scott didn't feel great early in the run.

"I was stiff going into the pit," says Scott. "Both Peter and Greg went by me."

Back on Alii Drive, Scott started to loosen up. "Jürgen and Kenny were coming back," he remembers.

Glah's heart monitor was telling him that his heart rate was dropping. "I didn't take in enough calories," says Glah. "A low heart rate means my blood sugar level was way too low."

Welch caught Glah just past eight miles.

"I said, 'Nice bike ride,'" remembers Welch. "Kenny said, 'This is where the race begins.'"

"I got on his shoulder, but I wasn't going to run hard up the hill on Palani Road," insists Glah. "Those guys had to be flying to make up two minutes on me in eight miles. I kept thinking, 'He's only gone sub-2:50 here once.' People come back. When Dave came by me he said, 'Be patient.'"

Words to live by if your name is Dave Scott. Now out on his turf, the Queen Kaahumanu Highway, Scott was moving in for the kill. In 1984 and 1987, he passed a fading Mark Allen on this very same stretch of barren nothingness to become Mr. October and the Lord of the Lava. Welch appeared vulnerable. In both 1991 and 1992, he had stretches where he was forced to walk. It is one thing to come off the bike in 10th place and run a sub-2:50 marathon to finish in the top five. It is quite another to do it with a chopper overhead, cameras in your face and a natural-born killer on your heels.

"I told myself, 'Be patient... be patient," remembers Scott. "I felt the best place to make a move was on the Natural Energy Lab downhill. I ran very hard there."

The lead shrank from 20 seconds to 12. With his target just up the road, Scott couldn't close the gap any further.

"Coming back out of the energy lab, I felt weary. His lead went from 20 to 40 to 52 seconds," he recalls. "I didn't feel dreadful... but I didn't feel crisp, either."

Welch could feel his momentum slipping

Above: "Who am I?" Greg Welch scolded himself while Dave Scott loomed full-frame in the rear-view mirror. "Who the hell am I?"
Opposite page: Paula Newby-Fraser wins her fourth title in a row. Photos by Lois Schwartz

away. "When Dave got to within 12 seconds, I knew that I really had to dig," says Welch. "I said, 'If you don't dig now, you never will. You can do anything you want to do.'"

After taking the right turn out of the lab, he finally allowed himself a quick glance back. He smiled and bounded to his toes.

On his seventh try, just like Allen, he knew his fantasy was coming true, and the biggest race in the triathlon galaxy was finally his.

"I've measured it," Welch admits. "After you come out of the Natural Energy Lab, it's exactly 10.67 kilometers to the finish. I knew I could do that."

Behind him, Scott was content. He finished four minutes back of Welch with an impressive 8:24:32. As Scott ran toward town, he turned to *Competitor* photographer Lois Schwartz and her motorcycle driver John Smith.

"So what do you think?" he asks.

"Unbelievable, Dave," says Smith.

"Yeah, I think I raised a few eyebrows here today," Scott replies.

He took the turn at the top of Palani Road and waved to his boys, Ryan and Drew. Ryan was only a baby and Drew wasn't born when their daddy lost to Allen way back in 1989 in one of the greatest races of all time. On this day, Ryan and Drew got to watch their daddy push someone to the brink of their endurance. Now they know what Daddy does.

As the sun rises
The Iron Hopefuls are enveloped
In a spectacular cocoon of blue.
This is their day,
Their day to become an Ironman.

Photo by Tracy Frankel

IRON HEART

The Ironman from the very beginning has been about changing perceptions of what the human body can accomplish and overcome. There were many doubters: 2.4, 112 and 26.2 all in one day? Impossible!

How wrong they were.

So when amputees Pat Griskus, Jim MacLaren, Paul Martin and Willie Stewart came to the Big Island the thought was why not? When Dick Hoyt wondered about pulling his son Rick in a raft, putting him on the handlebars for the bike ride and using a modified Baby Jogger for the run, there was little hesitation. Years earlier Dick had been told to institutionalize his son Rick. He refused. Instead they became an amazing team that finished the Ironman in style.

If someone with two arms and two legs can do it, why can't someone who happens to be missing a limb and may be using a prosthetic instead? Ironman is all about going beyond the boundaries, about never saying never. Jim MacLaren became the Babe Ruth of amputee athletes when he went 10:42 in Kona.

When Dr. Jon Franks came to Hawaii in 1992 to race the Ironman using a handcycle for the bike and a racing chair for the run, the question became can he make the cutoff times? The Ironman created a level playing field for wheelchair bound athletes. Make the cutoff times for the swim, the bike and the run and you're an Ironman. Franks didn't make the cutoff time on the bike and, in his first two attempts in Kona, neither did Australia's John MacLean. But in 1987, MacLean made the bike and the run cutoff in his third try and then former Navy SEAL Carlos Moleda took it to the next level. He went 10:55 in 1998, a time that would have won the Ironman overall in 1978 and 1979. Disabled? Not quite.

"When I'm racing the Ironman I feel free," says Carlos Moleda. "Out in the lava fields I'm an athlete just like everyone else."

It is a simple formula.
One heart
One goal
One leg
No limits.

Photo by Robert Oliver

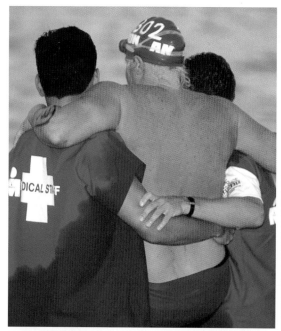

Top left: Randy "The Animal" Cadell, who was paralyzed, went on to become a top handcycle athlete and a perennial contender in Kona. In February 2005, Cadell was killed when he was hit by a car while out training. Photo by Robert Oliver

Top middle: Leandro Romans of Argentina went 14:11:36 in 1996 despite missing a leg. Photo by Lois Schwartz

Top right: Jim MacLaren set the course record for lower leg amputees with a 10:42 in 1989. Unbelievably, he was hit by a truck during a race in California in 1993 and became a quadriplegic. Photo by Lois Schwartz

Middle left: In 1997, on his third try, John MacLean became the first handcycle division athlete to officially complete the Ironman when he went 12:21:30. Photo by Lois Schwartz

Bottom left: In 2005, Jon "Blazeman" Blais was the first person to finish the Ironman with ALS, Lou Gehrig's Disease. He passed away at the age of 35 on May 27, 2007. Photo by John Segesta

Bottom right: Dick Hoyt (right) races with his son Rick (left). Team Hoyt had their best race in 1989 when Dick pulled, carried and pushed his son Rick 140.6 miles in 14:26:04. Photo by Lois Schwartz

Top left: An amputee Ironman hopeful takes a break during the marathon.
Top middle: Sarah Reinertsen, an above knee amputee, missed the bike cutoff in 2004, but came back to take care of her Unfinished Business in 2005. Photo by Rich Cruse
Top right: Major David Rozelle finished in 2006. Photo by Tim Mantoani
Middle left: Australia's John MacLean on the marathon course.

Bottom left: Former Navy SEAL Carlos Moleda, the four-time handcycle division champion and Ironman course record holder.
Bottom middle: Scott Rigsby became the first double below knee amputee to finish the Ironman in 2007. Photo by Rich Cruse
Bottom right: Marc Herremans of Belgium was sixth overall in the 2001 Ironman. The next winter he was in a bike crash and was paralyzed. Herremans came back to Kona to compete in and to eventually win the handcycle division. Photo by Robert Oliver

You are surrounded,
Yet so alone.
Alone to plan and dream
To hope and pray.

The day to come
Will have it all.
The highest highs
And the lowest lows.

The fact that it's hard
Is what makes it special.
It's also what makes it the Ironman.

Photo by Lois Schwartz

105

1995: MISSION IMPOSSIBLE

Above: The whole world was watching as Paula Newby-Fraser, The Queen of Kona, started to come apart.

Right: Thomas Hellriegel went by Mark Allen (pictured) like a jet and all Allen could do was hope the lead didn't get too big.

Photos by Lois Schwartz

The roar of the crowd crescendoed as the NBC helicopter spun into view. Puffy clouds sprinkled the heavens. Tim Twardzik of Mrs. T's Pierogies fame stood among the cheering throng massed at the finish line and scanned Alii Drive for the first sign of the victor. The announcement had already been made. Paula Newby-Fraser, the seven-time winner of the Gatorade Ironman, was about to win number eight.

Twardzik, one of Newby-Fraser's long-time friends and sponsors, would get to do the honors this year. After the announcement, Race Director Sharron Ackles turned to Twardzik and   handed him the lei that traditionally goes to the first male and female finisher.

"She   handed   me   the   lei   and   said, 'Congratulations,'" recalls Twardzik.

Moments later the world came crashing down.

"I was standing with Paul Huddle [Newby-Fraser's fiancé], when Ken Murrah from NBC came sprinting up," Twardzik remembers. "He yells, 'Karen Smyers has passed Paula! Karen's going to win this race!' I was in shock. All of a sudden I felt empty."

Empty or not, he knew what he had to do. Twardzik made eye contact with Race Director Ackles, but not a word was spoken. He took the lei and handed it silently back to Ackles. On this particular day it belonged to Karen Smyers.

Kona once belonged to Mark Allen. Between 1989 and 1993, he won the Gatorade Ironman each and every time. But this is an MTV-short-attention-span world of three-second sound bites. Allen took 1994 off so that he could recharge and spend some quality time with wife Julie and son Mats. In his absence, Greg Welch won the 1994 Ironman and Allen became a name from the past.

When Allen reappeared on race day 1995, he was wearing a blue one-piece swimsuit that he felt could save him a second every hundred meters in the swim. With the best men's field ever assembled and so much at stake — and at the age of 37 — Allen was

Above: It was his last Ironman and he was 13 minutes down with 26.2 miles to go. Five time champion Mark Allen had to pick up 30 seconds every single mile. When he did, it became the greatest comeback in Ironman history and would be the equivalent of Ted Williams hitting a home run in his last time at bat.
Photos by Lois Schwartz

willing to seize every advantage as he approached what many thought would be his last Iron-go-round in Kona. His "girly-man" outfit, as he called it, attracted the attention of top German triathlete Jürgen Zäck.

Zäck shook his head when he saw the getup. "Nice suit," he laughs.

Nice swim, Karen. Last year, Smyers was literally mugged in the mass swim start, losing her goggles and four minutes to Newby-Fraser. Out of sight, out of mind... Newby-Fraser won wire-to-wire. This year they came out of the water virtually together.

"I'm in the best shape of my life," Newby-Fraser insisted in mid-September. "I've probably doubled my mileage over other years."

To prove her dominance, Newby-Fraser had already won Ironman races in both Lanzarote and Germany earlier in the summer. To prove she's not crazy, on the Thursday before the race she made it clear that this would be her last one in Kona.

"This is my 27th Ironman, and my 11th here in Kona," she says. "This one is for me alone. I want to walk away feeling like I've done myself justice and walk away with a really good feeling."

As the bike ride heated up, Newby-Fraser could feel the pressure. Smyers, one of the premier short-distance triathletes in the world and a runner with sub-2:45 marathon credentials, was still right on her.

The women's field that confronted Newby-Fraser was a strong one. Two-time Nice champion and Ironrookie Isabelle Mouthon from France, always tough Sue Latshaw and last year's third-place finisher Fernanda Keller from Brazil were all fit and fired up. They needed to be — they were facing one of the toughest days in the history of the event.

At 6:30 in the morning, World Triathlon Corporation President David Yates received

a call. It was Rich Havens, the gentleman responsible for hanging banners in their appropriate places.

"David, we've got a problem," warns Havens. "The wind is howling out here on the course. There's no way I can hang the banners."

Hanging tough for the men were Greg Welch, Mark Allen, Rainer Mueller, Pauli Kiuru, Tim DeBoom, Rob Barel, Chuckie V and Cameron Widoff. They were in the lead pack, facing 45-mile-per-hour gusts out towards Hapuna on the Queen Kaahumanu Highway.

"There were 10-15 guys there, and I was assessing the situation," remembers Mark Allen. "I'd heard all the horror stories from the European Ironman where the Germans went off the front and put so much time on the field. I started looking around. There's a German, another German, a Holland guy, an Australian... there are two guys missing here."

Just then Jürgen Zäck, the bike course record holder, made his presence known.

"Here comes Jürgen, and my heart rate goes up 20 beats," continues Allen. "Then here comes someone else, Thomas Hellriegel. I didn't really get a chance to look at him. All of a sudden he and Jürgen were gone."

Part of the German army, 24-year-old Hellriegel spent the summer establishing a triathlon beachhead for himself. After winning in Lanzarote and finishing second at the European Ironman in Germany, he flew to Rome to win the Military Olympic Distance World Championships two weeks before Hawaii.

Hellriegel's style on the bike is all his own.

"I don't like waiting in a group," he says with a shrug. "I go out as hard as I can the whole time."

When asked if he thought about riding with his fellow countrymen Holger Lorenz or

Right: Paula Newby-Fraser had over 11 minutes on Karen Smyers at the end of the bike ride. But with just a few hundred yards to go in the marathon, her torrid pace caught up with her and she collapsed.
Photo by Rich Cruse

Jürgen Zäck, Hellriegel responds, "I don't think Jürgen wanted to ride with me."

The point is, no one could ride with him. With the wind in their faces, the chase pack averaged a tough 13-14 miles per hour on roads where they would normally be going 25.

By the turnaround in Hawi, Hellriegel had 3:20 on Zäck and 6:20 on the chase group.

"I figured I might be able to give up 6-8 minutes to Thomas during the bike," admits Allen. "He had that by the turn-around."

Newby-Fraser was pulling a Hellriegel on the women's field. After dropping Smyers, she proceeded to add to her lead with each mile.

"Mark Allen and I rode 40 miles out on the course earlier in the week," she says. "The wind was probably as bad, but I hardly noticed. I felt great on the bike. Frankly, it seemed easy."

How easy? On the way to Hawi she caught some of the top male pros, Alec Rukosuev and Ray Browning. She extended her lead after the turnaround. By the time she returned to Kona, her gap on Smyers was approaching 12 minutes.

"I thought I was riding well," says Smyers. "But Paula just kept getting further and further away."

As Hellriegel's lead advanced into the teens, Allen and the chase group could do nothing more than hope the torrid pace had at least taken something from the leader's legs.

Simon Lessing, the world's top male short-distance triathlete, was in town spectating. His assessment of Hellriegel, the runner, was less than good news for the chasers.

"I trained with him in South Africa," says Lessing. "He runs very well. And he trains in the Canary Islands, so he's used to the heat."

Thirteen minutes, 31 seconds. That's how big a lead Hellriegel had on the chase pack off the bike. Someone in that group would

109

have to outrun him by 30 seconds per mile to win the race. If Hellriegel could piece together a three-hour marathon, Welch, Allen or Rainer Mueller would have to run sub-2:47 to win. Red Barber, the Old Dodger broadcaster, would call that sittin' in the cat-bird seat.

"I thought we'd be about eight minutes back," says Welch. "I didn't know it had gotten to 12 or 13."

Not one to fluster, Hellriegel took off confidently.

"I did not want to go out too fast," he says. "I knew when the group started to run they would go out very fast. I thought maybe they would die in the end."

Allen spends a fair amount of his time addressing groups about taking challenges, about facing their fears. He often uses a visualization technique where he tells the athlete to concentrate on the pain, to imagine opening a door, facing that pain, dealing with it and then moving on. Early in the run, he had to dig down to a place very few people could ever go, a place where doubt, pain and fear simply do not exist. From the first

step of the marathon, Allen was a man on a mission.

"I had 12 minutes on Dave Scott back in 1984," recalls Allen. "But I was polite enough to start walking so he could catch me. I'm not saying the Germans aren't polite, but Thomas was running very fast."

So was Smyers. She started to slice and dice Newby-Fraser's off-the-bike lead almost immediately. With a cloud cover overhead, Smyers quickly shook off the effects of the hard ride. Last year, she had a similar deficit to overcome and came up far short. This year, Smyers looked leaner than ever.

"You don't want to be carrying any extra baggage in the lava fields," she points out.

Smyers checked her baggage at the door and headed out on the express train to the turnaround.

Still in control, Newby-Fraser was starting to feel the heat.

"Karen put on enough pressure to the point where I lost my focus and my center," admits Newby-Fraser.

As if Smyers wasn't a big enough problem, an aid station volunteer inadvertently flattened the Queen of Kona at about mile 21.

"I was flat on my back on the ground," Newby-Fraser remembers. "I didn't think much about it. I just got up and got going. I thought I'd better keep moving."

Smyers certainly was. She was eating up 30 seconds per mile, but it still looked like Newby-Fraser would be able to hang on for her third Ironman title of the year.

"I saw Karen with about three miles to go," remembers Smyer's husband Mike King, who was also racing. "She was still 2:05 down, meaning she had to make up 40 seconds per mile. Not impossible... but..."

The rest goes without saying — and highly unlikely. The veteran Newby-Fraser against third-year starter Smyers. A substantial lead, and not much real estate left.

But panic is a strange bedfellow. It whispers untruths into accepting ears. "You

don't need to drink," it tells you. "Just get to the top of Palani Hill and you're in," it insists.

"It's my own fault," admits Newby-Fraser. "It was a total rookie mistake. I know better. At the end of the race I had a full container of Carbo Burst that I didn't use. I ran past the aid stations. Instead of doing this race for myself, I started listening to other people. I know I should have stopped for 5-10 seconds at the aid stations. I know I should have used my Carbo Burst." Here she pauses, "But I didn't."

"When I saw Karen I remembered what Scott Molina yelled at her when she won the 1990 World Championship," remembers King. "You gotta want it."

Smyers caught a staggering Newby-Fraser just before she made the right turn onto Alii Drive, at most 300 yards from the finish.

"Plenty of room," laughs Smyers. Her 3:05:20 marathon was the second fastest ever, behind only Erin Baker's 3:04:13 in 1990. Newby-Fraser, out on her feet, sat down on a curb. Like a boxer who has just been smacked upside the head, she waited, hoping to regain her composure. After removing her shoes and getting some fluids and a water-bucket shower, Newby-Fraser showed her class by walking the last few hundred yards to the finish line 20 minutes later.

"I thought I was going to die out there," admits Newby-Fraser. "I was hoping that all I had to do was get to the top of Palani Drive and the rest would be downhill. It didn't quite work out that way. It proves once again that this race is never over 'til it's over."

Ask Thomas Hellriegel. He was running a sub-three-hour marathon, but he was still losing over 30 seconds per mile to a driven Mark Allen. By mile 13, Allen had disposed of Greg Welch, Cameron Widoff ("The first guy with dreadlocks I've ever raced against," says Allen), Rainer Mueller and Jürgen Zäck.

The lead was 4:10 at mile 16.

"I had to have absolute trust in my power and my ability to just continue to stay on the pace," insists Allen. "I could never once have an ounce of doubt about what I was doing out there." What he was doing out there was comparable to hitting a grand slam in the bottom of the ninth to win the seventh game of the World Series. In the glare of the media, with the NBC helicopter hovering overhead, he never faltered.

"When Thomas kept gaining ground on us during the bike, I had to make an executive decision," remembers Allen. "Do you panic and chase, or do you stay where you're at and get completely ready to have the run of your life."

The choice was obvious. He took the curtain and had the run of his life.

His mission was to drive his body to the very brink of destruction, if need be, while driving his opposition into collapse. Hellriegel was not cooperating.

"In the Natural Energy Lab, here comes the man I've never seen," says Allen. "I didn't think he was looking bad. When I came out of the energy lab, I told myself 'You've got to go NOW!'"

If Hellriegel felt pressure, he has a weird way of showing it. When Allen eventually caught him at 23 miles, Hellriegel surged back by him. Not your typical Kona rookie.

"I thought maybe Mark Allen would get tired," says Hellriegel. "I tried to stay with him, but he was too strong."

After a tough bike ride, Allen ran an amazing 2:42:09 marathon. Hellriegel ran 2:58:05... and lost. It's one thing to be off the front and run a fast marathon. It's another to HAVE to run 2:42 to win the race. If Allen had run 2:44.34, Hellriegel would have been the new King of Kona.

"This was special, my most satisfying win ever," says Allen. "I feel like I graduated this year."

With honors, big guy. If this turns out to be your last Ironman, if we never see you racing on the Kona Coast again, you left us with a memory we will never, ever forget.

They are denizens of the dark.
They understand
The key to solving the
Ironman puzzle is simple.
To win is to finish...
And to finish is to win.

Photo by Robert Oliver

IRON RIVALS

It was a simple request, really. I asked Mark Allen in mid summer 1989 if I could get a photo with him and Dave Scott for the cover of our pre-Ironman issue of Competitor magazine.

"Sure, no problem," said Allen. "Just have Dave fly out here to Boulder, Colorado and I'd be happy to do the shoot."

My next call was to Scott. Would he go to Boulder for the shoot?

"I'd be happy to do it," said 'The Man.' "Just have Mark come here to Davis, California."

Hmmmm. Obviously, I wasn't making much progress. So I did the next best thing. I hired photographer Dave Epperson and he took the same backdrop, drove to Colorado, drove to Davis and created our Showdown on the Kona Coast cover.

The following year, we put Paula Newby-Fraser and her arch rival Erin Baker in a studio for a photo shoot together in March, before the build up of pre-Ironman anxiety I thought. Wrongo. The tension between the two was thick even seven months before race day.

Over the years, we shot Allen with Greg Welch, Newby-Fraser with Karen Smyers, and Luc Van Lierde with Peter Reid. Since übercyclist Jürgen Zäck of Germany is an equal opportunity destroyer, we shot him as Zorro because he didn't have one particular rival. He basically wanted to leave his mark on everyone.

"I need to take the run out of the runner's legs," was his rationale. And he did just that.

The Iron Rivalries created a thread that winds its way through the history of Ironman and links athletes together forever. Kathleen McCartney and Julie Moss have become one because of the dramatic events of February 1982. The John Dunbar vs. Gordon Haller rematch of 1979 came to a screeching halt when a tavern owner from Southern California named Tom Warren throttled both of them. Scott Tinley and Dave Scott finished one-two in February 1982, October 1982, 1983 and 1984. Scott won three and Tinley one. The closest race in Ironman history? The 1983 race where Tinley finished 33 seconds back.

The Allen and Scott rivalry was born in 1984 when Scott roared from way off the pace to catch Allen on the Queen K Highway. Scott beat Allen in 1986 and again in 1987. In 1989, their rivalry would lead to the greatest race in Ironman history.

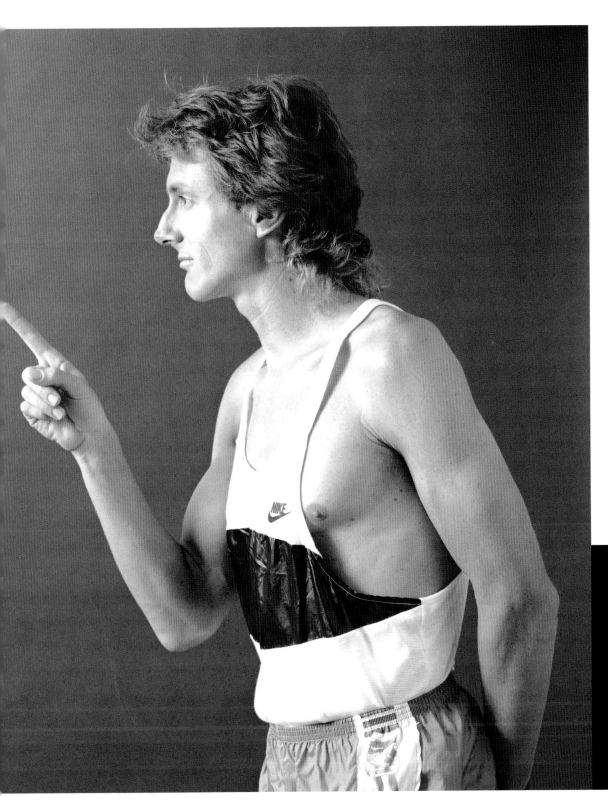

In 1989, after Mark Allen and
Dave Scott refused to travel for a photo
shoot, crack photographer
Dave Epperson first drove to Davis,
California to shoot Scott and then on to
Boulder, Colorado to shoot Allen. The pho-
tos were then put together for the dramatic
pre-Ironman Shootout on
the Kona Coast cover of Competitor
Magazine. Photo by Robert Oliver

IRON RIVALS

From left to right, top and bottom:

"No one pushes my buttons like Erin Baker (left)," says Paula Newby-Fraser (right). When they went to the starting line in the late 1980s and early 1990s, there was little doubt that one of the two would win. Photo by Melanie Carr

Below: Top cyclist Jürgen Zäck of Germany isn't the type of guy to have a rivalry with anyone in particular. He wants to leave the mark of Zäck on the entire pro field. "I want to make the good runners work hard on the bike," he says. And he always does. Photo by Tim Mantoani

Lori Bowden (left), Wendy Ingraham (center) and Heather Fuhr (right) were hard core rivals on the race course. But once the Ironman was over, the Spice Girls knew how to have a good time. Photo by Sean Arbabi

Between 1990 and 1993, Mark Allen's most feared rival was another great runner, Australia's Greg Welch. Photo by Melanie Carr

In 1998 Peter Reid (right) won and Luc Van Lierde (left) took second. In 1999, Van Lierde won with Reid second. Before the 2000 race, we anticipated "The Shootout on the Kona Coast". Photo by Tim Mantoani

Two Queens... one crown: Before the 1996 Ironman, seven-time champion Paula Newby-Fraser (left) and 1995 champion Karen Smyers posed together. Photo by Tim Mantoani

Going into the 2005 Ironman, there was a new kid on the block. Short course specialist and Olympic Silver Medalist Michellie Jones was coming to Kona for the very first time and going head-to-head with five time Ironman champion Natascha Badmann. Photo by Tim Mantoani

After the 2006 Ironman, a war of words between the first place finisher Normann Stadler and second place finisher Chris McCormack helped light the fire under this hot new rivalry. It didn't hurt that there seemed to be a genuine dislike between the two and the margin of victory that year was only 71 seconds. Photos by John Segesta

COVER STORY

Triathlon was a brand new addition to the endurance sports landscape in the late 1970s. By the early 1980s, though, *The Running News* of San Diego adapted to the phenomenon by changing its name to *Running and Triathlon News* (right). Publisher, editor and photographer Mike Plant was sold on the drama he witnessed each October on the Kona Coast of Hawaii and the growth potential for this new sport. He first learned of the event from his friend Bob Babbitt, who became one of Plant's writers and editors.

In 1987, when *Running and Triathlon News* closed down, Bob Babbitt and Lois Schwartz created *Competitor Magazine*, which focused on the Ironman and the athletes who helped to make the event so unique.

The Ironman Triathlon World Championship is showcased on these pages through the covers of *Running and Triathlon News* — 1982 through 1986 — and then *Competitor Magazine* — 1987 through 2007 (below). The idea of a cover photo is to freeze a special moment for eternity. The Ironman is blessed with 30 years of those indelible moments.

" You need to respect
the weather conditions here.
You have to know they are
stronger than you are.
When you believe you can
beat the wind... you lose."

Two-time Ironman Champion
Luc Van Lierde

Photo by Robert Oliver

1996: COOL HAND LUC

One king was showing. They all thought the other was face down in front of him. To call or not to call? Paul Newman as Cool Hand Luke. The other inmates in shackles and stripes argued about the merits of staying in or folding. Luke's facial expression never, ever changed.

"Kick a buck," he'd counter anytime someone would doubt him and his hand. "Kick a buck."

Finally, the price got too steep. He had scared them all off one at a time. As Luke pulled the pot towards him, the others scrambled to find the other king in his hand.

They never did. Nothing matched. Luke had bluffed... and won.

"You've got nuthin' Luke!" they yelled. "Absolutely nuthin'!" Luke smiled that "tell-me-something-I-don't-know" smile and piled up the bills.

"Sometimes nuthin' can be a real cool hand."

Flash forward 30 years. In Kona, on the Big Island, Luc Van Lierde of Belgium had nuthin.' No track record, no Ironman experience, no history, absolutely no expectations. No European had ever won the Ironman. Van Lierde had never even run a marathon before.

But Cool Hand Luke and Luc Van Lierde shared more than a name. They both sported number 37, Luke on his state-issue prison fatigues, Luc in magic-marker on every limb. And they're both absolutely fearless.

This summer was a great one for the often-injured Belgian star. He had a win in Nice, a win in Hungary at the European Championships, a second place in Muncie at the Long Distance World Championships and another second in Cleveland at the Olympic Distance World Championships. It makes for an impressive resumé, and it should have made for a lot of pre-race speculation.

It was his first time to the Big Dance, but you'd never know it. Even with three minutes in the box for drafting, Cool Hand Luc Van Lierde (#37) of Belgium still ran down Germany's Thomas Hellriegel (#2) and became the first male Iron Rookie to win his debut since Dave Scott in 1980. He also set a new course record of 8:04:08.
Photo by Rich Cruse

But Luc had never been to the Big Dance in Hawaii before. Resumes are nice, but in Hawaii they aren't usually worth the paper they are printed on. Tiki torch fodder. Volcano droppings. Lava slop. Speed, endurance and potential are just cards dealt from the middle of the deck. It's what you ante up come Ironday that ultimately matters.

A Night in the Box

After coming out of the water behind Wolfgang Dittrich and in the same time zone as Greg Welch, Cameron Widoff, Peter Reid, Kenny Glah and Tim DeBoom, 27-year-old Ironman rookie Luc Van Lierde set off in hot pursuit of Dittrich. Last year, the leaders were humbled by a blast furnace of 40-50 mph winds along the Queen K Highway that slowed them to a torturous crawl. They were more worried about staying upright than Bob Dole.

This year, the quaint seaside town of Hawi was eerily silent. The trees and brush, usually stooped over like a liquored-up, fez-sporting 70-year-old Shriner from their constant battle with the mumuku winds, stood surprisingly proud and tall on this late fall afternoon. Hot, but not my-skin-is-melting hot. Very little wind. If last year's Ironman was Howard Stern, this year's was Rush Limbaugh. This Ironman would be as different from last year's as nature could make it. Forget survival. Forget the wind tunnel. This year, it was crank-up-the-turbochargers and get it on.

Dittrich of Germany hadn't raced here since 1993. A knee problem kept him out of Kailua Bay and off the island. This year, however, the elder statesman of the German onslaught rode point for most of the trip to Hawi. Behind him were countrymen Thomas Hellriegel, last year's second-place finisher; perennial contender Jürgen Zäck; Holger Lorenz; Rainer Mueller-Horner, third-place finisher in 1995, and Lothar Leder, the first man to go under eight hours in an Ironman race, which he did last July in Roth, Germany.

On the way to Hawi, Hellriegel — with Van Lierde in tow — finally passed a fading Dittrich. Van Lierde had already been forced to execute a stop-and-go for blocking, an example of the new Ironman get-tough policy on two-wheel offenders. Van Lierde let Hellriegel know early on that he would be serving three minutes in the penalty box when they turned into the Kona Surf Hotel at the end of the 112-mile ride.

"He told me he had a penalty," remembers Hellriegel. "I couldn't understand, because he was the only one who could follow me."

And follow he did. Even as a first-timer to the Kona Coast, Van Lierde showed very little in the way of trepidation or fear of a course that has been known to grind up those who go too hard too soon.

"The wind is no problem for me," insists Van Lierde, who has yet to see real Ironman wind. "In Belgium, I live at the coast and there is a lot of wind. And I go two times a year to the Canary Islands, where there is a lot of wind. But the humidity was different."

He obviously wasn't afraid of Hellriegel, either. This is a guy who put 13 minutes on the field last year and was riding this time around at a course-record clip. By the time Hellriegel and Van Lierde hit Hawi, they had put 4:13 on Dittrich and 5:30 on 1994 champion Greg Welch, Tim DeBoom, Widoff, Kenny Glah and Canadian Peter Reid. Back another minute were Cristian Bustos, Holger Lorenz, Michael McCormack and Tony DeBoom. Rainer Mueller-Horner dropped out before Hawi, Lothar Leder was nine full minutes back, and six-time Ironman legend Dave Scott was in the Twilight Zone, a full 16 minutes back. It was apparent that this time he'd find Jimmy Hoffa before he'd find the leaders on the bike.

Nobody Eats 50 Eggs

On the way back from Hawi, Hellriegel and Van Lierde traded the lead.

"I tried to drop him on the bike," says Hellriegel, "but it didn't work. I had to ride together with him. I knew I was in good shape on the bike, and I knew we were going very fast. It would have been bad to ride slower, with all the rest of the guys."

"Slower" to Hellriegel means slower than the old bike course record, which he smashed this year by three full minutes.

Opposite page:
Top: The year before Paula Newby-Fraser (#43) tried to win the race from the front and blew up. This time around she decided to be the hunter, not the hunted. She ran side by side with Natascha Badmann of Switzerland (#100) who was racing in Hawaii for the first time. Eventually, the Queen of Kona won her eighth title. "It wasn't important for me to win today," said Newby-Fraser, "And I think that's why I did."

Bottom: Fernanda Keller of Brazil, shown here on the bike course, finished sixth.

This page, left: Dave Scott, 42, put together a 2:45:20 marathon to run his way into fifth place. After 10 appearances in Hawaii, his record stood at six wins, three second-place finishes and one fifth.

Photos by Lois Schwartz

egel and Van Lierde came into the
:ition together, but before running, Van
de had to do his three minutes "in the
'

n Lierde is a student of his craft. He
»s notes on all his competitors, their
igths and weaknesses, and he has
ied the Ironman.

watched what happened last year and
zed that anything is possible," he says.
ee minutes is nothing. I wasn't happy
I got the penalty, but I didn't panic.
n I started to run, my legs were so sore
ught I wasn't going to finish. So I start-
unning slowly and went very easy up the
few hills."

ellriegel's lead was up over five minutes.
ch was seven or eight back of Van
de. Bustos and his sub-2:50 potential
pped out during the run.

eid was competing in his third Ironman
e mid-July, running barely sub-three-
r pace and happy to be there. Peter
oko and Dave Scott were too far back to
e a run at the lead, even though Scott
; in the process of putting together a
marathon.

fter a 2:58 marathon in 1995, Hellriegel
s on pace to go much faster in 1996. But
specter of a 29-minute 10K guy sporting
ike swoosh running right behind him was
ugh to give anyone déjà vu. After all,
rk Allen came from nearly 13 minutes
:k to run Hellriegel down last year.

I started to gain time," says Van Lierde.
at because I was running faster, but
:ause Thomas was slowing down."

Coming out of the Natural Energy Lab,
a Lierde was two minutes down and
llriegel was dealing with hamstring prob-
1s.

The longest run of Van Lierde's life was
K, two weeks before race day. Now there
re only two minutes separating him from
llriegel and 10K to go.

'I twisted my hamstring at the energy lab
naround," admits Hellriegel. "After that, I
ed to run different."

Van Lierde remembered that Mark Allen
s about two minutes behind Hellriegel
ming out of the Natural Energy Lab last
ar.

"I said to myself, 'I need to gain some
time here,'" recalls Van Lierde. "What happened last year in the men's and the
women's races said to me that anything is
possible in the marathon here, even just 400
yards from the finish. The race is over at the
finish line, not 400 yards before, not 10K
before."

Van Lierde could tell that Greg Welch in
third place was too far back to catch him,
even if he crashed and burned. So he went
for the win.

"I thought 'I will be second here,'" Van
Lierde admits. "But here was a chance to
win. I had to take the risk. I took a risk, ran
harder and gained two minutes."

Like Mark Allen last year, he caught
Hellriegel at about mile 24.

"When I caught him, I stayed maybe 10
seconds behind," remembers Van Lierde.
"Then I accelerated by him. That hurt, of
course, but it's necessary to do that
because if you run, say, five seconds per
kilometer faster, then it would have been
possible for him to follow me."

Not on this day. For Hellriegel, it was the
old good news/bad news routine. The good
news? He swam a minute faster than last
year, broke the bike course record and ran
12 minutes faster than in 1995. Plus he
went under the existing Ironman course
record by more than a minute. The bad
news? He got passed at mile 24 for the second year in a row by a guy with a swoosh on
his chest.

Luc Van Lierde, the newest Cool Hand
Luc.

"For a first-timer to put all three together
like that," says Scott shaking his head. "For
him to swim 51 [minutes], ride 4:27 and run
2:41… that's frightening. I would never bet
on a first-timer winning here."

Luc Van Lierde would take that bet. He
smiles and pulls the $41,000 Ironman pot
towards him.

No king in his hand. Nuthin' on his résumé
about doing an Ironman before. Nuthin'
about racing on the Kona Coast. Nuthin' in
the marathon experience column.

Sometimes nuthin' can be a pretty cool
hand.

Above: Peter Reid of Canada had a
breakthrough race, finishing an impressive
fourth and breaking three hours
in the marathon (2:59:42).

Opposite: Jürgen Zäck prided himself
on making the pace tough on the bike.
The harder the conditions, the stronger
the wind, the better he liked it.

Photos by Lois Schwartz

" Most people lose their concentration
after about five hours. They give up.
It's not physical, it's mental.
When you come to Kona, it's like
racing on the moon."

Six-time Champion Dave Scott.

Photo by Tracy Frankel

EMILY

The room is hospital white, the floor polished squares of institutional linoleum. Sterile. Unforgiving. The smell of despair hangs in the air like a soggy cloth coat on a withered old man.

This is no place for a little girl. Barely five years old, she lies on her back, surrounded on all sides by large men and women wearing rubber gloves and thin blue masks.

FBI agent Bob Jordan strapped his frail little girl with the peach fuzz-covered head into the Baby Jogger for another training run around the neighborhood. They were a team. Team Jordan. Bob, Emily and Terry, who rode alongside on her bike or in-line skated until it was her turn to push Emily in her jogger.

Bob and Terry met at the Bay State Triathlon in 1988, and their relationship has been multi-sport-based ever since. Bob was racing that day and Terry was cheerleading. It was the start of something pretty wonderful.

"We always worked out together," remembers Terry. "When I was pregnant with Emily, I rode beside Bob on his long runs. We sorted out most of our major issues during those workouts. After Emily was born, we took turns pushing the Baby Jogger around Lake Miramar."

A short pause, "Then Emily started to talk…"

And she never stopped. So Terry stayed home while Bob and his little girl went out together for long talks and long runs.

After he tucked her into the Baby Jogger, Bob would look Emily in the eyes and smile.

"Who's the Ironman, Emily?"

She never hesitated, especially when he tickled her.

"Daddy's the Ironman!" giggled Emily. "Daddy's the Ironman!"

"What's an Ironman do, honey?"

"He swims, bikes and runs and runs, bikes and swims, Daddy!"

They'd both laugh and daddy would go about his business, putting in the miles with his little girl giggling the whole way.

"The two of them were great training buddies," says Terry. "They almost wore that Baby Jogger out."

Among the crowd of blue masks, there were two eyes that the little girl recognized — the ones that were welling up with tears. Her mom grasped her hand and started to tell her a story about Sally the caterpillar.

In February of 1996, at the age of four, Emily was diagnosed with leukemia.

That spring and summer, Bob and Emily trained together for the Vineman Triathlon, a full Ironman-distance event in the wine country of California. Bob had always wanted to be an Ironman, and had sent in his application for 10 straight years. For 10 straight years, he called the Ironman office on May 1 and received the same "better luck next year" news.

"Every year since 1985, I'd do this same pathetic lemming-like deal," recalls Bob. "I'd send my money in for the lottery, make my call and get my 'no.'"

That August, Terry gave birth to an 11 pound, 4 ounce baby boy who lived for all of two minutes.

"You'd think that a big baby means a healthy baby," says Bob softly. "We learned that's not always the case."

The child's name was Thomas and, to this day, the doctors couldn't tell you what went wrong.

Emily's leukemia progressed so quickly that Bob and Terry were forced to leave San Diego and move with Emily into the UCLA Medical Center. She was being prepared for a bone marrow transplant, the last of her dwindling chances for life. She was in the high-risk category, which meant that a donor had to be found… and soon.

"There was no donor available," says Bob, "And we knew that 20 percent of the kids die from the process of conditioning them for the bone marrow transplant. They have to bring the

patient down to base level zero and then introduce the new bone marrow."

"I look back now and wonder, why did we put her through all that?" says Terry. "It's an incredible process. No one allowed to visit... the isolation... But Emily was such a brave little person."

Terry was pregnant again, and the best chance of success for matching bone marrow was through a sibling. There are six points that doctors look to match when considering a donor. A match on four of the six is considered good. Emily's chances of survival without the transplant were now single digit.

Little Timothy was born early, but wasn't a match on any point.

"Sally the little caterpillar ate so much her belly became very big and began to hurt," Terry told Emily. *"It was so big she couldn't breathe. The little caterpillar tried rubbing her belly with one of her many, many feet but even that didn't help to make the pain go away."*

"At that point, we thought there was very little hope," says Bob. "Then they found a mother on the East Coast who had lost her baby, but had saved the umbilical cord."

The cord matched on five of the six points.

"We thought maybe this was our lost baby coming back to save Emily," remembers Bob.

On March 3, 1997, Emily received her transplant.

"When new bone marrow is injected, your body recognizes that something strange is being put into your system and fights itself," says Bob. "It's full-on-war... the host against the graft."

A war that raged inside their little girl.

"Her spirit and will through all of this never ceased to amaze me," says Bob.

On April 24, Bob Jordan left Emily's room and walked into a wall of light. It was his 46th birthday, and he was surprised by a bunch of strangers and fellow FBI employees congregated in a hospital meeting room.

"They hand me this letter and tell me it's from Emily," says Bob softly. "I figured it was a birthday card. You've got to understand. My little girl had been so sick. Whatever Emily had to say was very important to me."

He laughs. "I guess Ed Muskie and I are the only two men to cry on national TV."

The letter was indeed from Emily — with a little help from mom. It was addressed to the Ironman office in Florida and explained how Emily would like to see her dad get into the Ironman. She could be there with him. Strapped into the Baby Jogger, they could go on their long runs together again.

After barely making it through the letter, Bob Jordan was handed a plaque from the Ironman office. He had been accepted into the race.

"I could have fallen over," says Bob.

The men and women with the blue masks stood mesmerized as Terry told the story of Sally the little caterpillar. There was no movement in the operating room. The doctors and nurses, poised with their tubes and machines, were suddenly children, transfixed by the story. "One day, Sally decided that if she went to sleep, maybe her big belly and the pain would go away," *soothed Terry.* "So she wrapped herself up in her favorite yellow blanket and drifted off to sleep..."

Emily was having a tough go. Vomiting and diarrhea day and night. All her food came through an IV. She had open sores inside her mouth and on her bottom. When she went to the bathroom, parts of her stomach lining ended up in the bowl.

"The drugs attack the fastest-growing cells," explains Bob. "Like your hair and your stomach lining."

The little girl was having trouble breathing and her belly was swollen to twice its normal size. The doctors worried that she would asphyxiate.

Even when things were the worst, there was always a silver lining.

"I found something every day to be grateful for," Terry says. "The support of our friends and family. The hard work of all the doctors and nurses. It was important to me to maintain that sense of gratitude."

"We had to make a decision," says Bob. "The doctors felt Emily needed to have a machine breathing for her, and to do that she had to be knocked out because she would fight the machine."

There was one more consideration: If Emily was knocked out, there was a 75 percent chance she would never regain consciousness.

It was a Friday night. Emily slowly put her feet to the floor and moved away from the bed that had become her full-time home.

"Where are you going, Emily?" Bob asked softly.

His beautiful little girl with the big blue eyes didn't say a word. She couldn't breathe well, couldn't speak.

"Anything we can do for you, honey?"

Emily just came over to Bob and crawled up onto his lap so he could hold her.

"You learn to change your priorities from 'my child hit a triple' or 'my child was student of the month' to 'my child opened her eyes,' and 'my child squeezed my hand,'" says Bob. "I remember looking at her and thinking, 'I've been trying to get into the Ironman for 10 years and you, someone who can't even talk, pulled this thing off.'"

The doctors and nurses were still immersed in the story, which Terry was making up as she went along. "Sally the caterpillar woke up after many, many days asleep. She opened her eyes and realized her big belly was finally gone. She looked around for her yellow blanket, but that was gone, too! Instead, the yellow blanket had changed into wings and Sally the little caterpillar was now a beautiful butterfly."

Terry realized while she was telling the story that her little girl might not wake up from the procedure, that this might be the last time they would be together.

"The story was to let her know that when she woke up, she would be better. To me, this was a good story, no matter if she woke up or not," says Terry.

That night, Emily went into a coma. She never woke up.

"There is nothing worse than losing a child," says Terry. "But we're still grateful for many things. Emily was a blessing, and we had her for five-and-a-half years. Timothy was basically raised in Emily's hospital bed, so we have photos of Timothy with his big sister. The doctors were against it, but we told them, 'No Timothy, no transplant.' Emily was proud of us for that. She told anyone who would listen that her daddy said 'No Timothy, no transplant.' The highlight of her day was when Timothy showed up."

It is 8 a.m. on a Saturday a few months later. They are once again out at Lake Miramar, Bob stretching a little and tightening up his running shoes. Terry on her bike. Timothy squirming in the Baby Jogger.

Life goes on... and there's an Ironman to train for.

"Emily wouldn't want us to retreat from life," insists Terry. The threesome head out for their workout, the lake shimmering in the early morning sunlight.

Emily never leaves their thoughts.

"There is an eternal nature to our children," says Terry. "There was much more to Emily than her body."

Terry pauses, "Emily is closer to us now than our own breath."

Bob had an appointment with the lava fields of the Kona coast back in October 1997, and he wasn't swimming, riding or running alone.

"I know Emily was there with me every step of the way," says Bob.

1997: PASSING THE TORCH

BY TIM CARLSON

It's a long way from the lonely, brutal heat of the Queen K Highway on Ironman Day to the homestretch in Barcelona where Carl Lewis is quivering to get the stick to wrap up the gold in the 400 meter relay. But no matter how individual the Ironman is, no matter how the rules say clearly there are no pacers, no rabbits and no relay teams — still, a virtual baton was passed on Mile 12 of the 21st Ironman.

Unlike most passes on the course, where the overtaking runners dispatch their prey like matadors placing the knife between the shoulders of the bull, this handoff was done with love. Heather Fuhr, the shy Canadian from Edmonton, Alberta, caught up to her training partner, mentor, close friend — and, coincidentally, the legend who has won this race eight times — Paula Newby-Fraser.

Five weeks out of this year's event, Newby-Fraser went to do PR at the Malibu Triathlon and came back with a sore throat, which escalated to a fever, abscessed tooth, root canal and antibiotics. The infection traveled and one side of her face became horribly swollen. An oral surgeon prescribed a double dose of a second antibiotic, which did not work. Late one Friday night, friends called in an eye/ear/nose/throat specialist who found where the infection was hiding — her perotid.

"I had vowed I should not race when it happened like this, but..." says Newby-Fraser.

There was a lot of sponsor pressure for her to be in Hawaii, and Newby-Fraser takes her responsibilities seriously. Still, when she saw the salt cake on her body during the bike, she said to her agent, Murphy Reinschreiber, "I am cooked." She was just looking for the place to say her exit line.

Fuhr, with her gentle, self-effacing demeanor, survived her usual desultory swim, biked into position, and unleashed the giant within on the run. She came off the bike sixth, 8:10 behind Wendy Ingrahm, 4:45 behind Newby-Fraser.

In a dozen miles of the most brutal conditions in Ironman history, she blew by Fernanda Keller (mile two), Lori Bowden (mile seven), Sian Welch (mile nine) and now Newby-Fraser, who was fading.

Fuhr tried to re-light the spark, pretending they were just leaving Newby-Fraser's home in Encinitas and about to go for a Sunday run.

"Come on, Paula, let's go do our long run now," she says.

It didn't work. Newby-Fraser, relieved to see Heather finally arrive, said: "No, Heather, my day is done — and it's been done for a long time. It's all yours now, go and take it!"

This was the moment Newby-Fraser had been waiting for, and she dropped out just a mile down the road. She felt as if it were a relay and now Heather could take it ahead.

"I was going backwards, and after what happened to me in 1995, I knew what lay ahead. By mile 16 or 17, it would be a death march, I would be entering a place where I would be subjecting myself to serious injury," says Newby-Fraser. "I was finally free of the ego and the fear that people would say I was a quitter. I was quite comfortable retiring for this day out on the Queen K, because that was the place where I had left so many pieces of myself in the past. I didn't need that again."

What happened inside Fuhr was even more crucial to the day.

"It was emotionally difficult to leave Paula, but it took the pressure off me," says Fuhr. "I thought, 'OK, I have to show that all we

Above: Heather Fuhr passed her training partner and long-time friend Paula Newby-Fraser at about mile 10. Newby-Fraser dropped out a mile later. "When I passed her I said 'Come on Paula. Let's go for our long run now,'" remembers Fuhr. Newby-Fraser told her that her day was done, that it was time for Fuhr to go at it alone. She did just that, winning the Ironman title (opposite page).

Above: Lori Bowden passes Wendy Ingraham on her way to second place.

Opposite page:
Top: Jürgen Zäck once again had the fastest bike split, but his time he held on in the run to finish second, his best finish in Hawaii.

Bottom: In 1995, it was Mark Allen. In 1996, it was Luc Van Lierde. After two tough second-place finishes, Germany's Thomas Hellriegel (shown on the bike) finally won the big one.

Photos by Lois Schwartz

have done together in the past has worked. That even though she wouldn't finish on top, this would be a big part of her also.' If I could go ahead and win, we would both win. So it was my job to catch Wendy."

Wendy Ingraham was having a break-through day of her own. She controlled the women's race for nearly eight hours, leaving Kailua Bay with a brand-new swim record of 49:52 and leading throughout the 112 miles of the bike. When Fuhr passed Newby-Fraser, Ingraham was two minutes ahead on the run course.

Fuhr, three-time champion of Ironman Japan, but only sixth where it mattered, final-ly faced her fears of late-race collapses. She was determined to stand up and be counted at Kona. No more retreating, no more stay-ing comfortable. As part of a team, "Second place is no longer acceptable," she said, as she sped ahead and passed Ingraham at mile 15, taking a 20-second lead into the Natural Energy Lab Road.

Paula put it best: "It is a weird thing, but sometimes all these people believe in you — but it doesn't matter until you believe in your-self. Fuhr's husband and her parents and Paul [Huddle, Newby-Fraser's fiancé] and I and Murphy have all believed in Heather for years. Others have had their doubts. So when she showed she was ready, I was ecstatically happy."

Although she took the lead from Ingraham with 11 miles to go and led the rest of the way, Fuhr's story was not the most dramatic one in this, the most hotly contested women's race in years.

Ingraham, who began her Ironman string with a 10th place finish in 1991, dropped out on the marathon the next year with a stress fracture to her foot, then alternated fifth and fourth places the next four years, had learned how to win with a victory in the 1995 Ironman Australia. The irrepressible Ingraham had learned how to bike and run well enough to put Newby-Fraser under stress, and sessions with her boyfriend, mountain bike downhiller Kurt Stockton, had her ready to rumble.

Ingraham left Germany's Ute Mueckel in her dust coming out of the water, and actual-

ly built on her 2:12 edge early over Newby-Fraser, who exited Kailua Bay in 53:04.

Sian Welch, representing the Welch household since husband Greg, the 1994 champ, withdrew due to a blood condition, was here with a new sense of self, gained in the past year or so as she emerged healthy from horribly painful chronic plantar fasciitis and started showing she could win. She had raced short-course queen Michellie Jones head-to-head in Brazil and elsewhere, topping off a great year with a win at Shu's U.S. Pro Championship. Better than that, she had gotten over the trauma of last year's DQ for two blocking calls at the Hawaii Ironman, and her old feelings of insecurity about the distance.

"In order to win, you first have to believe it is possible," says Welch, reflecting on her old fades to ninth after a strong bike. "I have taken that step."

Beforehand, new race-husband Greg was proud of Sian but admitted privately a little concern about the short time she had to prepare for Hawaii.

"I am so proud of her however she does, and I just hope Sian gets through this feeling happy about her experience," says Greg, pausing. "That nothing traumatic happens."

Loving and eerily prophetic words. Welch was disappointed by her 56:16 swim, rode fast to move into third, then threw up on the climb to Hawi. Women started passing her back. Welch showed her new courage by not panicking, recovering, and starting to bike like a demon as she got close to the Kona Surf.

Welch passed Fuhr again and rode in a pack with Newby-Fraser and Lori Bowden, ready to rock on the run.

Bowden came in on a high with a 3:01 marathon to win Ironman Canada, the result of junking her old low-mileage coach and taking on the high-mileage work ethic of her fiancé, Peter Reid. Bowden slipped to a 1:04:31 swim in Kailua Bay, 14:51 behind Ingraham exiting the water, but blew the field away with a 5:15:26 bike, nearly eight minutes better than Fuhr, who was second fastest. Apparently, however, Bowden's killer legs were neutralized by that effort.

She started the run first of a three-woman pack with Newby-Fraser and Welch but, her legs fried by a bike far more intense than anyone else' on a day of killer mumuku winds, let Newby-Fraser and Welch go.

Brazil's exotic Fernanda Keller, third in '94 and '95, ignited by her best swim ever, a 57:27, had the best seat in the house as she left the bike-to-run transition with Fuhr. Fuhr actually had a discouraging race before hitting the run.

"I started passing people fast on the bike, but after Hawi a lot of women passed me back," she admits. "Sian Welch looked very strong and I could not hope to stay with her. Lori looked great. Finally, Fernanda passed me, but I found enough inside to hang on, about 100 meters behind, and I waited."

Taking her lesson from Luc Van Lierde's conservative strategy starting out on the run in 1996, Fuhr was content to target Keller's back for the first tough climbs out of the Kona Surf and back up from The Pit.

"I normally would have started out faster and then died, but I used Fernanda as a physical gauge to make myself slow down at first. I vowed not to catch her too quickly."

She finally edged past Keller at mile three of the run. Fuhr used the same strategy on Bowden, then half a mile ahead.

"I could see that Lori didn't have her same legs left after that bike ride," says Fuhr. "But I knew if I ran right up on her I would not have enough left for the end."

She finally edged by Bowden at mile seven, going up to Palani Hill. By then Fuhr was in a groove, on course to a fifth best-ever 3:06:45 marathon. Somehow, as winners often are, she was in another climatic zone.

"Honestly, it just didn't feel as hot for me," says Fuhr.

Bowden passed Ingraham in the Natural Energy Lab. Welch, recovering nicely, heard she was 3:40 down to Ingraham and third place leaving the energy lab and started to dig deep.

"Right then, I was on the edge, but I went harder," says Welch, in a prelude to disaster.

Fuhr herself had a rough patch in the energy lab.

"Last year, I faded badly there and dropped to 8:30 a mile all the way in," she remembers. "I heard Lori was five minutes back with 10K to go, and with her 3:01 at Canada, I knew my lead could easily evaporate.

Fuhr found inspiration from her husband Roch Frey at the energy lab, and held it together. Worried by the ghosts of Bowden's potential, she put the hammer down in the last few miles, just as Luc Van Lierde did last year when he passed Hellriegel.

Fuhr was almost scared by the tidal wave of emotions that engulfed her along Alii Drive as she finished in 9:31:41, while more Ironman destiny was unfolding behind her.

Bowden held on for a Canadian one-two finish, 10 minutes down. Then came another chapter in the Ironman Hall of Fame of psychodrama and heart-attack finishes.

By then Newby-Fraser was calling the finish on local TV.

"I saw Sian pass Wendy, who looked bad, coming to Palani Hill at mile 25. Sian looked bad, but I thought she would make it," says Newby-Fraser. "I said she was about to get third, just as her husband Greg did last year."

Ingraham, in fact, stopped to clutch and massage her legs, which had cramped badly. Running up just behind was Keller, who had skipped past the shuffling Newby-Fraser in the last few steps to gain third by a few seconds in 1995. This year, she had Ingraham in her sights and made the final pass as she turned on to Alii Drive.

Just ahead was the spectacle of Welch, wobbling under the banyan tree 200 yards from the end.

Keller had run a steady race and took third again.

"They say I am world champion of passing people in trouble on Alii Drive," smiles Keller, $20,000 richer.

Behind her was chaos that left people grasping for metaphors. Welch, looking behind her, seemed stunned when Keller went by; she fell to the ground.

"Fernanda seemed to take the wind out of her sails," says Newby-Fraser.

Welch dragged herself up, tried to run, but her legs buckled again. When she reached

It was the first "crawl off" in Ironman history.
Wendy Ingraham (left) and Sian Welch (right) both collapsed
a hundred yards before the finish, tried to stand, then realized
that there was no other way. When the dust had settled,
Ingraham had fourth with Welch in fifth.
Photos by Lois Schwartz

Opposite: Lori Bowden finishing in second place.
Photo by Robert Oliver

the finish line chute, she grabbed onto the fence with the banners and tried to use them to steady herself.

Announcer Mike Reilly said, "Here comes Wendy!" and Newby-Fraser was aghast.

"It was like something out of a cartoon. Wendy comes with her legs wide like a praying mantis. She cannot hold her back up straight and she is bent over like an old lady. Sian obviously tries to go forward and collapses."

A pregnant Karen Smyers is also calling the finish and staring with disbelief. "Sian tries to get up, and lurches to the left and bumps into Wendy and they both go down together."

They were 20 meters from the finish line, both on the carpet.

For one horrifying moment, first Sian, then Wendy try to get up, and fail. Up and down. Up and down. Newby-Fraser now really into being a witness to history, says, "I was stifling a laugh and crying at the same time, like it was some crazy Fellini movie."

Dan Empfield, whose own wife JulieAnne White collapsed after the 1993 Ironman, was also transfixed and grasping for metaphors.

"It was like *Rocky Two*, where Rocky Balboa and Apollo Creed both hit each other at the bell and are knocked out simultaneously and you wonder who would win."

In the middle of this surreal scene, so reminiscent of the Julie Moss crawl to the finish line in February of 1982, Ingraham didn't lose her clarity of mind nor her sense of humor.

"We were like Laurel and Hardy," she remembers. "My mind was very clear and telling my body what to do, only it wouldn't listen. It was like our heads were cut off."

Sian felt the same way. "Actually, it was kind of cool," she says.

Ingraham realized first it wasn't working.

"I finally decided to revert back to when I was three years old and started to crawl," she says.

In the face of this shocking, ultimate competitive effort, Reilly throttled back on the microphone and an eerie, relative silence gripped the crowd.

Welch's father, a doctor, had to restrain himself from rushing out and picking up his beloved daughter. Greg was stunned. Welch caught on a touch too late and crawled after Ingraham.

During this demented diaper dash in hydrodynamic bathing suits for the $15,000 fourth prize, a thought occurred simultaneously to Ingraham and Newby-Fraser: Why not stop, take Sian's hand, and cross the line together?

"If Wendy had done that she would have been immortal," says Newby-Fraser.

Ingraham has a better memory for the rules and history. In fact, Chicago marathon promoter Bob Bright was brought into the Ironman when they first issued prize money in 1986 and cautioned the pros then that they had to race to the finish line or face disqualification — to ensure that pros would not agree to split the money.

"I just knew that it was a race and we were supposed to compete to the finish line," says Ingraham. "So I crossed the line and then I held out my hand to help Sian cross."

Both Welch and Ingraham were carried off in the arms of their significant others, and both were well enough to go to the post-race press conference.

"Since Julie Moss started all of this 15 years ago and this was her last race in Hawaii, I guess Wendy and I did this as a tribute," laughs Welch.

Fuhr was pragmatic about the crawl off.

"Yes, it will give some fuel for people who already think this is an insane and crazy person's sport," says Fuhr. "But at the same time, it is obviously one of the most grueling sports in the world. I think it shows how strong we are as athletes and how far we can push ourselves — past the point where we can't even walk any longer."

Two days later, Fuhr sat in her condo with Newby-Fraser and finally let all her emotions run out.

"I thought I would break down at the finish line, so I kept it in," admits Fuhr.

Then, it all hit her and the tears were just streaming down her face.

"I was just happy," she says.

THE FIGHT FOR LIFE: JIM HOWLEY

It's May 1996 and the sun is setting behind the green hills that surround Lake San Antonio in Central California. Most of those watching old sol's hasta la vista are still splattered with sweat and tattooed with race numbers from their Wildflower Half Ironman adventure earlier in the day. They had gone head to head with 1.2 miles of swimming, 56 miles of cycling and 13.1 miles of running.

H2... Hills and Headwinds, are what make Wildflower such a worthy adversary.

The assembled multitude, the humbled conquerors, have either placed in their age division and are waiting to collect their award, or they are hoping beyond hope that their name will be drawn at random and they will own a spot in the coveted Gatorade Ironman bike rack. Only the winners of each age group are assured a spot in Kailua Bay in October.

The wind picks up and scatters leaves and burrito wrappers as the announcer drones on. Jim Howley, 34, who is working on his master's in clinical psychology, is one of those anxiously awaiting the lottery call. He knows the odds are bad but — trust me on this — he has definitely seen worse.

Howley has AIDS. Full-blown AIDS.

"Most people would expect him to be dead by now," says Dr. Gary Cohan, his physician for the past two years. For 12 years, Howley has been HIV positive. For nearly six years, he has had AIDS. The average "healthy" person has 800-1,000 T-cells, the guys that fight off infection. Howley has between four and eight. Not 400. Four.

He basically has absolutely no immune system.

"Jim is doing well," admits Dr. Cohan. "He has outlived the odds and he is living day to day. But you can't rebuild the immune system. All we can do is try to preserve the T-cells Jim has left."

Since he found out he had AIDS, Howley has run the Los Angeles Marathon five times and completed numerous triathlons, including this year's Wildflower event — with a pulled hamstring — finishing in a time of 6:39.

What usually happens to an AIDS patient is that they develop what Dr. Cohan refers to as the wasting syndrome.

"In healthy people, if they starve, they lose fat, which is non-essential," says Dr. Cohan, a board-certified internist and assistant clinical professor at UCLA. "When you have AIDS, the metabolic pathway is uncoupled and the body chews up lean body mass and vital organs. By working out, Jim has been able to keep his lean body mass."

In the past, exercise wasn't even a consideration for AIDS patients.

"We tended not to pay attention to exercise," says Dr. Cohan. "Exercise has never been encouraged. Frankly, it's been ignored. I've just started speaking about AIDS and exercise recently."

Jim Howley was told that the type of training he would need to do for the Ironman would kill someone with AIDS. He proved them all wrong when he completed the toughest day in sport. Photo by Lois Schwartz

Opposite page: Photo by Rich Cruse

Jim Howley (#125) shocked the world in 1996 when, with AIDS, he finished the Ironman in 14:47:22. To prove it wasn't a fluke, he came back in 1997 and went 13:14:55, over an hour and half faster.
Photo by Lois Schwartz

Howley does what no AIDS patient has done before. Each week, he runs 35 miles, cycles 150 and swims five to six miles. He takes 60 pills a day to help combat the ravages of AIDS.

"Since I have no immune system, I can get sick from tap water," says Howley. "The pills I take make me sick... but they also keep me from getting sick at the same time."

One of the pills he takes, Marinol, is a marijuana pill designed to give him the munchies so that he can eat enough to keep his weight up. At the moment, he is a robust 193 pounds.

When he first learned that he was HIV positive 12 years ago, Howley started doing 2-3 grams of cocaine a day and anything else that would make him feel good. When he took another test six years ago and found out that he had AIDS, he thought it was all over.

"[Doctors] told me not to even go into a crowded movie theater," he recalls. "That's how bad it was. I freaked out. I went home and decided that before I die, I want to do a triathlon. I went to a pool that day and wasn't able to swim to the other side."

His first triathlon was in Cerritos in 1990. "That race changed me forever. This has

been the best five years of my life because of triathlon."

His life has touched the entire Santa Barbara triathlon community. Gary Flacke, a long-time professional triathlete, remembers Howley showing up at Saturday morning 5K runs and always finishing last.

"He wasn't good at all," laughs Flacke. "But he was always so upbeat."

Howley has worked his way up to the middle of the pack and seems to be loving every minute of it.

"He is never bummed," admits Flacke. "I didn't know about Jim having AIDS for two years after I met him. I was so impressed with him as a person by that point, I admired him so much, that it didn't make a difference."

The goal now is Ironman, Hawaii. Last year would have been nice. This year would be awesome.

"He really wanted to get in last year," remembers Flacke. "When he didn't get in at Mike and Rob's Triathlon, you could tell he was close to tears."

Friends from the Santa Barbara Triathlon community got together and put up $30 each to enter Howley in the Ironman lottery and the Ironman passport club this year. They did it without his knowledge.

At dinner one night, his friends presented Howley with a card adorned with his name and the Ironman logo.

When he found out that he didn't get in through the lottery, he set off for Wildflower. The half Vineman is later this summer and if necessary, he'll go to Mike and Rob's Triathlon on August 13.

"There's not a question that he can finish Ironman," insists Flacke. "No way he wouldn't finish that race."

Ironman or no Ironman, Howley is already in a race. It's a race against time and it's a race to spread his message.

"Twelve years ago, when I first found out I was HIV positive, most guys were blowing their brains out," he says. "Now I'm getting calls from all over the world from other AIDS patients. Their doctors are telling them not to do anything. I'm trying to get them to buy bicycles, to start running or swimming. It works."

He pauses as the wind picks up around us.

"The switch is either on or off. If it's off, they're just going to go and die. I was forced to grab life. Basically, I train to stay alive."

A few weeks later, we speak again. At the end of our conversation, Howley says that he won't be able to swim, ride or run

for 10 days or so. Something about a minor eye problem.

Speaking with Dr. Cohan later that day, I ask about the eye situation. Typically, Jim has understated the problem.

"Jim has a sight-threatening eye infection," Dr. Cohan tells me. "We have to operate and then treat it with medication."

Without an immune system, Howley is a bacteria magnet. Little problems that our bodies, our T-cells, would take care of, can kill him.

Which makes what he has accomplished that much more amazing.

"He's an inspiration," says Dr. Cohan. "He's far and away the most active person — in terms of competition — of the over 1,000 AIDS patients I have worked with. Jim is one of those guys who can push the edge of the envelope."

The message Howley is sending to other AIDS patients?

"That you shouldn't live with one foot in the grave," says Dr. Cohan. "And that it ain't over 'til the Fat Lady sings."

The Fat Lady hasn't even begun to warm up her vocal chords yet. A certain someone still has to secure his spot in the biggest tri-show on earth.

It is so very personal.
Whether it's your
First or your 21st,
There is no feeling
like finishing the Ironman.
Photo by Robert Oliver

"Frankly Jürgen, I don't give a damn." Peter Reid.

Above: Peter Reid (#4) passes a fading Jürgen Zäck (#2).

Opposite page: It's a winning combination: Reid rode within a minute of 1997 champion Thomas Hellreigel and then ran faster than 1996 champion Luc Van Lierde.

Photos by Lois Schwartz

Yep. That's the quote. Short, sweet, to the point. As the mumuku winds played flip-me-over-into-the-lava-fields twister with the 1,500 Ironwannabes and dished out Sherman-marching-on-Atlanta-type havoc to egos and bike splits alike on Iron morning, Canadian Peter Reid was the guy sitting pretty in the eye of the storm.

As Jürgen Zäck cylced his way to the lead about an eon earlier than expected, Peter "albino boy" Reid kept his white hair, white outfit and white skin way the hell away from the lead. If Zäck wanted to put together a solo assault on Mt. Ironman, if he wanted to wear the funny hat, toot the whistle and engineer the Zäck Express from Kona to Hawi and back solo — "Hey," Reid must have been thinking, "Knock yourself out, big boy."

"Jürgen was set on being the fastest one out there today, on being first into the bike-run transition," says Reid in his best Mark Allen-ese. "I wanted to win this race... not be the first guy off the bike."

The windsock at the small heliport just short of Kawaihae told the story. It was standing at Viagra-enhanced attention and the lead cyclists, heads down, looked about as helpless as a San Diego Padres relief pitcher. Zäck was leading and played to the crowd. "Tough conditions," he seemed to be saying. "I laugh at tough conditions."

Zäck took one of the handlebars and pre-tended to be so bored by the swirling head-winds and the competition that he was casually buffing his nails on his skinsuit as the mumukus head-butted the field.

"I will pray for wind," Zäck says at the pre-press conference.

He must have been a good boy this year. His prayers were answered in spades.

Forty seconds behind Zäck was the course record-holder in Hawaii (8:04:08), the guy who set the overall Ironman record in Germany in 1997, Luc Van Lierde of Belgium. The 1996 champion was injured and did not race Ironman last year. But now he was back and looking a tad sur-prised by the wind.

How different was this race from the one he won in 1996? Van Lierde laughs.

"The easiest wind today was worse than the toughest wind in 1996."

Behind Van Lierde was three-time ITU World Champion Spencer Smith of Great Britain. A short-course specialist, a guy who flies on adrenaline, Smith was making his first attempt at the Ironman. He vowed to race smart, refusing to chase down anything and everything that came his way. Smith wore a heart monitor and tried to keep the governor on all day long.

"I raced exactly the way I wanted to," says Smith. "There were times when I thought I should go and I thought, 'No, stick to what you said you were going to do. You don't know enough about this race.' I played it safe and stayed within myself."

Until Zäck showed up.

"Jürgen came by me like a jet," remem-bers Smith. "I was with Luc at the time and was keeping my heart rate between 145 and 150. As soon as Jürgen came by, it went up to 165 and the wind was enormous. I thought, 'Jürgen, if you can keep this up and still run, you deserve this win. There is no way I can keep this pace.' He was as strong as an ox."

While the German Oxboy was just up ahead playing to the crowd, Reid was about two minutes back with 1997 champion Thomas Hellriegel riding steady. Hellriegel felt he was in even better shape than the past three years, when he finished second, second and first respectively.

"Is your fitness as good as last year?" he was asked. He smiled ear to ear, "I am so strong," he insisted.

Reid was flying blind, not quite so sure where his fitness was. Because he was diagnosed with an iron deficiency early in 1998, Reid spent the middle of this season in recovery mode. He did only one Ironman race, Ironman Australia, which he won in a sprint finish with Chris Leigh back in April.

"This year, a lot of my bike rides didn't go very well," admits Reid. "I lost lots of time on the bike and felt I wasn't the rider I used to be."

Reid wasn't sure about his readiness, was extremely nervous all week before Ironman and was hoping for a good bike ride.

"Within 10 pedal strokes I knew," he remembers. "I knew I had what I needed. The strength was there."

"We headed into the most incredible headwinds I have ever seen in my life," he continues. "That's where my cycling strength paid off. All the other guys struggled, and that's where I pulled away. The wind didn't faze me. The other guys were grimacing and having a tough time dealing with it, but it didn't bug me that much. While most of the other guys crumbled, I was just getting stronger all day long."

While he wasn't crumbling, Germany's Hellriegel certainly didn't have his "A" game.

"Was I keying off Thomas?" Reid continues. "Definitely. I keyed my entire ride off him. At one point on the way back from Hawi, I dropped him. Jürgen was just up the road and I'm like, 'I need Thomas.' Thomas rides so well and so smart, I just love keying my races off him when I'm feeling good. When I'm not, I'll never see the guy, because he's just so strong on the bike."

Hellriegel wasn't his usual Cyborg-type self on the bike.

"I could see from his facial expressions that he was struggling to keep my pace," says Reid. "But we both realized we didn't need to put out that extra effort to try and catch Jürgen."

Zäck had a little over two minutes on Reid and Hellriegel at the turnaround in Hawi, with Van Lierde leading Spencer Smith and the chase group another five minutes back. Then Zäck flatted on the way down the hill. He swears he wasn't going too hard.

"I was not riding all out," he insists. "I was surprised to find myself in the lead 45 minutes into the bike ride — and it was easy. It was not like last year, when I had to push hard to catch Hellriegel. I had about a three-minute lead when I flatted, and I rode 10 minutes on the flat before the support car showed up."

By that time, he had company.

Fast company.

On the way back to the Kona Surf bike-to-run transition area, after re-establishing his lead on Reid and Hellriegel, Zäck could only put another 1:40 on them. Back farther were the best runners in the field, Luc Van Lierde and Germany's Lothar Leder, but Reid never panicked. Two natural-born killers who eat up seven- and nine-minute leads for breakfast were breathing down his back, but Reid did his best Alfred E. Neuman "What me worry?" imitation and played his game.

He ran easily up the big hill out of the Kona Surf. Water bottle in hand, he stayed easy as he headed down the hill towards the turnaround at the bottom of the pit.

"I took my time going down the hill," he recalls. "I wouldn't let myself pick up my stride until I finished my water bottle. Then we passed Jürgen and I was with Thomas coming out of the pit. I could tell he was laboring to stay on my feet. The Hellriegel I know would have matched my pace the entire marathon. He would have given everything he had just to hang on. Thomas just let me easily get away."

Reid understands that some days you're hot, some days you're not. Last year, he was thinking about dropping out on the way back from Hawi. He decided not to, hung tough and finished fourth.

"I learned that day to never give up," he insists. "It's too bad, but I had to deal with that last year. That's how it is racing at the Ironman. Some days you wake up and just don't have it."

And sometimes you do. Reid never let up, never showed a chink in the armor, never let Leder or Van Lierde smell blood.

"The only way I could win this race was to be steady to good all day long," he says. "I had an awesome swim, great ride, and an incredible run. You can't have any major weaknesses here. Look at Chris Leigh [sixth place]. He missed the boat in the swim and he was never a factor."

Reid has been a factor for a long time. Fourth in 1996 and 1997 in Kona. Fourth in Ironman Europe in 1996. Two wins at Ironman Australia and one at Ironman Lanzarote. All of a sudden, the man who was dumbfounded by Paula Newby-Fraser's 21 Ironman victories around the globe was on the verge of his fourth. Neither Van Lierde nor Leder was making up much ground on Reid. Coming out of the Natural Energy Lab with 10K to go, he hadn't lost a second to

Van Lierde and only a few minutes to Leder.

"That was the longest six miles of my life," he laughs, reflecting on the final 10K. "I didn't want to become another statistic."

To avoid being a statistic, he spent six weeks that summer training in Boulder, Colorado with Tim DeBoom. They didn't race each other, they pushed each other. There's a fine line between the two.

"That's why I trained with Tim," insists Reid. "We'd decide on our heart-rate targets. We didn't race. We'd push each other to maintain these heart-rate zones. We understood each other so well. We'd be doing this long run and he'd try to talk to me. 'Tim, I'll talk to you in 15 minutes. I'm having a bad section here.' Twenty minutes later, I'd start talking and he'd go, 'Peter, I'm going through a tough spell. I'll talk to you later.'"

A win at Wildflower in 1996 jumpstarted Reid's career. A fourth in Germany at Ironman Europe later that summer after six weeks of living and training with a local family built his confidence... sort of. The family he was staying with scoffed at his training. The husband was a cyclist. The wife was an Ironman athlete. They both rode more miles every week than Reid did. They sneered at his workouts.

That's when Reid called his coach Roch Frey and asked whether he was doing enough in training. Hey, when the home-stay family is outworking you and dissing you, maybe it's time to up the ante.

Frey told Reid to ignore mom and dad and to stay the course. Reid did — and the rest is history.

On Ironday, Reid's fiancé Lori Bowden was also having a great race. She ran her way from way off the pace into second place for the second year in a row.

The two made eye contact as they passed going opposite directions on the road to Hawi. They passed again on Alii Drive, while Reid was heading out on the run and Bowden was heading towards home on the bike.

"I was running so strong," he says with a grin. "Because I wanted her to be so proud of me."

How could she not?

Peter Reid... Ironman champion. That's definitely something to be proud of!

1999: BIG HAIR DAY

Lori Bowden was the anointed one, the woman of destiny, the It Girl. She was a force of nature, unstoppable, invincible, in the zone. She was Shirley Temple curls meets Lance Armstrong lungs. She had "The Gift," like Paula, like Natascha. She'd win six or seven or eight more Ironman titles in Hawaii after this, just like Paula. Wow, some thought. Just imagine what they'll say about her if she actually wins one.

The hype, the buzz, the expectations surrounding the 32-year-old Canadian before the 1999 Ironman were overwhelming. The question seemed not whether she'd win, but rather "By How much?" The great Paula Newby-Fraser was retired and 1998 champion Natascha Badmann was prepping for the Olympics. And the even-faster-than-Lori running of 1997 champion Heather Fuhr was nullified by a Bowden-esque swim and so-so bike.

Far left: An ecstatic Lori Bowden ran the first ever sub-three-hour women's marathon in Kona to beat Karen Smyers.

Center: Karen Smyers and Lori Bowden.

Below: The happy couple. Peter Reid greets his Ironman champion wife Lori Bowden at the finish line.

Photos by Lois Schwartz

Top: *On the bike, Luc Van Lierde followed Thomas Hellriegel most of the day. Photo by Lois Schwartz*
Bottom: *The happy couple. Peter Reid passes his wife Lori Bowden during the marathon. Photo by Robert Oliver*

Someone forgot to tell 1995 Ironman champion Karen Smyers that the race was over before it began. Smyers had been away from the Ironman for two years due to childbirth and a couple of freak injuries. At 38, she's still a complete, dangerous athlete, solid in every discipline. Though short on Ironman mileage, she came back strong in '99 with some notable short-distance wins. On a perfect day, she can hang with Bowden, she says.

"But if it's not perfect, I'll be a sitting duck," Smyers admits beforehand.

Off the bike first, Smyers was passed early in the run by Beth Zinkand from Davis, California. Smyers caught her at mile three and moved back into lead. But she wasn't feeling quite that confident about her chances.

"About this time during the run, I realized that I needed to train more," says Smyers.

Another 3:05 marathon like the one she had put together when she won in 1985 wasn't in the cards today — and wouldn't win it anyway. The Bowden Express had pulled too far out of the station.

Old Kona saying: Bad conditions favor strong riders. Bowden had power-pedaled through the headwinds in a best-of-the-day 5:08:30, making up 6:31 on Smyers and leaving her just three minutes back as the run began.

When Smyers turned right at the Hot Corner (mile 7.4) and headed up steep Palani Road to the Queen Kaahumanu Highway, Bowden was 10 seconds behind her. By the time she reached the Queen K, she was in second place.

"I thought of running with Lori — until I saw how fast she was running," says Smyers who was thrilled with her comeback after a two year layoff.

"I saw Karen in the Natural Energy Lab, and she looked pretty good," remembers Bowden. "No lead seems big enough. So when I got back to the highway, I hauled."

She hauled fast enough to break Heather Fuhr's run course record by nearly five minutes, going 2:59:16.

Bowden broke the tape and then stood still, arms raised above her head, mouth wide open in ecstasy. Her husband, Peter Reid, first in 1998 and second today, stepped forward and raised her off the ground and into his arms. They wore matching temporary tattoos on their ankles.

She knew this wouldn't have happened without Reid. It was Reid who pushed her to do more miles, to make her training more consistent and to take advantage of her tremendous talent.

"I used to be happy to come here as an age grouper and get in the top 50," she admits.

"Then she met me," Reid says.

While the modest Bowden isn't known to wear ambition on her sleeve, she admits that Reid made her envious when he won the Ironman in 1998 and she didn't.

"After watching him announced all year as Ironman Champion Peter Reid, I really wanted to win this thing once," she says.

Some think she'll win it a lot more.

*They flip flopped the results from the year before. Luc Van Lierde
wins his second Ironman title this time around with Peter Reid in second.
Photo by Lois Schwartz*

IRON CELEBRITIES

Over the years, the lure of the Ironman has spread all the way to Hollywood and beyond. Getting to the finish line on Alii Drive has become the ultimate prize and there are no limits as to who wants to have that finisher's medal dangling around their neck.

Alexandra Paul (pictured) who starred on Baywatch, spent a full year training for the Ironman under the guidance of Scott Tinley.

Real Andrews played Detective Marcus Taggert from General Hospital.

Darryl Haley (New England Patriots) and Butch Johnson (Dallas Cowboys) both played in the NFL and both played in the Super Bowl. Haley has the distinction of being the first 300-pound Ironman finisher.

Maxine Bahns starred in the movies Brothers McMullen and She's the One.

Kevin Costner didn't do the Ironman. He joined the Ironman fan club and watched the race while on the Big Island filming Water World.

Tim Jacobs, the Undercover Ironman, was a Secret Service agent on President Clinton's Emergency Response Team, ERT.

David James Elliot was the star of the long running TV show JAG.

Lt. Andy Baldwin was an Ironman athlete before he starred on the 2007 show 'The Bachelor.'

Judy Molnar lost 130 pounds and, in her second attempt, finished the Ironman. While on a promotional tour for the Ironman, she appeared on the Rosie O'Donnell Show. O'Donnell was so impressed that Molnar was hired to create a program to empower overweight women called The Chub Club. She followed that up with a self-help book called, appropriately enough, You Don't Have To Be Thin To Win.

Baywatch star Alexandra Paul.
Photo by Lois Schwartz

IRON CELEBRITIES

Clockwise from left:

Maxine Bahns

Darryl Haley

Kevin Costner and Paula Newby-Fraser

Real Andrews

David James Elliott

Andy Baldwin

Tim Jacobs

Judy Molnar

Butch Johnson

You are heading towards the end of the Ironman swim and everything feels great. It's easy to get carried away. Remember to stay calm and patient. You're still 138.2 windy, hot and tough miles from the ultimate goal. The swim is over... but the Queen Ka'ahumanu Highway awaits.

Photo by Robert Oliver

2000: FREE WHEELIN'

It was late afternoon, and the sun had just started its daily drift toward the horizon. The wind suddenly calmed and the clouds overhead seemed to slow down to take in the action. David Bailey sat stone still on the Queen Kaahumanu Highway at the mouth of the Natural Energy Lab.

He was wrestling. No abdominal claw on Goldberg or a chair to the back of The Rock's noggin. Bailey was mind wrestling, trying to figure out that age-old question: Do I or don't I? It was Tuesday of Ironweek. A little late in the game to be adding over four miles to his last major push before race day.

To show how far the wheelers have come, wheelchair division course record holder Carlos Moleda's 10:55 winning time from last year would have won the first two Ironman events back in 1978 and 1979 overall and his marathon time of 2:17 in 1998 helped establish that black ribbon of highway that runs through the lava fields as his turf.

For the last two years in Kona, Bailey was schooled and tooled by Moleda. For the last two years, the former motocross champion lingered in the shadow cast by Moleda's broad shoulders. Moleda was looking at this as his last Ironman — and he wanted to go out with a bang.

"I've only gone about 80-85 pecent here," admits the former Navy SEAL who was paralyzed after getting shot in the back during a military operation in Central America. "I'm going to go as hard as I can for as long as I can." He paused and smiled. "No holding back this time."

Months before Moleda had uttered the words "sub 10:30." If Moleda was planning to go half an hour faster than ever before, Bailey was in for a tough day.

"Everything Carlos has said he was going to do here, he's done," says Bailey. "If he's thinking 10:30, then to beat him I've got to train to break 10:30, too."

Hence his trip to the Natural Energy Lab.

"I thought, 'I really don't want to go that far, but the Ironman could come down to this," remembers Bailey. "If I go down

Early in the handcycle, Carlos Moleda went by him like he was on a moped. But former motocross world champion David Bailey (right) never panicked. In his third try, on his mother's birthday, in the last few miles, he finally beat Moleda and won his first Ironman title.
Photos by Rich Cruse

"I did the whole bike like there was no marathon, to tell you the truth. I had no idea how I was going to do the marathon, even slowly. I mean, I can't walk. If I stop, I'm stuck."

David Bailey

there, then I know I am really committed to winning this race. I want to look at every bump, every pebble. I want to know the feel, I want to know what the light is like at this time of day. I want to know the wind. I want to visualize the race coming down to this... because it will come down to this."

The best stories at Ironman Hawaii are often those of personal battles — of two people facing each other down, of competitors bringing out the best in each other.

In 1998, Peter Reid's training partner in Boulder, Colorado was a guy named Tim DeBoom. They rode for hours and hours through the mountains without saying a word. They ran, rode and pushed each other to greatness and became the best of friends in the process. When Reid won that year, DeBoom was as happy as if he had won. When DeBoom had his breakthrough race last year and finished third, the first one to great him at the finish was second-place finisher Peter Reid.

But racing means you put your feelings on hold. Racing means every man for himself. Racing means beating everyone... including your buddy. So when Reid and DeBoom found themselves running side by side on Alii Drive with fast-fading German cycling ace Normann Stadler, the only thing between them and Kona glory, the war was on.

"Heading down into the pit, who's on my heels but my buddy Tim DeBoom," recalls Reid. "Three miles later, Tim is still right there. I tried a little trick and stopped to pee to let him go by. That worked for a little bit, but soon Tim was right back on my feet."

Ironday turned ugly early this time around.

"It was so hot, I started dumping water on my head 10 miles into the bike ride," remembers DeBoom.

Then came the wind. A steady 40-45 miles per hour gale on the Queen K Highway on the way out and even worse up to the turnaround. It was pouring rain out at Hawi.

Just your typical October fun run in the lava fields.

"The crosswinds were so bad," says Reid. "I saw this one age grouper get blown across the road on his bike, over the guardrail and out into the lava fields."

The howling winds forced many riders to walk their bikes up the stair-step climb to Hawi. Sister Madonna Buder, 70, ended up with a broken collarbone and over 20 stitches.

Both Reid and DeBoom passed Stadler before mile 14. By the time they headed into the Natural Energy Lab, Reid felt in control.

"My lead was 3:20 in the energy lab over Tim," says Reid. "I felt I could hold that the rest of the way."

Ahhh, to have a good lead late in the Ironman. Wave to the crowd and savor the taste. That's what Natascha Badmann was up to. The 1998 champion sat out the 1999 Ironman trying to make the Swiss Olympic team. After realizing she was better suited for going long, she attacked the Ironman bike course this year with a vengeance and put over 17 minutes between herself and her biggest threat, 1999 champion Lori Bowden of Canada. Yeah, she gave up time in the marathon, but Badmann could afford to do the Rose Parade wave and give Bowden back 14 minutes. It looks close on the stat sheet — 2:40 down at the end — but Badmann was never in trouble, smiling and laughing her way to her second Ironman title.

Not so for Reid.

"I left the energy lab with not a whole lot of energy left," says Reid.

DeBoom shrunk the lead to 1:50 as they emerged from the energy lab, and the magic arrow was starting to point his way.

"The first part of the run, I felt really bad," remembers DeBoom. "When I ran up Palani, I saw [1994 champion] Greg Welch standing on the side of the road. 'What should I do?' I asked him. He told me to eat everything."

He did. And he kept dumping water on himself and putting ice in his shirt.

"Coming up out of the energy lab, I felt so much cooler. Once I got out, I really picked it up," says DeBoom.

Reid could tell. But DeBoom was still flying blind. "I was getting conflicting splits," recalls DeBoom. "I couldn't see Peter and that's not good."

It was good for Reid, who was starting to crumble.

"When you're leading, you don't get splits," he says. "With four miles to go, I saw a friend of mine on the side of the road. He goes, 'You may want to dig deep NOW!' I was trying to find some sort of running form. I was using my arms and my hips... anything I could think of. You've got to be creative out there."

When the sun came out from behind the clouds, DeBoom started to melt. The lead, which had been cut to 1:30, went the other way and eventually went back to two minutes.

"This was the toughest race I have ever done," insists the now two-time champion Reid. "In 1998, everything went right for me all day long and I was able to enjoy that last

magical stretch down Alii Drive. This year, I didn't even see Alii Drive. All I wanted was to see that white line at the finish and to see my feet across it. I crossed that line, and I was completely worked. There was nothing left. It's a great way to finish the Ironman, because it makes you realize how hard this race really is. It was a fight all the way to the finish."

There was still another battle to be decided.

"Coming into this year, I knew this would be a fight," admits Bailey. "I didn't like Carlos. I totally respect his ability and his times over here, but he had something I wanted and I couldn't like him."

After the swim, Bailey and Moleda were a second apart.

"Going up the first hill out of the swim, Carlos went by me like he was on a moped," remembers Bailey. "I thought, 'If that's how fast he's going all day, it's over.' We went through 21 miles in an hour flat and I was losing sight of him."

After the 112-mile handcycle, Moleda was up by about a minute. There were times in the wind on the way to Hawi that they were going all of five miles per hour. Into the run, Moleda quickly put five minutes on Bailey.

"I did the whole bike like there was no marathon, to tell you the truth." says Bailey. "I had no idea how I was going to do the marathon, even slowly. I mean, I can't walk. If I stop, I'm stuck."

Bailey felt lousy for the first five miles of the run.

"I just scooped up all the things that have happened to me, how much I have wanted to win this race going back to 1986 when I saw the Ironman for the first time," he says. "Carlos was coming out of the pit as I was going in. My heart and my spirit were just about broken. I decided there was no way I was going to leave anything extra out there. I'm going to go into the medical van or win."

When he came by the Hard Rock Café about seven miles into the marathon, Bailey saw his mom, his wife and his kids.

"I could tell they were thinking it was over..." he remembers. 'Well, at least he tried."

At the top of Palani, he had a quick conversation with himself.

"I got mad," says Bailey. "I thought, 'Come on, man... I don't want to lose this again. Not like this. I had it. He's right there.'"

On the Queen K Highway, Bailey finally got into a groove and started to eat into Moleda's lead. At mile 14, he was four minutes back. At 16, it was down to 2:40.

"Mark Allen talks about being in a place where you just don't feel the heat, a sort of inner calm," says Bailey. "I always thought 'Yeah, whatever... I guess so...' but I've never experienced it before. Until now, I was hitting the push rims just right. Everything was working for me. I was ducking under the wind and I was in a zone."

He gained 10 seconds... then 15 more. Moleda had gone as hard as he could for as long as he could, but he was starting to fall apart.

"Carlos tried to win the race on the bike," says Bailey. "He dug himself a hole and bonked in the marathon.

"When you're picking up time, your mind completely changes," continues Bailey. "You do everything right, you make all the right decisions."

He was 1:30 down going into the Natural Energy Lab.

"Okay," Bailey says to himself, "This is why I came out here on Tuesday. Now, go to work."

After two disappointments in Kona, a third in 1998 and a second in 1999, Bailey was finally having the Ironman race he always felt he should have.

"His game was to go off the front and never see me," says Bailey. "Mine was to be in the race, to be a problem all day long."

Coming out of the energy lab, Moleda's lead was down to 20 seconds. Bailey gathered himself for the final pass.

"I don't care how much this hurts," he says to himself. "I'll give it my best performance. I'll try and show how strong I am. I was crying. I was screaming. I'm sure Carlos could tell how much I wanted this."

Bailey passed Moleda with less than four miles to go.

"I had to go by hard," insists Bailey. "Carlos just does not give up. He is the toughest competitor I have ever raced against. It killed me to go by him. I said to myself, 'This is going to hurt worse than anything I have ever done. I've got to show him nothing but strength... I have to break his spirit.'"

Suddenly, there was nothing in front of Bailey but a white line and an empty road. His eyes started to mist up as he hammered toward town. Tears dribbled down his cheeks for the last two miles.

He had paid his dues and come back to have the race of his life.

"If I had just come over here for the first time and had a great race and won it, I don't think I would have the respect for the island and the conditions and the heat and the stuff that just comes up out of nowhere and bites you in the butt," reflects Baily. "That feeling coming down Alii Drive first is something I have been visualizing for a lot of years."

He had made a deal with himself before the race: "I decided that no matter how bad it gets out there, I'm just going to shake hands with it," says Bailey. "I was comfortable with the idea that it was going to hurt."

Bailey smiles as he plays with his finishers medal.

"The fact that it hurts is what makes it special. That's what makes it the Ironman."

*Because the 2001 Ironman happened
to occur so close to the September 11 tragedy,
Tim DeBoom knew he was racing
for something much bigger on Ironday.
Mark Allen was the last American male
to win the Ironman back in 1995.
"The people weren't chanting 'Go Tim',"
he recalls, "They were chanting 'Go USA!
Go USA!' It gave me goosebumps."*

*Tim DeBoom
2001 Ironman Champion*

Photo by Robert Oliver

2001: TEMPTATION ISLAND

Previous page: Tim DeBoom stayed patient all day long on the bike. He knew that while Steve Larsen might win the bike ride, the ultimate goal was to win the race.

Above: Cameron Brown (#22) led Peter Reid (#1) and Thomas Hellriegel (#5) early in the run. Brown took second, Hellriegel took third while two-time champion Reid dropped out.

Opposite page: When you win the Ironman you become the target for next year, the guy carrying the torch. Announcer Mike Reilly greets first-time champion Tim DeBoom.

Photos by Robert Oliver

Tim DeBoom needs it. Badly.
Sure, he's happy for
his friend Peter Reid.
But fair is fair.
He has waited in the shadows
long enough.
His year, his life and his career
are wrapped around this one day.
Win it. That is his mantra.
Just win it.

The date was October 14, 2000. They embraced at the finish line. What could be better? Two training partners, two buddies taking first and second place at the most important triathlon on earth. But as they dripped sweat on each other, their thoughts were oh, so different.

"I was thinking, 'I lost the Ironman by two lousy minutes,'" remembers Tim DeBoom. "I knew that every time I went out for a ride or a run or a swim for the next 12 months, that two minutes would both haunt me and push me. Two minutes? You've got to be kidding."

Peter Reid, on the other hand, saw the same two minutes, but it told him an entirely different story.

"Winning that race was so hard knowing that Tim was coming back on me," remembers Reid. "Every step was agony. It was so much tougher than my first win in Hawaii. I decided that 2001 would not be close. I would train so hard that I wouldn't just win the Ironman, I'd dominate."

Be careful what you wish for. It's an oxymoron. When you use the word 'dominate' and 'Ironman' in the same sentence, caution is in order. Kona is a magical place that is both dangerous and beautiful at the same time. Over time, you learn that it is important to tread lightly on Madame Pele's turf. The wind howls, the heat bakes and the body suffers. That is a given. But when will the wind start to swirl? Will the day dawn calm and stay that way? Or will the Mumuku Winds devour your best laid plans and leave you — and them — mutilated on the side of the Queen Kaahumanu Highway.

The Ironman doesn't offer perks to former champions like two-time winner Reid. Just like everyone else, there is but one option: One foot, then the other. Repeat. And pray you get there first.

After the 2000 race, Reid had begun training full time with Lance Armstrong's main man, Chris Carmichael. If Reid rode faster than ever before, the Ironman would be over by the time he got off the bike. The run would simply be a parade lap. Wave to the crowd, kiss some babies, collect his $70,000 and become a three-time champion. It all sounded so perfect.

"I never took any time off after last year's Ironman," admits the Canadian. "I was doing more in November than I had ever done in my life. I was so pumped up from my win that everything seemed so easy. I was so psyched. I was doing six-hour rides all alone in the pouring rain and loving it. I had won by just a little over two minutes. No way that was going to happen again."

Carmichael's philosophy might be great

for a cyclist like Lance Armstrong, but it didn't work for someone who had to balance running, swimming and cycling. Reid went backwards on the bike and wore himself out with his huge mileage and long training days.

By the time Wildflower rolled around in early May, Reid was totally toasted. He had dug himself a Grand Canyon-sized hole that he would spend the rest of the season trying to burrow out of. By June he had gone back to his original coach, Roch Frey.

"It was too much," says Reid. "My cycling suffered and my weight dropped. In the past when I won Ironman, I was at 164 pounds. This year when I arrived in Kona I came in at 158."

Tim DeBoom, on the other hand, was a man on a mission. A little over two minutes — 129 ticks of the clock to be exact. That was the motivation, that was the impetus.

"There wasn't a day that went by where I didn't think about it," says DeBoom.

The plan was to get an Ironman out of the way early, in April in Australia. But DeBoom overheated in the swim and, his body steaming, had to be pulled from the water. He returned to the states and immediately signed up for Ironman California in May. He ended up going head-to-head with his older brother Tony before surging away around 18 miles into the marathon.

"Getting my first Ironman win was big for me," he insists. "It made me feel like everything was falling into place for Kona."

Things were not falling into place for defending champion Reid. He dropped out of Ironman Europe in Germany and decided to fill the void and build his confidence by going back to Ironman Canada where he was the defending champion. Canada was a scant five weeks before Kona.

"I didn't think it would be a problem to recover," says Reid. He won easily. "Everything in Canada went perfectly and going into Ironman I felt great."

Kona. The Big Kahuna. The one Ironman where everyone would be: two-time champion Luc Van Lierde along with Germany's best, including 1997 champion Thomas Hellriegel, Lothar Leder, Jürgen Zäck and Normann Stadler. When the top prize is $70,000, top athletes gear their entire season around traveling to the Kona Coast for the infamous dance with the devil.

The alarm went off for DeBoom early in the Ironman bike ride when he was pulled over by lead marshal Charlie Crawford. That meant he had to do a stand down on the side of the road and then a three-minute stretch in the 'sin bin' at the end of the bike ride.

"It was a tough situation to deal with," remembers DeBoom. "Last year I dropped

my chain and had to go hard to catch up. That uses up extra energy. I knew that meant I needed to eat more. I felt that I needed to ride hard to get a couple of minutes on Peter, Lothar and Luc to make up for my three-minute penalty."

At Waikoloa, Germans Andreas Niedrig and Lothar Leder led, but Van Lierde, Reid, DeBoom, Stadler, Spencer Smith, Hellriegel and the other players were right there — except for one: the X Factor known as Steve Larsen.

Larsen started out as a roadie and was a teammate of Tour de France Champion Lance Armstrong on the Motorola Team in the mid 1990s. He came over to triathlon from the sport of mountain biking where he was a two-time NORBA National Champion and immediately made an impact. He was fourth in his first-ever road triathlon at Wildflower.

"When he passed me on the bike, I thought he was just some roadie out for a ride," remembers Jürgen Zäck the day before Ironman. "Cam Widoff goes, 'Hey…he's in the race.' I was pretty impressed by the way he rode by us. But that was Wildflower and that was in May." Big smile. "This is not Wildflower. This is not May. This is the Ironman."

Since Wildflower, Larsen has won both the Vineman Half Ironman — running a sub-1:15 half marathon — and Ironman Lake Placid where he ran a 2:57 marathon after obliterating the field on the bike.

Larsen came out of the water on Ironday 12 minutes behind the leader in 240th place. He was hoping to swim 57 or 58 minutes. Instead he was 1:00:45.

"I was concerned, thinking I was too far behind," he recalls. "But it turns out everyone was off by about two or three minutes. I was really only eight down. I might have been too hasty early and gone too hard."

On his hot new 27" Lotus with the 56x11 monster gear on the front, he went through the field faster than a Sumo convention through a Denny's all-you-can-eat buffet.

"I was taking some chances out there," he says. "I was really hanging it out in the tailwind section."

Ahhhhhhhhh, tailwinds. On this particular day, they were as rare as body fat in Kailua

Bay. How windy was it, you ask?

Let's listen to one Kimberly Arsenault of Toronto, Canada who was doing her first Ironman in Hawaii. On the way to Kawaihae she was blown completely off her bike by one of the 45-mile-per-hour gusts. She lay on the ground and, one hand on her brake hood, attempted to stand up. The bike blew into the air like a kite and was hovering at a 45-degree angle pointed to the sky as the 5'2" 100-pound Arsenault attempted to hang on for dear life.

"I was trying to get my hand on the handlebar to bring the bike to the ground, but the wind was too strong," Arsenault remembers.

This is a 22-pound bike and, yes, the wind is keeping the damn thing airborne.

"I'm thinking this is stupid," she says. "I never swear and I must have used the 'f' word 1,000 times that day." Eventually, a marshal showed up and helped her lower her Cervelo to earth. "He says 'You are a hazard right now and I'm here to help.' He held the bike down so that I could get back on. I was going about 11 kilometers an hour on the flats. It was awful."

Larsen had no time to worry about the gusts. He was busy outsplitting the field by almost 12 minutes.

"He went by me like a rocket," says Normann Stadler. "I couldn't believe he was going that fast. I thought I had no legs, but I was going 35K per hour when he went by. He put 200-300 yards on me in 20 seconds."

Thomas Hellriegel was equally impressed. "I liked his pedal stroke," Hellriegel admits. "It was very nice to watch."

He didn't get to watch it for long as Larsen hammered his way toward the lead. Peter Reid was more concerned about Tim DeBoom. And DeBoom? He couldn't have answered the challenge if he wanted to.

"At the point Steve passed me I was feeling so crappy I couldn't even think of going with him," says DeBoom. "I wanted to make sure I had a lead on Peter going into the run. Because I knew I was going to lose three minutes to him in the penalty box."

At 80 miles, Larsen had gone by everyone except Normann Stadler. By mile 95, Larsen was leading, but he was running out of road. He was hoping to have upwards of 10 minutes by the end of the ride on DeBoom, Reid and Van Lierde. By the end of the ride, he had about five minutes on them. And just over one mile into the run, he had 4:45 on Reid, 6:00 on Stadler and 7:28 on DeBoom.

DeBoom caught his old training partner along Alii Drive and tried to get Reid to run with him. It was no use.

"I said, 'Let's go Pete' when I passed him," remembers DeBoom. "The hardest thing in the world is to struggle and have a bad day. Pete had one of those days anyone can have here."

"I tried to run with Thomas Hellriegel and then Lothar Leder, but nothing worked," Reid says. "I'm disappointed in myself for not finishing, but I just didn't have it."

DeBoom did. He was in hot pursuit of a cramping Steve Larsen. Out on the Queen K Highway, about the 10-mile mark, DeBoom made it official and eased by to take a lead he would never relinquish.

"I tried to race smart," he says. "Usually I try to catch the leaders on the bike. I wasn't even thinking about Steve beforehand and nothing he did was going to change the way I raced."

Nope. This time he let Larsen go, took his three-minute penalty, and then fashioned a 2:45:54 marathon, the fastest of the day, to win his first Ironman Hawaii title.

"When I passed Steve, the sun seemed to intensify," DeBoom admits. "I suffered."

So did Larsen, who was doing his second-ever marathon 10 weeks after his first at Ironman Lake Placid. He paid the price.

"My expectations were high for myself," says Larsen. "I was in a position to win. I needed to seal the deal at the end there, but I didn't. I learned a lot and hopefully I'll figure out what made the wheels come off 10 miles into the marathon."

The wheels come off for everyone, Steve. The temptation is to go hard too soon. Maybe scorch past 239 people in 112 miles. Or skip your special needs bag. Or change your bike position. Or go too hard too early. Or to do another Ironman five weeks before Kona.

Tim DeBoom learned his lesson well.

Sit back, be patient and take what the island gives you. When you get greedy, when you give in to temptation, you pay.

Pressure. It is something to dread or to savor.
It comes with being the defending champion.
On this day, Tim DeBoom (pictured) will be the target,
The one they will follow all day long.
He knows that while winning once is great...
Winning twice is even better.

Photo by Robert Oliver

2002: THE ROOKIE

Aussie Chris McCormack has won it all: a short course world title, Wildflower, Ironman Australia, Escape from Alcatraz. He likes to lead early and he likes to lead late. Make your move and say your goodbyes. Thanks for playing and don't forget your lovely parting gifts. Strategy has never been part of the Chris McCormack game plan. Keep it simple. The fastest and most aggressive guy wins, so strap 'em up tight and let's go.

On Ironman morning, the rain was coming down in buckets. The swim became one of the toughest in history.

"The swells were huge," remembers two-time champion Peter Reid. "You'd be with a group of guys and then a swell would hit and no one would be around you. Then the swell would hit again and we'd all be right together. It was really strange. Even with the boats out there, I didn't even see the turnaround until we were almost on top of it."

The rain slacked off during the swim, but it doubled the effort during the first hour of the bike ride.

"I went to the front because I didn't want to be caught in a drafting situation," says rookie McCormack. "I wasn't planning on leading."

But 30 miles into the bike ride there he was, just like in a short-course race, leading the way. He looked easy, relaxed. Before he knew it he had 30 seconds on defending champion Tim DeBoom, Reid, New Zealand's Cameron Brown and the rest of the Pips. That's right....The Pips.

It's business as usual on the Kona Coast. The defending champion — this time Tim DeBoom — is the equivalent of

Top: A happy Natascha Badmann blowing the women's field apart during the bike ride.
Middle: Cameron Brown of New Zealand had his second great race in a row in Hawaii. Second in 2001....third in 2002.
Bottom: Peter Reid (left) was happy just to be in the game after gaining 25 pounds and announcing his retirement earlier in the year. In the marathon he ran with his old training buddy Tim DeBoom before DeBoom pulled away.
"Coming in second was the bonus," he insisted afterwards. "Just finishing was all that mattered."

Opposite page: The Rookie, Chris McCormack, talked beforehand about eventually winning six Ironman titles. Early on in the bike ride he was smiling and happy. Before dropping out in the marathon, he was cramping and miserable. Welcome to the Ironman, rook!

Photos by Robert Oliver

Gladys Knight. All the characters hanging his every gear change are affectionat called The Pips. He makes a move, th make a move. He stands pat, so do they.

McCormack has never been a Pip. No He likes to blaze his own trail. But Ironm history says that it pays to be a Pip. M Allen learned over time that it was better hang with Dave Scott then it was to try a ride or run away from the guy.

"I planned to ride with the group," insi McCormack. "I have watched the race many times I know that going off the front your own is suicidal in Hawaii. When I go gap, I didn't feel like I was riding hard a felt I could handle the pace."

DeBoom knew better. He went from 10 to third to second to first in four years. Th Ironman is about paying your dues, abo putting in your time in the lava fields. Sur Luc Van Lierde of Belgium won it in 1996 his first attempt, but you have to go back Dave Scott in 1980 to find the last rookie win in Hawaii. DeBoom was staying in co trol and knew the runners were with hir The cyclists (Thomas Hellriegel, Jürge Zäck and Normann Stadler) were now wor ing with McCormack to build the lead. B DeBoom has learned over time to follo your plan and never deviate.

"I was hoping that they might be going little too hard," admits DeBoom.

Peter Reid was sure of it.

"When I saw them coming back from Ha their mouths were open from the effort. thought they were going way too hard wa too early."

McCormack couldn't disagree mor

veryone is saying that I went too hard on
e bike and left my running legs out on the
een Highway," says McCormack. "That's
solute rubbish."

Rubbish? Natascha Badmann was mak-
g rubbish of the women's field for the
urth time. She went through the women's
ld like Sherman through Atlanta and built
big enough lead to mail in the marathon.
nazingly, she made ground on the male
os on the out and back to Hawi. The
uestion wasn't if she'd win, but by how
uch?

McCormack was doing the same math.
et's see," he says to himself, "I've got
ght minutes on the field off the bike. If I
n a 2:58 marathon, DeBoom or Reid or
rown have to run 2:50 to beat me. I
ought 'This race is mine. They're never
bing to catch me.'"

In this case 'Never' came pretty darn
rly. Hellriegel went by McCormack before
ey made it to Pay and Save Hill and the
arade was on. DeBoom, Reid and Brown
aced past the cramping McCormack and
ll three caught 1997 champion Hellriegel
ho held on to fourth. DeBoom took his
econd win in a row proving that patience is
ndeed an Iron virtue.

"I thought, 'I have a shot here to win this,'
nsists McCormack. 'Then I started cramp-
ng. Mentally I was alert and ready to go. I
vanted to push forward, but my legs would-
't let me. It was the most frustrating
moment of my career. I thought, 'Man, this
s a nightmare.'"

No Chris, it's much more than a night-
nare. It's the Ironman.

2003: LOST AND FOUND

"My body started to fall apart. I was so far into the overtraining syndrome that mentally, physically, emotionally and psychologically I was cooked. I was done. I needed to get away and I didn't know if I was going to come back."

- Peter Reid

Going in to the 25th Anniversary race, both Tim DeBoom (1) and Peter Reid (2) had two wins each. But Reid caught DeBoom in the marathon and had a two-minute lead when DeBoom stopped at an aid station about 13 miles in and dropped out. He ended up in the hospital where he passed a kidney stone. Reid, in the meantime, ended up with win number three.
Photo by Robert Oliver

It is early afternoon. Two-time Ironman champion Peter Reid is relaxing in Starbucks. He is wearing his motorcycle leathers and there is powdered sugar on his sleeves and on his chest with a few crumbs clinging to his lips from the treat or three that he has been busy inhaling. If there was a mirror handy he would notice that his belly is bigger than it has been in years.

Check that. His belly is bigger than it's been....EVER.

Instead of pushing himself through his usual bike routes near his home outside of Victoria, B.C., like he would have been a few short months before, he has spent his retirement weeks flying through his old cycling routes on his motorcycle, his hand on the wide-open throttle and his mind in another world.

Reid first won the Ironman in 1998 on what he called a magical day. He said that it was a trip down Kona's famed Alii Drive that would stay with him until the day he died.

Two years later he won again, but this time it was different. He crossed the finish line with a 2:09 lead over-second place finisher Tim DeBoom. But in Reid's obsessive mind, winning was no where near good enough.

"I won, but I wasn't satisfied," Reid admits. "I crossed the line thinking 'That was too close.' I didn't sit back to savor the win. The next day I was already planning my assault for 2001. That was the beginning of the end."

Shortly after returning to the home he shared with his wife, 1999 Ironman champion Lori Bowden, in British Columbia, he got right back to work and started riding, running and swimming like it was the middle of the next season. By the time he got to his first race, he was totally toasted.

"My body started to fall apart. I was so far into the overtraining syndrome that mentally, physically, emotionally and psychologically I was cooked. I was done. I needed to get away and I didn't know if I was going to come back."

He had dropped out of the 2001 Ironman during the marathon while his friend and former training partner Tim DeBoom won in Kona for the very first time.

Back to the summer of 2002...As Reid sat surrounded by remnants of his fat-laden snack, his good friend and chiropractor Rob Hasegawa approached him. He had watched Reid spiral downhill to the point where he simply couldn't take it anymore. He had pulled an article from Inside Triathlon Magazine by Mark Allen called '18 Weeks to your First Ironman.' And now he was placing it in front of the two-time Ironman champion and telling him to push the donut aside and get back in the saddle again. He could see his friend was going backwards fast.

"Peter" he said. "Go back to Hawaii to finish the damn thing. Then quit the sport with some closure."

Reid picked up the article off the table. He was only 15 weeks from the 2002 Ironman so he was already three weeks in the hole. But what the heck? If he followed Allen's program, maybe he'd get his fat butt back into shape.

Over the next 15 weeks he lost 25 pounds

This page, top: One of the best battles of the day came when Lori Bowden of Canada (54) caught up to the leader, Nina Kraft of Germany. Eventually Bowden eased away to win her second title.

Bottom: Two time champion Tim DeBoom collapsed in the medical van during the marathon. He was passing a kidney stone.

Opposite page, top: It's a select club. Only five people have won more than two Ironman Triathlon World Championship titles: Paula Newby-Fraser (8), Dave Scott (6), Mark Allen (6), Natascha Badmann (4) and now Peter Reid (3).

Middle: Rutger Beke of Belgium surprised everyone- including himself- with his second place finish.

Bottom: German star Normann Stadler was first off the bike and led the marathon until Peter Reid passed him the lava fields. Stadler ended up fourth.

Photos by Robert Oliver

but did only five hard, intense workouts: two short triathlons, two hard swim workouts with Olympic triathlon champion Simon Whitfield and one 10K road race. Everything else was slow and steady.

"The love of the sport started to come back," admits Reid. "In the beginning I just loved to mix it up with the big boys. Then it got to the point where I was scared to lose, where I was more worried about what my sponsors thought than following my passion."

He came to Kona in 2002 with absolutely no pressure.

"It was an easy day," he continues. "I never dug deep. My only pressure was to finish. I felt that if I got to Alii Drive that would be good enough."

Tim DeBoom won for the second time with Reid firmly in second. When they passed each other in the Natural Energy Lab (Reid heading in and DeBoom heading out) there was Mr. Serious Peter Reid with this huge smile on his face.

"Tim must have thought I was crazy," remembers Reid. "He probably thought I was trying to tell him with that look that I was going to run him down. What I was really saying was 'Man, I am so happy to be back doing what I love.' I had forgotten all about the love of the sport."

He took time off after the 2002 race to savor his second-place finish.

"Probably too much time," laughs Reid. "It took me awhile this spring and summer to get my back in shape." He finished fourth in Ironman Germany in Frankfurt. "I thought I should have won," he says.

Back home in Canada he gave a call to six-time Ironman World Champion Mark Allen to bounce some ideas off of him.

"Mark's training was never very complicated," says Reid. "He always listened to his body and did what felt right. He told me not to plan too much, because if you do you won't listen to your body. I mapped out a plan and felt if I could complete it, I'd be super fit. Going into Ironman I was supremely confident because I knew I did sessions that I felt no one else would be doing."

Allen was called the Zen Master because of his ability to focus on race day and to tune out any and every distraction that could keep him from winning.

"Mark was always so mentally tough on race day," says Reid, "and I wanted to be just as tough."

He flew to Kona in mid-September and went up to 5,600 feet for two weeks of hard, solo training. He was Rocky training for a rumble with Apollo Creed. No TV. No training partners. No wasted time.

"I did some amazing runs and rides up at altitude and didn't train on the Ironman course," says Reid.

On race day 2003, he did everything right. He usually comes out of the water between 40th and 50th place. This year he was fourth or fifth onto his bike.

"I ruined a lot of people's days," he laughs. "Tim [DeBoom] was in absolute shock when I pulled up next to him 10K into the bike ride."

When Chris McCormack, the two-time Ironman Australia champion, caught up he said 'I thought you were Luke Bell. What are you doing here so early?'

Chris Legh bridged up to the leaders about 50K into the ride. He usually rides with Reid as they hammer their way through

the field on the Queen K Highway. He said something to Reid as well about his great swim.

Every comment was swallowed whole and then ignored. "I didn't respond to anyone," Reid admits. "I was in the total Zen mode. "Their words gave me strength. If someone came up next to me on the bike, I punched it to let them know I was strong."

Normann Stadler of Germany was leading, but the pack of DeBoom, Reid, Ironman rookie Rutger Beke, New Zealand Ironman champion Cameron Brown, Jürgen Zack, Cameron Widoff, Thomas Hellriegel, Chris Legh and 24-year-old Luke Bell was in the same ZIP code. With mellower than normal wind conditions, cycling star Steve Larsen, who was fighting an infection, made up very little ground in the first 85 miles of the ride and pulled the plug, knowing this would not be his day.

Reid knew it as well. Why? Because this one belonged to him. After grabbing Cameron Brown's run bag by mistake, he and Brown started the run an extra minute down to DeBoom and the others.

"I emptied my bag and this pair of Nikes tumbles out," he remembers. "Nikes? I've been with Reebok for 10 years. I had to run and find Cam and switch bags. I knew that if you give Tim some slack, he'll go. 'I've got to get up there quick,' I said to myself."

Quick? How often do you see runners in an Ironman marathon with both feet OFF the ground. Give up? UHHHHH...try NEVER. Not just one shot, mind you. Photo after photo after photo. Peter Reid leaping off the pavement like frickin' Bambi in search of DeBoom.

"I was surprised how quickly I caught Tim," he says. "The next thing I knew I had caught Normann and was leading the race."

When he headed down into the Natural Energy Lab a little more than 16 miles into the marathon, Mark Allen yelled to Reid that DeBoom was out.

"I thought Mark meant that he was out of contention," says Reid, "not out of the race. Tim doesn't pull out of races. If he's out, he's out on a stretcher."

Which was exactly the case. About two minutes back of Reid, DeBoom stopped at an aid station and then collapsed. It turns out he needed to be taken to the hospital because he was passing a kidney stone.

"People thought I'd be psyched Tim was out," says Reid. "No way. I wanted to beat him...to beat him at this best."

As Reid was on his way out of the Natural Energy Lab, Cameron Brown was heading in the opposite direction.

"Cam's quick little feet have been catching me all summer long," says Reid. "I learned in Germany how quickly it all can change. One minute I was in second place, the next fourth."

Between Reid and Brown was Rutger Beke, the newcomer from Belgium who was in second place and incredibly happy to be there. He wasn't planning any sprints to the front anytime soon.

"I was thinking in the Natural Energy Lab that if I get passed by Cameron Brown, that's okay, I'll still be in third," says Beke. "Coming off the bike I figured if I could out run four guys from our group I'd be in the top 10. I didn't believe it. I said to myself at the end 'SH__! You're second!' I was so excited I jumped in the air 1500 meters from the finish and almost cramped."

Reid came across the finish line first for the third time in his life. The first time was magical. The second time was torture. The third? While it felt good to win, it felt better to honor those close to him who were rock-solid and never wavered.

"Some people never gave up on me, even when I did," says Reid.

"I'll never forget that."

2004: SOLITARY CONFINEMENT

It is a Thursday night in September. Three-time Ironman Triathlon World Champion Peter Reid is in a cabin by himself at 6,000 feet up on Mauna Kea. No television, no computer, no radio, no distractions. For a few weeks each September, Reid disappears. He leaves his home in Victoria, British Columbia and heads to Kona to be a hermit, for what he calls solitary confinement.

The air is still. In the distance Reid hears a muffled explosion that brings him to his feet. The next explosion sounds even closer. Is the Big Island under attack? What the heck is going on? The noise ceases, and it becomes deathly quiet once again. Eventually Reid falls asleep.

He drives the 50 minutes to the pool the next morning and asks around before the workout.

"What the heck was going on last night?"

Calmly, one of the locals fills him in.

"Thursday night is bomb night at the military base," says the stranger casually. "It happens every week."

How appropriate. A few weeks later, this time on a blustery Saturday, Reid and his Iron-compatriots would be bombed into submission by übercyclist Normann Stadler of Germany, who systematically destroyed the field. By the time he dismounted and started the marathon that day, Reid heard that Stadler's lead was an unbelievable 24 minutes and 10 seconds.

Stadler was on Alii Drive a few miles into the run. Since no officials were on the course giving splits, he had been flying blind since the bike turnaround in Hawi. At that point, he knew he had a substantial lead over Reid, Tim DeBoom, Simon Lessing, Faris Al- Sultan, Luke Bell and the others.

"I've never seen anyone that far ahead at Hawi," admits Reid.

But that big a lead? Stadler had no idea.

"When someone told me that my lead was 15 minutes on second place and 22 minutes on Peter, I thought that I did a short course; that I must have missed a turn," laughs Stadler.

Reid wasn't laughing. He had called his coach and mentor Mark Allen in late August and asked him how he could gracefully get out of defending his title on October 16. He simply was not going to be ready.

"Mark told me how Scott Molina went to Palm Springs out of shape in 1988, crammed in 11 hard days of training, then won the Ironman. So I thought, 'Okay, maybe I can do this.'"

Reid goes to Kona for two and half weeks in September to answer the whys: Why do I do the Ironman? Why am I doing this to myself?

"That time alone allows me to reflect on my life," says Reid. "I learn to focus on mental drive and to answer all of my doubts. I answer the whys in September so that I don't have to deal with them on race day."

This year, for the first time, he brought a training partner with him, Björn Andersson of Sweden.

"The first day we swam together and it was great," remembers Reid. "Then we went out on the bike. I was in my small ring and he was in his 58 x 12."

They rode for 10 minutes before Andersson dropped Reid for the first time. Then he did it again, and again and again. Six times in all. By the end of the ride, Reid's already compromised confidence level had dropped to a level just below thin mint.

"I called Mark and told him what happened," says Reid. "He goes, 'You can't train with Björn anymore. I guarantee he'll burn out by race day.'" So for the rest of the time Reid rode, ran and swam on his own.

Last year, Reid came to the race in great shape. He surprised everyone in the lead group with a faster-than-usual swim, but when someone tried to compliment him on it, Reid wasn't buying in.

"I wasn't going to give away any energy," admits Reid. "I never acknowledged anyone all day long. My focus was total. It was 100 percent on me and winning the Ironman."

This year, Reid felt he went into Ironman in the worst shape of his career and his demeanor beared that out. While last year he didn't give away energy on the bike, this time around he seemed bothered and angry all day long.

"I was the lead for this group of 10 guys and I could never get anyone to share time at the front," Reid admits. "I was yelling 'come on, let's go,' but no one would help out. This year was all about mental strength. I fought all day long, one centimeter at a time."

His thought was that Stadler would gain 10-12 minutes by the end of the ride, just like the top cyclists had done in past years, and Reid would run him down, just like last year. Stadler led off the bike in 2003 before dropping to fourth during the run. Steve Larsen led off the bike in 2001 and Tim DeBoom ran him down. While Natascha Badmann has been able to ride off the front and win the Ironman on the bike for the women four times, the men's race has turned tactical over the years with the best runner in the field playing it cautiously on the bike before taking charge in the marathon.

Stadler had spent six weeks in San Diego training hard, watching his diet and staying away from chocolate — all for this day. The night before the race, the decision had been made that no officials would be on the course giving any of the athletes splits. If Stadler could get a gap, there was a chance that the chase group would stay with Reid and DeBoom rather than go after him.

And that's exactly what happened. With the number one on his chest and three wins on his resumé, Reid was the obvious target. Why would anyone in the chase pack want to get away from Peter Reid? The guy has a good chance to win and is the defending champion. Chase Stadler? Why? Reid knows what he's doing. We'll stay right here. Plus, with the wind in their faces all day long, the ride was hard enough without trying to play Super Hero and go off the front.

From 90 miles to the finish of the ride, the chase pack tends to let up to get ready for the daunting task of running 26.2 miles in middle of the day sauna-like conditions. Stadler knew that if he pushed that last 20 miles, he could really add to his lead and, maybe, just maybe, win the Ironman on the bike.

"24:10"

When Reid heard that number, he didn't panic.

"When I started the marathon I thought, 'This is the Ironman, anything can happen.'" He remembered that in 1995 Mark Allen spotted Germany's Thomas Hellriegel 13 minutes ahead and ran him down.

"I thought one guy at a time," says Reid. "And who's next?"

At mile five, a German spectator yelled to Reid that if he could keep his pace, he could get second. "No," snapped Reid as he stared him down, "first."

Reid saw Stadler coming out of the Natural Energy Lab with about six miles to go and still thought he had a chance.

"Normann looked good, but not great," remembers Reid. "If he walked one mile, I'd be right there. I kept fighting the whole way."

Stadler saw that he still had 17 minutes on Reid coming out of the Natural Energy Lab. Reid out split Stadler 2:46:10 to 2:57:53 in the marathon and cut the lead to 10:11 by the end.

But it was too little, too late.

Years ago, another great German cyclist, Jürgen Zäck, professed on the Ironman stage that his goal in pushing the pace on the bike was to take the run out of the great runner's legs. Six-time champion Mark Allen then took the microphone and countered, "Jürgen wants to win the bike ride. My goal is to win the race."

After crossing the Ironman finish line on October 16, Normann Stadler broke down in tears of happiness.

Why? Because he had just done both.

2004: Fall from Grace

BY DON NORCROSS

Nina Kraft headed down the finishing chute on Alii Drive of the Ironman Triathlon World Championship in Hawaii — all alone in first place and more than 15 minutes in front of Natascha Badmann. The sun was shining, music was blaring and fans were screaming and ringing cowbells, but Kraft did not celebrate. She didn't thrust her arms skyward. She didn't high-five fans. She didn't let out a joyous, ear-piercing shriek. The last 10, 15 yards, Kraft walked across the finish line.

This is a woman who had come so achingly close to winning triathlon's most revered race — third in 2001, second in 2002, third in 2003. When her day finally arrived, Kraft brought her hands up to her face and placed them on her cheeks, almost as if she was embarrassed by the lopsided victory.

Now we know why. She cheated.

Kraft tested positive for EPO and her victory was nullified. Badmann was elevated to her fifth Ironman Hawaii victory and now Nina Kraft's triathlon career likely is history.

Admitting her guilt on German television the day after her positive test became public, Kraft did not make excuses.

"I never really rejoiced over the victory in Hawaii," Kraft said. "I was ashamed the entire time, especially in front of my family. I cheated."

"I think you have to give her credit," said Heather Fuhr, who vaulted to second place. "She's probably the first (athlete) to say, 'I screwed up. I did it.' Give her credit at least for that."

Kraft turns 36 in December. The German Triathlon Union is expected to slap her with a two-year ban. By then, Kraft will be 38 and probably persona non grata.

"A lot of people will not forgive me, and I do not think they will want to see me in triathlon again," she said.

Kraft's positive test stunned the triathlon world, angered many and made people question her previous accomplishments, which include four Ironman-distance victories. She won Ironman Germany the past two years by a whopping 19 and 18 minutes.

"Who's to say Nina wasn't doing drugs then?" said Greg Welch, winner of the 1994 Ironman Hawaii.

"She has deceived everyone," said Normann Stadler, a fellow German and winner of this year's men's race.

"Who can sponsors trust now?" said Germany's Lothar Leder, four times a top-five finisher at Kona.

Eight-time Ironman Hawaii champion Paula Newby-Fraser suspected Kraft had used drugs after watching Kraft fly away on the bike.

"Her bike ride was ridiculous," Newby-Fraser said. "There she was, blowing away the competition, riding past professional men with no attention to aerodynamics. No professional athlete looking for that edge is going to have jewelry hanging off them, a bike pump hanging off the side of the bike, their helmet on crooked (not even wearing an aero helmet) and water bottles in the front and all down the tube. Yet there she is, blowing everyone's doors off. I thought, 'Oh, my God. This is not right.' "

Kraft has always cut a mysterious air, hanging in the background, always shadowed by her Svengali/boyfriend/coach Martin Malleier. Yet no one ever questioned her athleticism and boldness. Her first road race? A three-hour, 11-minute marathon. The first triathlon she finished? Ironman Germany in a respectable 10 hours, 30 minutes back in 1997.

But that same lust to think big, go for broke and a willingness to roll the dice, ultimately proved to be her downfall. Last year at Kona, she felt she was unfairly assessed a three-minute drafting penalty on the bike, a call that rattled her emotionally and which Kraft thinks cost her the victory.

"Last year," Kraft said on German TV, "I would have won that race, if I had not gotten a time punishment."

After becoming the only female triathlete to break nine hours this year at her Frankfurt victory last July, Kraft seemed destined to make the leap to heralded Ironman Triathlon World Champion. But Malleier espoused a conspiracy theory. He thought referees were against Kraft and that she would again be assessed a drafting penalty (which, indeed, she was.) And the Svengali didn't want to take chances.

"Even if you have a penalty, (by taking EPO) you can win," Malleier said he told Kraft. Malleier says he pressured Kraft into using EPO and that for a long time she refused. Eventually she caved in.

Said Malleier, "If you have someone always speaking about these things, putting mental pressure on you, by the end of the day, one day, you will say, 'OK, I'll do it.'"

Malleier said Kraft used EPO from "about 2 1/2 to three weeks" before the race, then stopped five days out. Asked if Kraft had ever previously taken performance-enhancing drugs, Malleier said, "No, no, no. It was my fault (she took EPO). I put the pressure on her. She is (normally) not a person to ever take anything."

Welch said Malleier's pressure doesn't absolve Kraft of blame.

"At the end of the day, Nina's got to take the drug," Welch said. "She could have said, 'No, Martin. I'm not a drug cheat. I'm going to do this the hard way.' "

Badmann has now won Ironman Hawaii four of the past five years. But sadly, Kraft's drug use denied fans and photographers the delightful sight of Badmann skipping, pirouetting, high-fiving and blowing kisses along Alii Drive.

From 2000 through 2002, the Swiss Miss dominated the race, pedaling away on the bike, then cruising in the marathon to 3-, 4- and 7 1/2-minute victories. The past two years, Badmann illustrated her grit. She was throwing up early on the run last year, then collected herself and finished second.

The effervescent Badmann likes to joke that an angel sits on one shoulder during Ironman and a devil is perched on the other.

"This time, the devil was so big," Badmann said. "I didn't know it could be this big."

On the bike, where she normally pierces through the wind, Badmann labored.

"I was struggling," she said. "I couldn't sit on the bike. (She said her, uhh, groin area was hurting.) I had no power. I never came close to what I normally can show. I just felt uncomfortable."

On a day when the Mumuku winds blew nearly 30 mph, wickedly changing directions so that they were almost always a headwind or crosswind, and the temperature climbed to near 90, Badmann officially won in 9 hours, 50 minutes, 4 seconds. Indicative of the taxing conditions, it's the slowest women's winning time in 19 years. Joanne Ernst won the 1985 race in 10:25:22. Kraft finished in 9:33:25.

"That was a little bit odd right there," Welch said of Kraft's near 17-minute margin. "But I still hadn't thought she'd done drugs."

Still, the day was memorable for one Kona veteran. Heather Fuhr, who turns 37 in January and had struggled so long at Kona after her 1997 victory, vaulted to second after Kraft's dis-

Natascha Badmann (41) ended up winning her fifth Ironman title, though denied her triumphant finish, when Nina Kraft (left) was disqualified for using EPO. Photo by Robert Oliver.

qualification. Australia's Kate Major, 26, the former pro squash player, moved up to third.

But the 2004 women's race will not be remembered for Badmann's determination. Or Fuhr's comeback. Or Major's ascendancy. It will be remembered for Nina Kraft's fall from grace.

"Nina's probably a talented enough athlete that she could have won without (EPO)," Fuhr said. "Now, we'll never know."

When Kraft's positive drug test became public, Welch kept thinking about how pained she must have felt when accepting the winner's trophy in front of a huge crowd at the awards banquet. "Inside, she must have felt horrible," Welch said. "She knows she cheated. When I thought about that, right that minute, I was sick to my stomach. I really feel sorry for her. She knows she's good enough to win it without drugs."

Welch paused for a moment, reflected on what Kraft's world must be like now, and said, "How can you carry that guilt with you all the time?"

The race is young,
the day just beginning.
A few strokes in,
you'll swear you are
in the world's largest
aquarium. Is there a
more beautiful swim in
the sport of triathlon?
We think not.

Photo by Robert Oliver

2005: THE JOY OF SIX

BY DON NORCROSS

Right opposite: Michellie Jones had a dream a few weeks before the Ford Ironman that she lost the race by two minutes to Natascha Badmann (above). That's exactly what happened. In a phenomenal rookie performance, Jones led off the bike, took second and went 9:11:51.
Photos by Rich Cruse

There were other women racing at Ironman Hawaii— 466 others to be precise. At that euphoric, late-night party atmosphere along Alii Drive—where native Hawaiians dressed in grass skirts and floral prints hula dance and pound the drums, where rock music blares, schwag flies through the air and thousands squeeze tight to celebrate life—Sarah Reinertsen sent tears down the spectators' cheeks, becoming the first woman with a prosthetic limb to finish the race.

In the race's final hour, Sister Madonna Buder at 76 became the oldest woman to finish Ironman Hawaii. Talk about faith. Barely 30 minutes after the midnight finishing hour, Sister Buder rested, exhausted and passed out atop a cement bench not 75 yards from the finish line.

Hours earlier, when the sun was still baking, 27-year-old Aussie Kate Major further validated what seems to be a given: Eventually, the laurel wreath will be placed upon the former squash star's head. In her knock-knock-knock, I'm-coming rise, Major has finished 12th-9th-3rd-3rd the past four years on the Big Island.

But on the subject of which female would cross the finish line first at the 2005 Ford Ironman Triathlon World Championship, it came down to two women: Michellie Jones and Natascha Badmann.

Two remarkable women, so talented yet so different: Jones, five-feet-10, regal, polished, professional. Badmann, five-feet-four, emotional, effervescent; her heart, soul and emotions exposed for all to see. Jones, the Olympic-distance darling. Badmann, the longer the better. Jones, raised in a warm home with a twin sister. Badmann, who will only say of her childhood, "Some things with my family were not how it should be." Jones, the Ironman Hawaii rookie. Badmann, trying to join the rank of legends and win the race a sixth time.

Badmann, who turns 39 in December, and Jones, 36, came to Kona with opposite agendas; Badmann to reclaim what was rightfully hers. For she might have won the Ironman Triathlon World Championship the year before, but the title was impersonal and perfunctory, like a business transaction, given to her by default only after Nina Kraft tested positive for EPO. Badmann cashed the $100,000 paycheck but didn't reap the thing she values most: soaking up the fans' love and adulation along Alii Drive. What good is it being queen if you can't dance while blowing kisses, touching hands and pirouetting down triathlon's most famed runway?

"The most hurting was not getting flowers," Badmann says. "Some people look at it and say, 'C'mon, she got her paycheck.' That's not what I race for. That's never what I raced for. Coming down Alii Drive, this is the paycheck."

As for Jones, she came to Kona with her eyes wide open, wanting to soak up the wonder that is Ironman Hawaii. She had been there once before, exactly 10 years earlier, at the height of her

Olympic-distance domination, curious to see what all the fuss was about. During her 1995 visit, she made the mistake of checking out the medical tent where, ironically, she would return 10 years later.

"It looked like something out of M*A*S*H," Jones recalls of the 1995 scene. "So many people did not look good. To me, it was like, 'No way I could do that.' "

She vowed to never race an Ironman. But things change. Jones' Australia triathlon federation turned its back on her in 2004, in essence saying, "Thanks for the 2000 Olympic silver, but your time has come and gone." Not ready to pose that "What now?" post-professional athletic question—her competitive fires not yet doused and expertly guided by her husband/coach/agent/bike mechanic/soul mate Pete Coulson—Jones moved to the long stuff.

And so on October 15, 2005, the two women converged—Natascha Badmann, wanting to etch her name among the greats and wallow in the applause one more time and Michellie Jones, in only her second Ironman race, needing to answer the Big Island's siren song.

"I had no idea how I'd go," says Jones.

Race-Day Match-Up

The swim is not Badmann's strength. When she took up endurance sports more than 15 years ago, her coach/life partner Toni Hasler looked at Badmann's stroke then said, "After 15 minutes, Natascha had to leave the pool. She couldn't drink all the water." This year at Kona, Badmann got lost with a group at the turnaround, swam a bit off course, recovered and stepped out of Kailua Bay in one hour, two minutes, 30 seconds. By then, Jones was dry, clipped into her bike and pedaling about town. Her swim: 54 minutes, 55 seconds.

The bike figured to be a fascinating battle between the two stars. Badmann has owned the Queen K Highway for years, typically recovering from a mediocre swim, then pedaling off and disappearing among the men. Jones, though, is hell on wheels. Coulson is a world champion masters track cyclist and pushed Jones hard during the summer. So hard that some women stopped riding with her. Says Triathlete Magazine co-publisher John Duke, "Michellie was just throttling those girls."

Jones assumed the women's lead at about Mile 28 of the bike and when she did everyone thought, "When does Natascha catch up? By the turnaround at Hawi? Sooner? On the return trip along the Queen K?" The answer? She never caught up—at least not on the bike.

"I'm passing people, thinking, 'Woah, I must be riding okay,'" says Jones.

Okay?

Badmann's bike split was only two minutes faster than Jones.' Worse yet, for Badmann, she was cited for a penalty and had to sit four minutes in the Sin Bin, meaning Jones' lead was closer to 10 minutes by the time Badmann finished serving her penalty.

Of her predicament, Badmann says, "If you had asked me before the race if I could [make up] 10 minutes, I'd say, 'Not against her.'"

For all her greatness, the unanswered question about Badmann at Hawaii was this: Can she run? The Swiss Miss had so dominated the women's field on the bike that she had never been pushed during the marathon. Rounding up a few seconds, she had gone 3:12, 3:14 and 3:13 the previous three years. This year, that just wouldn't get it done.

Jones, though, was running just the second marathon of her life and the first one had not been pretty. At Ironman Florida to wrap up 2004, Jones suffered digestive problems after consuming excess calories on the bike. Bloated, she limped home in 3:28, still good enough to win.

Jones' running issues were not as pronounced this time. But by about Mile 10, she was obviously feeling some pain. As it turns out, what might have cost her a stunning victory in her maiden Ironman Hawaii was a small pothole on the streets of San Francisco. Racing at the Escape From Alcatraz Triathlon in late June (one week after a half-Ironman win on the Big Island) Jones rolled over a pothole, crashed and suffered frightening injuries: two broken ribs, a concussion and a stress fracture to her right hip.

She could not run for more than a month; and come early August, Jones and Coulson wondered if they had run out of time to prepare for Hawaii. She recovered, but the injury robbed her of road mileage.

The word on five-time champion Natascha Badmann (in yellow), was that she had to have a lead off the bike to win the Ford Ironman World Championship, and that while she was the best cyclist in the business, her running was suspect. This year, she proved that theory wrong when she put together a 3:06:25 marathon to catch Olympic Silver Medalist Michellie Jones and win her sixth Ironman World title. Photos by Rich Cruse.

This page: It was a day of firsts. Sarah Reinertsen became the first above knee amputee woman to finish the Ford Ironman World Championship and the amazing Jon "Blazeman" Blais finished as well despite the fact that he was the first person with ALS, Lou Gehrig's disease, to attempt the Ironman. Photos by Rich Cruse

Right opposite: After finishing third the year before, Faris Al-Sultan of Germany ran his way to the lead and the win. Photos by Rich Cruse

Slowly, methodically, Badmann gained ground and finally, at about Mile 18, came The Pass.

"When I passed her, I said, `You did a great job all day,' " recalls Badmann. "She said, `Yeah, Natascha. Just go.' "

And so on a late Saturday afternoon, with the sun shining brightly, Badmann got her long-awaited wish. She danced down Alii Drive, smiling, waving, blowing kisses. She mugged for the photographers afterwards, spreading her arms wide and tilting her head waaaaay back as if doing the limbo. The wreath was placed atop her head and the flowers draped around her neck.

"I still haven't found the right words to describe all my feelings," says Badmann.

Hers is a remarkable tale, the stuff that should be set to cinema with maybe Renee Zellweger playing the leading role. A mother days before turning 18, she was an overweight secretary stuck in the 9-5 world who started exercising to lose the pounds. Her supervisor at the time (Coach Hasler) spotted her talents. It wasn't long before she was transformed into Paula Newby-Fraser's successor.

About winning Ironman Hawaii for the sixth time and joining the rank of legends Newby-Fraser, Mark Allen and Dave Scott as the only triathletes with six Hawaii titles (Newby-Fraser owns eight), Badmann says, "I'm very proud. It's something I never thought about where I could be one day. When I started [exercising], I couldn't run two miles. I was overweight. I never thought I'd go to Hawaii."

Badmann's winning time: 9:09:30. Jones finished second in 9:11:51. Badmann's marathon split: 3:06:25, eclipsing her previous Hawaii best by more than three minutes. Jones' marathon split: 3:18:13, a 10-and-a-half-minute improvement over her Ironman Florida effort.

"Natascha did have to run her fastest marathon," Jones says. "At least I made her work for it."

Jones worked, too, so hard that despite temperatures still in the 80s, she experienced chills after the race. So while Badmann was soaking up the post-race attention, a sun-burned Jones slipped off to the medical tent. She took fluids for a while, then was told that if she wanted to stay much longer she'd have to receive intravenous fluids. Needles give Jones the heeby-jeebies, so she exited.

About Badmann's marathon performance, Competitor Magazine co-publisher Bob Babbitt says, "We thought Natascha never runs fast. Now we know she never had to run fast. She proved what kind of champion she is. She doesn't need to win on the bike to win the race."

Badmann collected $110,000 for the victory. Jones earned $55,000, plus another $10,000 in bike premes. (Technically, the second preme was awarded on the run, but it came about one kilometer into the marathon.)

About 10 days before the race, just after settling on the Big Island, Jones had a dream. She had finished second, to Badmann, by two minutes. Lottery players worldwide will now be hounding Jones, wondering if she ever dreams numbers.

"Man," jokes Jones, "I should have dreamed I won."

In a way, she did. She won immense respect, confirming for all that on triathlon's biggest stage her career will not be measured solely by the Olympic distance. Like a fleet wide receiver, she can go long. Best yet, she liked it, and promises to come back for seconds.

"C'mon," says Jones, "you come so close, you better do it again."

When you are racing the Ironman, there are moments when you are the hunter... and moments when you are the hunted.

Photo by Rich Cruse

195

Above: After the Ford Ironman Coeur d'Alene, Major Rozelle completed the 2006 Ford Ironman World Championship in Kona in 12:46:27. Photo courtesy ASI Photo Cycling

Opposite page: Photo by Rich Cruse

It was June 21, 2003, a typical steamy day in Hit (pronounced Heat), Iraq, as Capt. David Rozelle got into his Humvee to lead his men out on a mission. He had been told earlier that week by the local leaders that, because he had helped to shut down the black market in guns, ammunition and gas, there was now a price on his head — $1,000 to the person who takes him out. He was warned to not join his men when they went out on patrol. "Your men will be safe, but you will be attacked."

Not going with his men was never an option for Rozelle, a man who feels that a real leader leads from the front. "There was no way I would ever stay behind," he says. "What type of message does that send to your men?"

Not far into the mission, his Humvee drove over an anti-tank land mine, lifting it off the ground and blowing the front end apart. The 100-pound right tire and wheel landed 100 meters away. Rozelle, who was sitting right above where the explosion was centered, was bleeding profusely from his arms, legs and face. Two of his men ran to him and evacuated him from the scene. Within two hours, Rozelle was in a hospital outside of Baghdad where the doctor gave him two options.

"He told me that there were no muscles, tendons or ligaments left to support the lower part of my right leg," recalls Rozelle. "He told me he could try to save the lower leg but that I'd have a club foot that would be worthless and eventually I'd want to have it removed." He laughs. "That was actually an option he gave me. The other was that he would save as much of the leg as he could, amputate the rest and I would be back running on a prosthetic within a year."

After making option two a reality, Rozelle was flown to Walter Reed Army hospital in Washington, D.C. where the 220-pound former rugby player now weighed a paltry 170. When his mom walked into the room, they both hugged and cried. Then she brought up an incident that occurred at a running race when he was younger.

"My mom reminded me that I was really hurting and that she came up to me with about two miles to go and told me that she was going to run with me and finish together," remembers Rozelle. "Then she told me, 'I'm here now and we're going to do it again. I'll be with you the whole way.'"

Rozelle ended up back home in Ft. Collins, Colorado, trying to deal with life as an amputee. It was a struggle. To deal with the real pain and the phantom pain that goes with limb loss — non-existent toes itching, cramps in a calf muscle that is no longer there — Rozelle did anything he could to make the pain disappear.

"We're human and sometimes we're weak," admits Rozelle. Morphine made the pain go away, so he would set his alarm to get his fix every two hours. When he wasn't on morphine, whisky was his self-medication of choice.

"I wasn't a good husband or a good father," he continues. "I stayed up late, woke up late and watched television all day. I couldn't even drive."

Then a letter arrived that changed everything. It was the last letter he wrote to his wife, Kim, from Iraq. At the time he wrote the letter she was due to have their first child, Forrest, any day.

"When I read that letter, I realized the pain my wife would have felt if she had received it after I died," says Rozelle. "I knew I was in denial, that I was addicted to morphine and that my total focus was on myself."

He eliminated morphine cold turkey, dealt with two horrendous weeks of withdrawl, and then found a new addiction. "I started working out 3-5 hours a day and then completed my first triathlon. There is no greater feeling in the world."

Rozelle went from one minute of jumping rope to 15. He learned to swim again and got on a mountain bike. He took Spin classes and rode his bike to and from the gym. Then he did the Pueblo Triathlon on his walking foot and ended up on crutches for a few weeks as a result. But he didn't care. The weight was coming off and he was once again the old David Rozelle.

In late October 2004, he did the 1.2-mile swim at the San Diego Triathlon Challenge. The next week, he ran the New York City Marathon. By Thanksgiving, he passed the physical to get back into active duty and resume his command in Iraq. Go back? David, haven't you given enough?

"It's hard to explain the sense of duty I feel as an army officer," he says. "My obligation was to go back with my men. I was healed and ready to go emotionally and physically. I wanted to prove to my fellow soldiers that this was not going to bring me down and I wanted to take my life over again from exactly where I left it two years ago."

Brave. Rifles. Veterans. Those are words Rozelle used with his men often. "During the Mexican wars," he explains, "General Scott said those three words to his men after their first major victory. It means that we have been baptized in blood and fire and come out as steel. It is an expression that I live by. I am stronger and more powerful because of what I have gone through."

No other soldier who has lost a limb in battle had ever gone back to his command with a prosthetic. In March of 2005, Rozelle proved that he had indeed come out as steel by becoming the first. Then his focus shifted from steel to Iron.

When he returned to the states after his second tour of duty in early June 2005, the man, now Major Rozelle, began working with the soldiers at Walter Reed Army Hospital who came back from battle missing limbs or in a wheelchair. The program he spearheads for the Challenged Athletes Foundation (CAF) is called Operation Rebound.

This past June, Rozelle completed the Ford Ironman Coeur d'Alene in 13:55:01. At the finish line, he stood strong and saluted his soldiers.

"It was important for me to look strong and powerful coming across the line," says Rozelle. "My soldiers need to know that if I can do it so can they."

Where there's a wheel...
There's a way..
Photo by John Segesta

Above: Chris McCormack and Normann Stadler congratulate each other on a great race where they ended up only 71 seconds apart at the end. In a post-event interview, Stadler accused McCormack of drafting on the bike. The next night McCormack confronted Stadler with those quotes and a rivalry was born!

Right: Norman Stadler celebrates his Ironman victory. McCormack didn't think that Stadler's 10-minute lead off the bike would hold up. He was wrong. Even though he ran a 2:46:02 marathon, Macca couldn't run Stadler down.

Photos by Rich Cruse

Normann Stadler of Germany did more than win the 2006 Ford Ironman World Championship in Hawaii.

In the process, he created an Ironrivalry with Australia's Chris McCormack that will last forever.

It was two days before the Ford Ironman World Championship in Kona, Hawaii. I was standing at the back of the outdoor gathering of all the professional triathletes right as the pre-event briefing concluded. My cell phone rang and my eyes lit up. One of my favorite athletes of all time was on the line. New Zealand's Rod Dixon was one of the most versatile runners of all time, taking home the 1500-meter bronze medalist from the 1972 Olympics and winning the 1983 New York City Marathon.

When Dixon won the marathon, he did it the hard way. Geoff Smith from England led from early on, and Dixon had to pull out all the stops to catch Smith in the final few hundred yards to win one of the closest and most dramatic marathons in history. His winning margin? Only nine seconds.

As the athletes started to filter out of the pre-event area, Chris McCormack from Australia walked by me. Knowing that he's a student of running, cycling and triathlon history, I grabbed McCormack and put him on the phone with Dixon. After a few "good lucks," Dixon asked McCormack if he was ready to go.

"I'm ready to go, mate," McCormack responded. "This could be my day."

How ironic: Dixon comes from behind in the last mile to win the New York City Marathon in 1983. Thirteen years later, McCormack and Germany's Normann Stadler stage another classic one-on-one duel on the Kona Coast that comes down to the last mile as well.

In the entire buffet that is the Ford Ironman Triathlon World Championship, the swim is a measly cocktail weenie — a bite-size appetizer before a much bigger meal. It's said that you can't win the Ironman during the opening 2.4-mile swim, but you can certainly lose it. Get your goggles knocked off, cramp up... there are a number of ways it can go south in a big way. Stadler did his very best to win the Ironman in the swim.

Swimming against the current on the way back from the turnaround, the pace slowed to a crawl and the largest pack in Ironman history emerged from the warm waters of the Pacific together. In the mass of arms and legs that sprinted out of Kailua Bay together, there was Stadler, the best cyclist on the triathlon planet, right there with a big smile on his face about 30 seconds down to defending champion Faris Al-Sultan and less than 15 seconds down on McCormack.

"When we got to the airport, we had an update on where everyone was," remembers McCormack. "They said the leader was two minutes up the road. I said 'Who's the leader?' They said 'Normann Stadler.' I was in shock. I had no idea Normann was already in front of us."

In front and flying. Stadler won in 2004, but last year had two flats. The last time he was visible in Kona, he was flinging his Kuota bike into the lava fields after being unable to get the sew-up off his wheel.

The scene is still embedded in many of our minds. In fact, a friend of ours has a young son who has one great imitation in his repertoire. He picked it up after watching last year's NBC coverage of the Ironman. All you have to do is say, "Do your Normann impression" and on cue he puckers up his face and screams at the top of his lungs: "Too much GLUEEEEEEEEEEEEEE!!!"

So the question was out there: Was this guy too fragile to win his second Ironman title? He melted down as defending champion in 2005 and really hadn't had a good race since his 2004 win. Three-time champion Peter Reid questioned Stadler's running ability in a pre-race interview, wondering if he could win again running a 2:57:51 marathon. Not a bad question, by the way. Since 1984, the only marathons slower than Stadler's for the

winners were Scott Tinley's 3:01:33 in 1985 and Scott Molina's 3:02:42 in 1988.

But Stadler was doing his best to minimize the marathon. If he built a 10-minute lead and ran the same 2:57, someone would have to run sub-2:47 to beat him. As every good runner knows, it's one thing to run a 2:49 like McCormack did in 2005 —the fastest run of the day, by the way — to salvage a lousy race and finish sixth overall. It's quite another story to run that fast when you need every second to win and can't afford to have one bad mile.

McCormack has had a lot of bad miles in Kona. The fact that he has won Ironman events in Australia and Ironman-distance events in Roth, Germany, never seemed to carry over to the lava fields. In 2002, he led off the bike and blew to the moon nine miles into the run. In 2003, he finished but walked most of the marathon. In 2004, he dropped out again, this time in the Natural Energy Lab. And the guy who picked him up and drove him back to town? Six-time Ironman World Champion Mark Allen.

"Mark told me that I'd live to fight another day," remembers McCormack. "I said, 'Mark, at least when you blew up over here you finished second or third. I can't even finish the bloody race.'"

Then Allen shared a secret: He'd been working with Peter Reid, and Reid called him in a panic after seeing that McCormack had run in the low 2:40s in Roth and had gone under eight hours there. Allen asked Reid to send him some photos of McCormack from the race and then told Reid to relax.

"He told Peter that there was no way I could be fit for Ironman Australia in the spring, fit again for Roth and then fit for Ironman in October, that it was physically impossible," says McCormack. "He told me that if I wanted to be ready for Kona that I needed to be fat in July."

So in 2005 and 2006, McCormack went to Roth 10 pounds overweight and still won both times. Then he built up for Hawaii and finally had that great closing run at the 2005 Ironman.

"I was down by the pier after the race," remembers Reid, "and I saw Chris. I could tell from the look in his eyes that he finally got it, that he was now ready to be a factor in Kona."

The factor was sitting with Faris Al-Sultan, Luke Bell and Chris Lieto in the chase pack behind Stadler. Lieto started to move away and McCormack started to go with him. Then he reconsidered.

"'Mate, that's not the right move to make right now,' I said to myself. 'I think Chris is going to get hung out to dry. Be patient,'" recalls McCormack.

His patience paid off when he got off the bike 10 minutes down, even though Stadler had obliterated the bike course record with a 4:18:24.

"I seriously thought that my main competition on the run was going to be Cam Brown," says McCormack. "Normann's best run there was just under 2:58, and I knew I could run under 2:47. When Normann has gone really hard on the bike, he's run over three hours. I thought that 10 minutes was just not going to be enough time for him."

At the top of Palani Hill, McCormack was still eight minutes back of Stadler with Al-Sultan two minutes back of McCormack.

"I was clipping off six-minute miles and had taken 90 seconds out of Normann," says McCormack. "There's no way I could run a 2:55 marathon after a 4:18 bike ride. Normann's not that good a runner. He's got to pay for going so hard on the bike."

But Stadler was not crumbling. He was giving up time but holding form.

"At the top of Palani, I made the decision that I had to go for it," says McCormack. "I knew I could blow up and finish fifth, but I didn't care. When I came out of the Natural Energy Lab and was still four minutes down, I dropped my fuel belt and said, 'Mate, you've got to go as hard as you can for this last 10K. This is your destiny. It's going to be beautiful. You're going to be just like Mark Allen and catch the German in the last mile. The crowd will go crazy!'"

The lead went from four minutes to three minutes to two minutes and eventually just under a minute. Then it was over.

"When it was 48 seconds, I looked up ahead and could see two Normanns," recalls McCormack. "I had spent every single piece of energy I had." He laughs. "People keep telling me that if the race was another mile I would have caught him. If the race was another mile I don't know if I would have finished the bloody thing. I had absolutely nothing left.

Seventy-one seconds. That was the final

gap. A stop to pee. Sitting too long in transition. Rubbing on sunscreen. Seventy-one seconds — the third closest finish for the men in the history of the event.

Normann Stadler had used the anger from the lack of respect he was feeling to fuel his 8:11:56, the fastest winning time since Luc Van Lierde 10 years ago and the fifth fastest winning time in history. After the race, Stadler went out of his way to say that McCormack had drafted during the bike ride and should be ashamed of his second-place finish. McCormack was anything but.

"Normann surprised me," insists McCormack. "I didn't realize he was that good. Normann rode like a man possessed. I give him full credit. When you lose to a world champion on his best day ever, there's not much you can do about it."

Except plan to change the order of the finish next year.

"Normann doesn't understand that his lack of respect for me just gave me a reason to get up for swim workouts at five every morning," says McCormack. "The key to beating Normann is to get in his face and make him angry, nervous and scared. I think he's fragile. I'll stay on him all season and he'll crack. I don't think I have to beat him; he'll beat himself."

I don't know about that one, Macca. He's the defending world champion and you're not. The scoreboard reads: Normann Stadler two Ford Ironman World Championship titles, Chris McCormack zero.

Fortunately for us, the next "Ironshowdown" is less than 12 months away.

I can hardly wait.

A left turn from the Queen K Highway takes you towards the run turnaround in the Natural Energy Lab. When you emerge, you will be about 6.2 miles from the greatest finish line on earth.

Photo by John Segesta

CHEAP BIKE: CORY FOULK

It was October of 1996 and as Cory Foulk wheeled his 61-pound monstrosity towards the Ironman World Championship bike corral, every eye in the house was on him. He was the proverbial brown pair of dress shoes hanging out with the black tuxedo or Dave Scott trying to sneak into the Pot Belly Hall of Fame.

The bike racks were filled with rows and rows of tricked-out rides. Cory's steed, however, definitely stood out. It was a neon yellow Schwinn Typhoon single-speed with solid green knobbies and coaster brakes.

"When I rolled it into the bike transition area for check in, the first thing they made me do was take my kick stand off," Cory laughs. "Then when they realized my tires were too thick to fit in the rack, I had to put the kick stand back on."

The total cost for the bike was $15... with the basket.

"It cost me more for the three cans of spray paint it took to cover the bike," he insists. He also had rainbow straws put on the bike spokes to add just a hint of color along with streamers coming out the end of the handlebars and the foam flames attached to his helmet.

That's not to mention the tie-dyed Speedo and the Fred Kahuna Aloha Shirt that he raced in.

So why go retro at Ironman? Cory loves the sport and lives on the Big Island, but he felt that triathletes and the event had gotten a little too serious. "I just wanted to go out there and have a little fun," he says.

And he did.

After coming out of the water, he started making up some serious ground. When you've got a 61-pound neon yellow beast with one gear, you're forced to work pretty hard on the uphills. But those downhills are SWEET!

He did the bike ride, believe it or not, barefoot.

"The pedals got a little hot, but it wasn't a problem," he recalls. "I had plenty of cargo space in my basket to carry water and ice to cool my feet down. Plus, I had a pair of tennis shoes in the basket in case I needed them to push the bike up some of the grades."

He never needed them.

When it came to nutrition, Cory was on top of that as well. He had 10 pounds of Jolly Ranchers in the basket to munch on along the way or to toss to the adoring crowds in town or at the aid stations.

"That bag cost me two dollars at a pre-Halloween sale," he laughs.

During the bike ride, he would stop along the way to call the local radio station and give race updates.

"The station gave me a roll of quarters that I kept in the basket," he says. "I was climbing the hill to Hawi, passing guys even though I had only one gear. But it was the right gear for that hill. I get to the turnaround, pull over, drop the kickstand and run over to the Laundromat to use the pay phone. I see these guys I just passed going by my bike, kickstand down, sitting there on the shoulder. They're just shaking their heads."

After the call, Cory was back on the prowl — this time on the downhill.

"I was back on my American-made big rig and BOOM!, I blow by them again and I'm going so fast I just about suck their sunglasses off," he says. As he flew by, his feet were up on the basket and he looked like he was back in grammar school.

He was having the time of his life.

Cory has one picture that he loves. It shows a couple of athletes trying to draft off of him.

"I am towering over the course on this thing, and they are all tucked in behind me," he recalls. "Big draft. You could draft this bike from 40 yards out."

His bike split was 8:50:21 (including both transitions) and his total time was 15:46:57 (with a 1:29:40 swim and 5:26:56 run). Not bad when you consider that his bike weighed practically three times everyone else's.

You will see Cory Foulk at the starting line in Kona on October 13 — but this time with a racing bike, hot wheels, an aero helmet and, hey, maybe even a pair of bike shoes.

"Back then," he says, "I wanted to prove that you don't need ten grand to do the Ironman."

A big smile. "All you need is some sunscreen, a little spray paint and a really cheap bike."

> "I just wanted
> to go out there
> and have a little fun."

> "I had plenty of cargo space
> in my basket to carry water
> and ice to cool my feet
> down. Plus, I had a pair of
> tennis shoes in the basket
> in case I needed them to
> push the bike up some
> of the grades."

> "When I rolled it into the
> bike transition area for
> check in, the first thing they
> made me do was take my
> kick stand off. Then when
> they realized my tires were
> too thick to fit in the rack,
> I had to put the
> kick stand back on."

> "I wanted to prove that
> you don't need ten grand
> to do the Ironman."

In 2007, Cory Foulk dressed for Ironman success. He wore the latest racing outfit, rode the hottest bike and was aerodynamic from head-to-toe. Not so in 1996. Back then Cory was definitely the rebel with a cause who wanted to turn back the hands of time to see if someone on a cruiser bike could actually finish the Ironman. Photo courtesy Cory Foulk

2007: THE LIST

> **"Sean and I would watch the coverage of the Ironman over and over again and my dad would walk by and laugh at us. He'd say, 'Boys, why do you keep watching that same show? Here's what's going to happen. Mark Allen will break away from Dave Scott and finally win.' Then he'd walk away shaking his head."**
>
> *Chris McCormack*

Sean Maroney and Chris McCormack sat down to create The List. They were 18-year-old soul mates who had fallen hard for the sport of triathlon. They dreamed of one day being the best in the world, just like their heroes Mark Allen and Dave Scott.

"We had read all of the magazines and seen all of the television coverage," recalls McCormack. "There was the Escape from Alcatraz, St. Croix, Chicago… 37 races in total."

Their goal was to one day win every single one of those races. At the top of The List was the Ironman, the most important one of all.

"Sean and I would watch the coverage of the Ironman over and over again and my dad would walk by and laugh at us," remembers McCormack. "He'd say, 'Boys, why do you keep watching that same show? Here's what's going to happen. Mark Allen will break away from Dave Scott and finally win.' Then he'd walk away shaking his head."

Young Sean and Chris didn't care. They were intrigued with the classic colors of the Big Island of Hawaii, the contrast between the bluest blues of the ocean and the blackest blacks of the lava fields. Legendary commentators Phil Liggett and Al Trautwig, along with a great musical score, sucked them in again and again.

"It looked so inviting," says McCormack. "I couldn't wait to one day give it a go."

By early in the new century, McCormack had won the ITU World Olympic Distance Championship, Ironman Australia, Quelle Roth and had crossed off every other event on the master list. Except one.

McCormack was gearing up for the 2002 Ford Ironman World Championship and Maroney had qualified as well. Besides eventually winning the Ironman, the two buddies also had made a secret pact. They wanted to lead the Ironman bike ride at the turnaround in Hawi.

In early June, Maroney was at a party in Honolulu and somehow, someway, fell to his death. McCormack was devastated. When he went to the Big Island in October to attempt to cross off the last event on the master list and to, hopefully, cement his Hall of Fame resumé, he was racing for both of them.

At a pre-race media event, McCormack told anyone who would listen that he was hoping to win the Ironman six times, just like his idols Dave Scott and Mark Allen. Some felt he was cocky and had a big mouth. Dave Scott? He felt McCormack may want to win number one before talking about number six.

On race day, McCormack found himself with the two German leaders, Thomas Hellriegel and Jürgen Zäck, as they approached Hawi.

"I asked them if it was okay if I led at the turnaround," says McCormack. When they nodded yes, he rounded the cone and looked skyward.

"We're leading the Ironman," he said to Maroney. "We're leading the Ironman!"

But about nine miles into the marathon, McCormack was walking the Ironman. Then

Chris McCormack runs by American Chris Lieto during the marathon. Lieto ended up in sixth place, his highest finish ever, with a time of 8:26:49. Photo by Rich Cruse

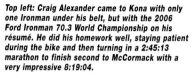

he was out of the Ironman. The following year (2003), he walked most of the marathon but still fininshed. And the year after that, in 2004, he dropped out again, this time in the Natural Energy Lab. Mark Allen happened to be out there in a car for NBC and picked up the totally distraught McCormack.

"He told me that I'd live to race another day," recalls McCormack. "I was upset. I said, 'At least when you had a bad day here you took second or third. I can't even finish the bloody race.'"

Allen then told him that Ironman champion Peter Reid, who Allen worked with, had been worried about McCormack after seeing his amazing split times from a July Ironman-distance race in Germany.

"He told Peter not to worry about me," says McCormack. "He told him that I was too skinny, that there was no way I could be that fit in April, July and October."

McCormack is an astute student of the sport. The following year, in 2005, he won the Quelle race in July even though he was 10 pounds overweight. Then he ran 2:49 off the bike in Kona and took sixth. In 2006, it was 2:46 off the bike and a second place by 71 seconds to Normann Stadler.

After last year's race, Allen agreed to look at McCormack's workouts and make a few suggestions.

"He told me that he was impressed with my workouts and how detailed my training diary was," says McCormack. "He suggested that I move to Boulder and train at altitude and that I add some longer runs of two-and-a-half hours. But the main thing Mark did for me was understand. He tried to beat Dave Scott in Kona six times before finally winning. Like me, he had won every other race on the planet, but he needed that win in Kona to really

Tim DeBoom (bottom left, photo by John Segesta) and Luc Van Lierde (bottom right, photo by Rich Cruse) each have two Ironman World Championship titles, but neither had been a factor in Kona in quite some time. In 2007 DeBoom and Van Lierde turned back the hands of time, taking fourth and eighth respectively.

This page: McCormack had been waiting 20 years for this moment. He was finally going to win the most important race in his sport, the Ford Ironman World Championship. So what does the guy do? He forgets to take out the sponges that he had dropped down the front of his racing outfit to keep himself cool, and now he has to live forever with the fact that he is the only Ironman World Champion in history with Man Cans. Photo by Rich Cruse

secure his legacy. I had nightmares about not winning this race and he could relate. He told me two things: Seize the moment and don't be scare to win. I repeated those over and over and over again on race day."

He needed to. Even though two-time champion Normann Stadler was throwing up and had to drop out of the race on the bike and 2005 champion Faris Al Sultan was so sick that he didn't even start, McCormack could see that the battle for the win was going to be intense.

Two-time champion Tim DeBoom was pushing the pace on the bike. Craig Alexander, the 2006 Ford Ironman 70.3 World Champion, was doing his first Ironman in Kona and having a stellar day. And two-time champion Luc Van Lierde, the course record holder, was hanging tough as well.

As McCormack sized up the pack, he felt those three had the best ability to run with him. With about 14 miles to go on the bike, Van Lierde pulled up next to McCormack.

"You're going to win this race," said Van Lierde. "Be smart in the marathon. This is your day."

Those words told McCormack that Van Lierde was not running for the win. After a number of years of injuries, Van Lierde was content to be in the hunt and hopefully finish on the podium.

Not so for DeBoom. This is a proud two-time champion who knows only one way to race and that is all out from the gun. McCormack knew that DeBoom would still be there when the marathon turned ugly and headed out onto the Queen K Highway.

Chris Lieto and Torbjorn Sindballe were leading at the end of the bike, but McCormack felt that there wasn't much chance they would be leading at the finish. He would concentrate on DeBoom and Alexander, one of the very best pure runners in the sport and a fellow Aussie.

At mile one, he heard that Alexander was 15 seconds back and DeBoom was 30. The first mile split? Five minutes, 40 seconds. Ditto for miles two and three.

"I said to myself, 'Is this stupid?'" recalls McCormack. "But Crowie (Alexander) was running the same pace and so was Tim."

At the first run turnaround on Alii Drive, he was able to see his pursuers for the first time.

"Crowie looked magic and Tim looked great. I thought, 'If you blow up, they've got to blow up, too,'" recalls McCormack. "But I was feeling good and was committed to the pace. The last thing I wanted to do was give them the opportunity to run on my shoulder."

The fast pace was eating quickly into the lead of Lieto and Sindballe, but by the Natural Energy Lab McCormack was in the lead. But the race was still way too close for comfort.

"I saw Crowie as I was coming the other way and he looked a little ragged. I saw him take a glance over his shoulder, which meant that he was worried about Tim. That gave me confidence," says McCormack.

Earlier, it all almost came crumbling down as he moved into the Natural Energy Lab. In his sixth attempt, he was feeling the pressure to win this year or give up the ghost.

"I took second last year," says McCormack. "If I dropped back to third or fourth, I didn't know if I could handle coming back again. There was no going backwards. There was only one position left and I have to deliver this year."

A photographer was standing in his way as he headed downhill and when the photographer tried to back up, he tripped and fell across McCormack's knees.

"I just gave him a stiff arm to keep him from taking me down," he recalls. "I kept saying, 'Please don't cramp, please don't cramp.'"

He didn't. But from all of the Ironman videos McCormack had watched, he knew that Pauli Kiuru was passed by Mark Allen in the Natural Energy Lab and that Allen had caught Thomas Hellriegel on his way back to town. He couldn't slack off for a minute.

"I ran a 6:24 mile coming out of the Natural Energy Lab and just told myself to do that again and again," says McCormack.

As he reached the top of Palani, he knew his lead was secure. He was on his way to a 2:42:02 marathon and he needed it all. Alexander was putting on a running exhibition of his own, and his 2:45:13 put the pressure on McCormack all day long. But now he had over three minutes and could savor the biggest win of his life.

"My mom died in 1999, and she and Sean were with me all day long," he says. "Coming down Palani, I realized that I had finally done it, that I had been dreaming of this for 20 years. It was very personal, almost surreal. I don't remember faces in the crowd, and the run down Alii Drive and crossing the finish line is a blur. It was such a relief after 10 years of hard work. If I had not won this year, it might have crushed me."

His 75-year-old dad was at the finish. A year ago, he had been in the medical tent with his son and couldn't believe what the young man was willing to put his body through to try and win the Ironman.

"He told me that I should forget about this race," recalls McCormack. "He said, 'You don't need to prove anything to me, son. I am just so proud of you. This sport is too hard.' With an IV in my arm I told my dad I wanted to try one more time."

His dad is totally old school. As McCormack headed to the finish, he saw his dad with tears in his eyes.

"The only other time I've seen him cry in my life was when my mom died," says McCormack. "That's when I lost it."

Mark Allen had told him to seize the moment and to not be scared to win. On his way to the medical tent he saw Allen with a smile on his face.

"I nodded and he nodded back," says McCormack. "Neither of us needed to say anything."

It was time to finally cross the Ironman off The List.

"I was hoping to finish top ten in Kona. I'm as surprised to have won as everyone else."

"I did my first triathlon in 2004 on a borrowed bike and a surf wetsuit."

"Six weeks before Ironman Korea my coach Brett Sutton asked if I wanted to do an Ironman. I asked 'Do you think I'm ready, boss?' He said yes. Then I went to Korea and won. Six weeks later I won the World Championship."

"I didn't have anything to lose in Kona. No one had any idea who I was."

"I was hoping I would feel good off the bike in Kona. Luckily I had my run legs in my transition bag."

Chrissy Wellington
2007 Ford Ironman World Champion

JON BLAIS: BLAZEMAN

"The bold don't live forever, but the timid don't live at all."

Only one man knew in his heart that someone with ALS could finish the Ironman. That man was Jon "Blazeman" Blais. Photo by John Segesta

It arrived in the mail the other day. It's a photo from the 2000 Ironman California at Camp Pendleton. There is a bicycle belonging to double above-knee amputee Rudy Garcia Tolson on a trainer with Rudy's bike legs leaning up against the front wheel. Surrounding the image are the words, "What's it going to be today, Blazeman... Victory or Death?"

Jon "Blazeman" Blais used the photo as a way to inspire himself to get out of the house and get in his training — also to motivate his students to reach for the stars. A special education teacher at Aseltine in San Diego, Blais had dove into the sport of triathlon full-bore at the age of 14 while living on the east coast and never backed off. Being in San Diego gave him every opportunity to run, bike and swim his brains out every day of the year. He didn't just teach the kids he worked with, he believed in them.

"I was full of piss and vinegar as a kid," he says. "So I guess I was able to relate to kids who were a lot like me."

As a kid one day he decided to dress up as condom man and throw condoms to the crowd. A trip to the principal's office quickly followed. "That was pretty funny," he admits.

He was always on the cutting edge, teaching the kids to rock climb and using heart-rate training so they could learn about their bodies and empower themselves.

"A lot of these kids try to avoid success," he continues. "They stay in their comfort zone and sabotage any chances they might have."

Blais built his following by believing in kids before they believed in themselves. That's what set him apart, what made him special.

In 2003, he competed in 20 triathlons; but in October of that year he started not feeling quite right. When he was working at school, his body would start twitching a lot and he found himself swimming off course.

"I'd be at the La Jolla Cove and I just couldn't swim a straight line," he says.

In January of 2005, he was at a party with some friends and he had trouble holding on to his beer bottle.

"I'm a southpaw and hold my beer in my left hand," he remembers. "All of a sudden, I had to hold my beer in my right hand." In February, he crashed hard on his mountain bike in San Clemente Canyon and ended up with 15 staples in his head.

"I never would have had such a stupid accident if I hadn't started to lose control of my hands," he insists.

Being the teacher, he went online and researched the symptoms.

"I'd stay up all night researching all the possibilities," he says. Blais knew that he had ALS (Lou Gehrig's Disease) before the doctors did. He was diagnosed on May 2, 2005. Gehrig's last game of his 2,130 consecutive game streak? May 2, 1939.

"If you have twitching and muscle wasting in more than one limb, you have ALS," he says. "No question about it."

He had to call his mom at 2 a.m. to tell her that her son had ALS. When you are diagnosed with ALS, it is a death sentence and you are given 2-5 years — if you're lucky. There is no treatment and there is no cure.

"About 150,000 people die of ALS every year, 411 a day and 17 per hour," Blais continues. "About 350,000 live with it every day. There is no beating ALS. No one has ever done anything but walk away and die."

But Jon Blais is not the type of guy to receive a death sentence and simply disappear.

"I knew that I had to raise awareness and funds to fight ALS," he says." I knew I wasn't going to win this battle, but I wanted to go out like a warrior. People who knew 'The Blazeman' knew I had to go down fighting."

Anyone who witnessed Blais at the 2005 Ford Ironman saw the heart of the man. He hadn't been able to train since 2003. He had gained weight and his body was deteriorating rapidly. He rode the bike for a few minutes in August for the NBC crew and then again after he arrived in Kona. That was it. He was racing the toughest race on earth on guts and guts alone.

In his prime, Blais would have swam the 2.4 miles in about 1:05. He was hoping for 1:30. Instead he went 1:50 because he was only able to use one arm and his body was cramping badly. On the bike he couldn't get out of the saddle, his upper torso felt like a brick and his quads and calves were seizing up with every turn of the pedals. At the turnaround in Hawi, a race official told him that he wasn't going to make the 5:30 p.m. cutoff time for the bike.

"I had just opened my special needs bag," he laughs, "so I chucked my banana bread at him. There was no way I was going to miss that cutoff."

The NBC camera crew that had been following him earlier had disappeared, as his chances of starting the marathon continued to dwindle.

"They took off," he remembers. "They gave up on me and went to film another story."

Fortunately, Blais doesn't believe in giving up — on the kids he teaches or the dreams he's living. By mile 80, he was back on pace and the camera crew was there to capture him finishing the bike and starting the marathon with his parents, 20 friends and the entire world there to witness a miracle in the making.

Before the race, Mike Reilly, the voice of the Ironman, had asked Blais what he was going to do at the finish line. A handstand? A cartwheel? A Greg Welch-style leap? But Blais told Reilly that he didn't know if he was going to finish and that Reilly might have to log roll his sorry butt across the line.

So when he approached the line, that's exactly what The Blazeman did. In the same way he has dealt with his disease, he proudly took his time, dropped to the ground and log rolled ever so slowly towards the finish of the race and ever closer to the finish of his life.

He savored every second of the journey. To the very end he will be the teacher. He is teaching us all about a disease that is insidious and totally ignored. He is teaching us how to handle adversity. But most of all he is teaching us to never, ever give up.

"You can choose to be pissed off, or pissed on," he laughs.

The Blazeman always chooses the former.

Jon "Blazeman" Blais passed away on Sunday, May 27, 2007. He was only 35 years old.

The sun may be setting, but for so many still out on the Ironman run course, the challenge to get to that finish shines brighter than ever.

Photo by John Segesta

IRON PEOPLE

The race for the win at the 2007 Ford Ironman World Championship was over. Chris McCormack and Chrissie Wellington were crowned champions. But who are the folks that balance their work and their families with their passion for the Ironman? Along with photographer Rich Cruse, we sought to capture a cross section of age-group participants who do just that.

Alex Piquer, 37 (#1169), from Austin, Texas, posing with his wife Jennifer and their son Eli. "It's my first. I got in to Kona through the lottery three days after my son Eli was born." (Finish Time: 13:09:49) "What an incredible experience. There is a power to this event that's beyond anything I could have imagined."

Benoit Bernard, 41 (#902), from La Plaine, Reunion Island. "This was my 20th Ironman and my fourth in Kona." (Finish Time: 11:36:36) "My best friend Gerard passed away two days ago. He had been sick for a long time, so I knew it was coming. But it was very hard to lose him. This race was for Gerard."

Andrea Putz, 24 (#1828), from Fond Du Lac, Wisconsin, posing with her husband Ben and her father-in-law Steve. "This was my third Ironman but my first in Kona." (Finish Time: 12:44:28) "The day had its moments, that's for sure. My toes were rubbing and driving me crazy, so I took my running shoes off and carried them for miles 22-25. The Ironman is always an adventure within an adventure."

Bob Sinclair, 47 (#572), from Minnamurra, Australia, with his wife Noelene and his daughters Kate (15) and Jane (12). "I have done Ironman Australia 15 times and Ironman New Zealand twice. This is my very first time in Hawaii." (Finish Time: 13:11:07) "My race number, 572, is symbolic because I'm the 57th person to have completed Ironman Australia 10 times, and I have been here to Kona to watch this race twice. When I got into Kona, my wife had me quit my job so that I could train full time; and she bought me a new bike. I am one lucky man. I had a ball and loved it all!"

Dale, 28 (#1683), and Dave, 32 (#1499) Fediuk, from Kailua-Kona, Hawaii, with dad Don and mom Penny. "This was my first one and my brother's second," says Dale. (Finish Time: 12:38:49) The brothers were out there to support their dad, who is dealing with Parkinson's Disease. Were you there at the finish line, Dad? "You bet I was," says Don. "It was a great feeling to see my sons cross that line together."

Gerald Geier, 46 (#180), from Höchstadt, Germany. "This is my eighth Ironman, but my first in Kona." (Finish Time: 12:15:04) Geier was in a motorcycle accident back in 1985 and lost his lower leg. He found that sport was essential in getting his life back in order. "When you are able to finish something like the Ironman, you realize that anything is possible."

Tim DeBoom, 36 (#12 in hat), from Boulder, Colorado, shown with his buddy Greg Mecca (far left), his brother Tony and wife Nicole (Finish Time: 8:22:33). DeBoom came to Kona with something to prove. As a two-time champion in 2001 and 2002, he hadn't really been a factor in Kona since 2003 when had to be pulled from the course, having fallen ill due to a kidney stone. "A lot of people felt that I wouldn't be a factor here this year," says DeBoom. After pushing the pace on the bike and running a 2:48:29 marathon, resulting in a fourth-place finish, he and his family and friends would have to disagree.

Felix Welzel, 25 (#1738), from Braunschweig, Germany. "This is my third Ironman but my first in Kona." (Finish Time: 12:02:50) "I was running through the course smiling and laughing the whole time because being here was like a dream. Even when I was walking, doing the Ironman in Hawaii was still a dream come true."

Jason Park, 36 (#1215), from San Juan Capistrano, California, with the 2007 Champion Chis Mc Cormack (right). "This is my fourth Ironman and my first in Kona." (Finish Time: 14:14:42) At 6'6" and 220 pounds, Park is one of the bigger triathletes on the planet. "I was out there a long time," he admits. "It was definitely an amazing experience, an absolute dream come true."

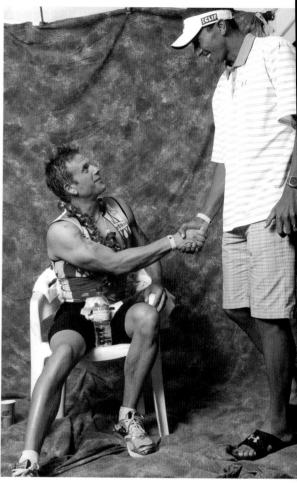

Luis Alvarez, 45 (#668), from Mexico City, Mexico. "This was 51st Ironman and my fifth one this year. I'm the only person to have done every Ironman event in the world." (Finish Time: 13:20:55) "What makes this race so special is that you have to qualify to get here. I love it!"

John Brenkus, 36 (#172), from Calabasas, California. "This is my third Ironman but my first in Kona." (Finish Time: 14:01:05) Brenkus was working on a feature story for the show he hosts on the FOX Sports Network called 'Sports Science.' The camera crew was following both Brenkus and soon-to-be Ironman champion Chris McCormack (right). "This was the hardest thing I have done but my biggest personal accomplishment ever."

Mia Richter, 25 (#1786), from Iowa City, Iowa. (Finish Time: 11:41:16) She was on her way to Kona in 2006 and happened to meet Jon Blais on the flight over from Chicago. Blais — aka Blazeman — was returning to the Ironman after finishing the race the year before despite having Lou Gehrig's Disease. "He couldn't hold a glass or the straw with his hands, so I helped him drink his Coke. I spent my entire race thinking of Jon." She hugged Blais at the finish last year, and it was a moment she will never forget. This year, she came back to Kona to honor Blazeman's memory. "This is about Jon," she continues. " I carried his picture with me. The high point of the day was rolling across that finish line for Jon. "I looked up at the sky and said, 'We did it, buddy. We did it!'"

Katie Bolling, 31 (#1618), from Northfield, Illinois, posing with her husband Chris and her mom Barb. "This is my third Ironman, but my first in Kona." (Finish Time: 11:48:45)

Bolling had a stress fracture in her foot, but that didn't concern her. The year 2007 had been tough for her entire family. Her husband Chris had broken his neck in a bike crash back in May and her mom Barb had been diagnosed with breast cancer on July 17. They both insisted that Katie not pull out of the race because of them but to keep training and to finish for them. She did just that.

Stacy Taylor, 41 (#171), from Fairfax, Virginia, with her daughter Lindsey. "This is my very first Ironman. I got in through the lottery." (Finish Time: 13:43:50)

Lindsey shipped off to boot camp on August 9 and wants to fly Apache or Blackhawk helicopters. "I e-mailed her commander to see if she could come to watch me race," says Taylor. "I expected a no, but I got a yes!" Lindsey flew in from Columbia, South Carolina, the night before the race to watch her mom complete the toughest day in sport. "I am so proud of her," says Lindsey. "Seeing my mom complete the Ironman makes me realize how strong I can be."

After sunset the distractions drift away and the Ironman becomes very raw. One step at a time. One moment at a time. One mile at a time. Then repeat.

Photo by John Segesta

IRON THANKS

Above, from left to right:

Peter Read Miller shot the Ironman in 1979 for a major feature in Sports Illustrated. It was the exposure that put the Ironman on the map. Photo by Tracy Frankel.

Lois Schwartz with driver John Smith.

Mike Plant with his wife Cathy.

Tracy Frankel in a helicopter high above the Ironman start.

Rich Cruse at the Ironman finish line.

Robert Oliver setting up one of his awesome underwater shots. Photo by John Russell

Dave Epperson started shooting the Ironman in the early 1980s. Photo by Robert Oliver

Carol Hogan at the 1981 Ironman.

John Segesta, smokin' photographer.

I have been blessed to have stumbled upon an event that would immediately change my life. To me, the Ironman has been a gift. I get to watch these wonderful, dramatic, heroic stories unfold each and every October. I get there before 5 a.m. on race morning so I can see the athletes as they march into the lights that bathe the pier in the pre-race darkness. Some smile, some laugh, some cry. They hug and shake and wonder: What will this day bring?

Pro and age grouper alike know better than to underestimate the 140.6-mile task at hand. They share that bond. It is a daunting challenge and one they will cherish forever. But for the moment there is fear, trepidation and anticipation. My long-time training buddy Jack Wilson calls that pre-race feeling "crank". There is the crank — or butterflies — you feel before a short triathlon or a 5K. Then there is the crank associated with a marathon. And, finally, there is the crank daddy known as the Ironman where it seems like the entire butterfly world has set up home and is aflutter in your belly.

They come to Kona to feel that crank and to see where they stand. Not so much against other people, but against themselves. At some point on Ironday it comes down to you against you. How much can you handle and how badly do you want the lights of Alii Drive.

I look back and remember Tom Warren taking Ned Overend and I under his wing and showing us that we could really do this Ironman thing. It was so laid back in the early days that I remember playing catch with Scott Tinley with a small football in 1985 while he was on his way to his second win. I remember being in the pro meeting in 1987. I was sitting right next to Dave Scott and Mark Allen and neither made eye contact with the other. You could cut the tension in the room with a knife.

In 1989, we had a huge entourage of vehicles surrounding Scott and Allen, but it was quiet enough to hear a pin drop. They were still side by side 24 miles into the marathon and I think we all realized how special the moment was, that we were witnessing history.

As I look through the completed book, what really sticks out is the magnificent talent of one Lois Schwartz. We both worked at *Running and Triathlon News* and co-founded *Competitor Magazine*. Although she would get sick every single year from riding backwards on a motorcycle for 17 hours in the heat and humidity, you would never know it from her work. *IronWar, The Equalizer* and so many others are great images that capture the drama of the moment.

To the athletes who have been so generous with their time and words; to Jim Howley, Bob and Terry Jordan, Klaus Barth and everyone else who allowed me to tell their stories; to Lew Friedland, Priscilla Fraiegari and The World Triathlon Corporation for allowing me to be part of the family; and to Lois Schwartz, Robert Oliver, Rich Cruse, Tracy Frankel, David Epperson, Carol Hogan and Peter Read Miller for freezing the essence of the Ironman for eternity through their incredible photography.

To my long-time collaborator Catherine Grawin, simply the best graphic artist on the planet. Her layouts and her use of color and images have been known to stop you dead in your tracks. She has the uncanny ability to take words and images and make them jump right off the page. Also, a big thanks to Diana Babb for taking the time to edit the copy.

And to Mike Plant, my friend and mentor, who led the way. From him I learned that writing isn't simply stating the facts, it's picking a story and making it personal; it's taking the reader inside the event through your eyes.

The story of the Ironman is one I have immersed myself in for the past 27 years. Thanks to all those who showed me the way.

— Bob Babbitt

You can't do it alone.
The Ironman
Is all about support.
From your friends
From your family
From your training partners.
And, on Ironday,
From your extended family;
The 7,000 Ironman volunteers.

Photos by Lois Schwartz

1978-2007 IRON STATS

The First and Last. The first-ever champion, Gordon Haller (left), won the Ironman 29 years ago on February 18, 1978 on the island of Oahu. There were only 15 entrants in that first ever Ironman Triathlon.

Australia's Chris McCormack (right) was all of 18 years old when he set the goal of one day winning the Ford Ironman World Championship. On October 13, 2007 that dream finally came true on his sixth attempt in Kona.

Photo by Tim Carlson

verall 1st Place - Men

Year	Name	Swim	Bike	Run	Total
7	Chris McCormack	51:48	4:37:32	2:42:02	8:15:34
6	Normann Stadler	54:05	4:18:23	2:55:03	8:11:56
5	Faris Al-Sultan	49:54	4:25:24	2:54:51	8:14:17
4	Normann Stadler	54:27	4:37:58	2:57:53	8:33:29
3	Peter Reid	50:36	4:40:04	2:47:38	8:22:35
2	Timothy DeBoom	52:02	4:45:21	2:50:22	8:29:56
1	Timothy DeBoom	52:01	4:48:17	2:45:54	8:31:18
0	Peter Reid	51:45	4:39:32	2:48:10	8:21:00
9	Luc Van Lierde	50:38	4:41:26	2:42:46	8:17:17
8	Peter Reid	52:04	4:42:23	2:47:31	8:24:20
7	Thomas Hellriegel	53:08	4:47:57	2:51:56	8:33:01
6	Luc Van Lierde	51:36	4:30:44	2:41:48	*8:04:08
5	Mark Allen	51:50	4:46:35	2:42:09	8:20:34
4	Greg Welch	50:22	4:41:07	2:48:58	8:20:27
3	Mark Allen	50:40	4:29:00	2:48:05	8:07:45
2	Mark Allen	51:27	4:35:23	2:42:18	8:09:08
1	Mark Allen	50:14	4:46:07	2:42:09	8:18:32
0	Mark Allen	51:43	4:43:45	2:52:48	8:28:17
9	Mark Allen	51:17	4:37:52	2:40:04	8:09:15
8	Scott Molina	51:28	4:36:50	3:02:42	8:31:00
7	Dave Scott	50:57	4:53:48	2:49:26	8:34:13
6	Dave Scott	50:53	4:48:32	2:49:11	8:28:37
5	Scott Tinley	55:13	4:54:07	3:01:33	8:50:54
4	Dave Scott	50:21	5:10:49	2:53:00	8:54:20
3	Dave Scott	50:52	5:10:48	3:04:16	9:05:57
2	Dave Scott	50:52	5:10:16	3:07:15	9:08:23
82	Scott Tinley	1:10:45	5:05:11	3:03:45	9:19:41
81	John Howard	1:11:12	5:03:29	3:23:48	9:38:29
80	Dave Scott	51:00	5:03:00	3:50:33	9:24:33
79	Tom Warren	1:06:15	6:19:00	3:51:00	11:15:56
78	Gordon Haller	1:20:40	6:56:00	3:30:00	11:46:40

ourse Record

o races took place in 1982 (February and October)

verall 1st Place - Women

ear	Name	Swim	Bike	Run	Total
07	Chrissie Wellington	58:09	5:06:15	2:59:58	9:08:45
06	Michellie Jones	54:29	5:06:09	3:13:08	9:18:31
05	Natascha Badmann	1:02:30	4:52:00	3:06:25	9:09:30
04	Natascha Badmann	1:01:36	5:31:37	3:11:45	9:50:04
03	Lori Bowden	56:51	5:09:00	3:02:10	9:11:55
02	Natascha Badmann	56:51	4:52:26	3:12:58	9:07:54
01	Natascha Badmann	59:55	5:16:07	3:09:33	9:28:37
00	Natascha Badmann	58:04	5:06:42	3:19:02	9:26:16
999	Lori Bowden	1:02:23	5:08:30	2:59:16	9:13:02
998	Natascha Badmann	56:02	5:10:00	3:14:50	9:24:16
997	Heather Fuhr	1:01:47	5:23:11	3:06:45	9:31:43
996	Paula Newby-Fraser	55:30	5:01:34	3:09:45	9:06:49
995	Karen Smyers	53:37	5:17:49	3:05:20	9:16:46
994	Paula Newby-Fraser	54:19	5:02:25	3:23:30	9:20:14
993	Paula Newby-Fraser	53:29	4:48:30	3:16:24	8:58:23
992	Paula Newby-Fraser	53:30	4:56:34	3:05:24	*8:55:28
991	Paula Newby-Fraser	54:59	5:05:47	3:07:05	9:07:52
990	Erin Baker	56:37	5:12:52	3:04:13	9:13:42
989	Paula Newby-Fraser	54:19	5:01:00	3:05:37	9:00:56
988	Paula Newby-Fraser	56:38	4:57:13	3:07:09	9:01:01
987	Erin Baker	57:42	5:26:34	3:11:08	9:35:25
986	Paula Newby-Fraser	57:03	5:32:05	3:20:05	9:49:14
985	Joanne Ernst	1:01:42	5:39:13	3:44:26	10:25:22
984	Sylviane Puntous	1:00:45	5:50:36	3:33:51	10:25:13
983	Sylviane Puntous	1:00:28	6:20:40	3:22:28	10:43:36
1982+	Julie Leach	1:04:57	5:50:36	3:58:35	10:54:08
1982+	Kathleen McCartney	1:32:00	5:51:12	3:46:28	11:09:40
1981	Linda Sweeney	1:02:07	6:53:28	4:04:57	12:00:32
1980	Robin Beck	1:20:00	6:05:00	3:56:24	11:21:24
1979	Lyn Lemaire	1:16:20	6:30:00	5:10:00	12:55:38
1978	-	-	-	-	-

* Course Record

+ Two races took place in 1982 (February and October)

Fastest Course Times

(Big Island Course)

Swim

1998	Lars Jorgensen (USA)	46:41
1999	Jodi Jackson (USA)	48:43

Bike

Bike

2006	Normann Stadler (GER)	4:18:23
1993	Paula Newby-Fraser (ZIM)	4:48:30*

Run

1989	Mark Allen (USA)	2:40:04
1999	Lori Bowden (CAN)	2:59:16

Course Record

1996	Luc Van Lierde (BEL)	8:04:08
1992	Paula Newby-Fraser (ZIM)	8:55:28

Age Group Record Holders

Men's Division

18-24	8:55:02	Vassilis Krommidas	24	1994
25-29	8:41:02	Maximilian Longree	25	2006
30-34	8:45:59	Igor Kogoj	34	1993
35-39	8:47:02	Jim Beuselinck	39	2006
40-44	8:58:55	Bent Anderson	42	2006
45-49	9:11:56	Brian Keast	45	2007
50-54	9:26:23	Kevin Moats	51	2006
55-59	9:47:29	Reinhold Humbold	57	2005
60-64	10:40:49	Takahisa Mitsumori	62	2005
65-69	11:29:45	Milos Kostic	65	2006
70-74	12:59:02	Bob Scott	71	2001
75-79	13:27:50	Bob Scott	75	2005
80+	16:21:55	Robert McKeague	80	2005

Women's Division

18-24	9:49:33	Kate Major	24	2002
25-29	9:47:40	Bree Wee	27	year?
30-34	9:51:12	Donna E. Kay	30	1993
35-39	10:00:58	Vicki Jones	35	2006
40-44	10:03:06	Donna Kay-Ness	43	2006
45-49	10:26:22	Donna Smyers	48	2005
50-54	10:35:59	Laura Sophiea	50	2005
55-59	11:43:33	Sandi Wiebe	55	2005
60-64	12:34:52	Mariana Phipps	61	2005
65-69	13:54:25	Jan Miller	67	2005
70-74	15:19:19	Ethel Autorino	70	2000
75+	15:54:16	Madona Buder	75	2005

1978

Original finishers

Plc	Name	Swim	Bike	Run	Total
1st	Gordon Haller	1:20:40	6:56:00	3:30:00	11:46:40
2nd	John Dunbar	1:00:15	7:04:00	4:03:00	12:20:27
3rd	Dave Orlowski	1:09:15	7:51:00	4:59:00	13:59:13
4th	Ian D. Emberson	1:01:40	7:47:00	5:15:00	14:03:25
5th	Sterling F. Lewis	1:02:30	7:47:00	5:15:00	14:04:35
6th	Tom Knoll	2:13:05	8:19:00	4:13:00	14:45:11
7th	Henry Forest	1:36:42	8:47:00	5:06:00	15:30:14
8th	Frank Day	1:44:20	8:45:00	6:09:00	16:38:31
9th	John Collins	1:31:15	9:15:00	6:14:00	17:00:38
10th	Archie Hapai	57:35	8:06:00	8:20:00	17:24:22
11th	Dan Hendrickson	1:35:35	11:39:00	6:48:00	20:03:28
12th	Harold Irving	1:05:30	11:04:00	8:00:00	21:00:38

(No women competed in 1978)

1979

Top 5 Men

Plc	Name	Swim	Bike	Run	Total
1st	Tom Warren	1:06:15	6:19:00	3:51:00	11:15:56
2nd	John Dunbar	1:09:55	6:51:00	4:03:00	12:03:56
3rd	Ian Emberson	1:02:35	6:53:00	4:28:00	12:23:30
4th	Gordon Haller	1:51:59	6:57:00	3:43:00	12:31:53
5th	Ron Seiple	1:58:47	6:47:00	4:57:00	13:43:00

Top Woman

Plc	Name	Swim	Bike	Run	Total
1st	Lyn Lemaire	1:16:20	6:30:00	5:10:00	12:55:38

(Only one woman competed in 1979)

1980 (NOTE: Event held in Honolulu, Hawaii)

Top 5 Men

Plc	Name	Swim	Bike	Run	Total
1st	Dave Scott	51:00	5:03:00	3:30:33	9:24:33
2nd	Chuck Neumann	1:02:00	5:38:00	3:44:41	10:24:41
3rd	John Howard	1:51:00	4:28:00	4:13:36	10:32:36
4th	Tom Warren	1:00:00	5:40:00	4:09:16	10:49:16
5th	Thomas Boughey	55:00	5:43:00	4:19:07	10:57:07

Top Women

Plc	Name	Swim	Bike	Run	Total
1st	Robin Beck	1:20:00	6:05:00	3:56:24	11:21:24
2nd	Eve Anderson	1:30:00	7:48:00	6:22:59	15:40:59

Continued...

Missy LeStrange has finished the Ironman 20 times and has 14 age group wins. Her best time came in 1993 when she went 10:05:24.
Photo by Lois Schwartz

1981 (NOTE: Course moved to Kailua-Kona, Hawaii)

Top 10 Men

Plc	Name	Swim	Bike	Run	Total
1st	John Howard	1:11:12	5:03:29	3:23:48	9:38:29
2nd	Tom Warren	59:40	5:37:09	3:27:49	10:04:38
3rd	Scott Tinley	1:05:34	5:47:52	3:19:21	10:12:47
4th	Thomas Boughey	56:26	5:57:00	3:30:14	10:23:40
5th	Dennis Hansen	1:03:48	6:01:45	3:21:10	10:26:43
6th	Dante Dettamanti	1:01:09	5:36:15	3:41:38	10:29:02
7th	James Butterfield	1:27:48	5:58:30	3:05:08	10:31:26
8th	Jonathan Durst	58:07	5:33:47	4:02:17	10:34:11
9th	Conrad Kress	1:02:26	5:49:40	3:46:09	10:38:15
10th	Ronald Krueper	1:02:56	6:00:57	3:25:28	10:39:11

Top 10 Women

Plc	Name	Swim	Bike	Run	Total
1st	Linda Sweeney	1:02:07	6:53:28	4:04:57	12:00:32
2nd	Sally Edwards	1:28:30	6:58:36	4:10:19	12:37:25
3rd	Lyn Brooks	1:20:07	7:13:11	4:08:57	12:42:15
4th	Cynthia Marks	1:11:07	7:33:02	4:16:42	13:00:51
5th	Kika Walker	1:08:17	7:21:47	5:03:25	13:33:29
6th	Nancy Kummen	1:51:17	6:26:06	5:16:43	13:34:16
7th	Georgia Gatch	1:05:37	7:23:36	5:51:47	14:21:00
8th	Carol Laplant	1:45:27	7:43:49	4:54:59	14:24:15
9th	Christa Obara	2:10:44	7:48:50	4:44:33	14:44:07
10th	Patricia Specht	1:57:06	7:41:13	5:11:49	14:50:08

February 1982

Top 10 Men

Plc	Name	Swim	Bike	Run	Total
1st	Scott Tinley	1:10:45	5:05:11	3:03:45	9:19:41
2nd	Dave Scott	58:39	5:17:16	3:21:02	9:36:57
3rd	Jeff Tinley	1:13:02	5:27:45	3:12:29	9:53:16
4th	Mark Sisson	1:18:18	5:21:23	3:17:34	9:57:15
5th	Reed Gregerson	1:05:00	5:31:54	3:25:43	10:02:37
6th	Jeff Jones	1:03:40	5:33:27	3:33:32	10:10:39
7th	Greg Reddan	1:04:30	5:52:53	3:16:28	10:13:51
8th	Kim Bushong	58:29	5:08:11	4:09:04	10:15:44
9th	Thomas Boughey	1:02:00	5:39:54	3:35:24	10:17:18
10th	Tom Warren	1:03:41	5:26:03	3:48:22	10:18:06

Top 10 Women

Plc	Name	Swim	Bike	Run	Total
1st	Kathleen McCartney	1:32:00	5:51:12	3:46:28	11:09:40
2nd	Julie Moss	1:11:00	5:53:39	4:05:30	11:10:09
3rd*	Lyn Brooks	1:19:30	6:38:02	3:53:29	11:51:00
3rd*	Sally Edwards	1:36:30	6:30:06	3:44:24	11:51:00
5th	Cheryl Lloyd	1:23:31	6:01:50	4:32:38	11:57:58
6th	Claire McCarty	1:20:01	6:21:33	4:16:24	11:57:58
7th	Cherry Stockton	1:44:35	6:06:47	4:09:15	12:00:37
8th	Eva Oberth	1:19:48	6:27:41	4:26:03	12:13:32
9th	Darlene Ann Drumm	1:15:17	6:32:08	4:32:28	12:19:53
10th	Shawn Wilson	1:01:27	6:26:04	4:58:03	12:25:34

*Tie

October 1982

Top 10 Men

Plc	Name	Swim	Bike	Run	Total
1st	Dave Scott	50:52	5:10:16	3:07:15	9:08:23
2nd	Scott Tinley	1:00:58	5:18:09	3:09:21	9:28:28
3rd	Jeff Tinley	58:05	5:21:05	3:17:43	9:36:53
4th	Scott Molina	52:48	5:26:20	3:31:15	9:50:23
5th	Jody Durst	55:41	5:23:33	3:33:29	9:52:43
6th	Kurt Madden	56:16	5:35:16	3:33:04	10:04:36
7th	George Yates	1:07:42	5:26:20	3:33:18	10:07:20
8th	Dean Harper	53:30	5:47:06	3:27:19	10:07:55
9th	Reed Gregerson	55:32	5:38:38	3:34:14	10:08:24
10th	Ferdy Massimino	53:32	5:28:51	3:47:44	10:10:07

Top 10 Women

Plc	Name	Swim	Bike	Run	Total
1st	Julie Leach	1:04:57	5:50:36	3:58:35	10:54:08
2nd	JoAnn Dahlkoetter	1:14:04	6:02:29	3:41:48	10:58:21
3rd	Sally Edwards	1:15:38	6:19:27	3:27:55	11:03:00
4th	Kathleen McCartney	1:14:05	5:51:43	4:05:05	11:10:53
5th	Lyn Brooks	1:09:24	6:34:03	3:34:47	11:18:14
6th	Ardis Bow	59:37	6:03:42	4:18:39	11:21:58
7th	Darlene Ann Drumm	1:09:33	6:07:37	4:12:45	11:29:55
8th	Kathie Rivers	1:08:15	6:09:02	4:15:15	11:32:32
9th	Jennifer Hinshaw	53:26	6:06:51	4:37:51	11:38:08
10th	Cheryl Lloyd	1:11:35	5:52:21	4:36:03	11:39:59
11th	Mary Jane Henning	1:04:32	6:32:15	4:04:12	11:40:59
12th	Hilary Matte	1:17:27	6:23:03	4:04:31	11:45:01
13th	Mireille Gradeff-Casiano	1:08:18	6:20:32	4:22:06	11:50:56
14th	Julie Moss	1:00:57	6:02:04	4:53:17	11:56:18
15th	Jenny Lamott	53:24	6:14:41	4:49:52	11:57:57

1983

Top 10 Men

Plc	Name	Swim	Bike	Run	Total
1st	Dave Scott	50:52	5:10:48	3:04:16	9:05:57
2nd	Scott Tinley	57:24	5:03:58	3:05:08	9:06:30
3rd	Mark Allen	52:08	5:13:32	3:15:26	9:21:06
4th	Marc Thompson	1:01:20	5:20:49	3:26:57	9:49:07
5th	Robert Roller	53:30	5:32:13	3:30:38	9:56:23
6th	Mark MacIntyre	1:03:29	5:52:59	3:00:47	9:57:16
7th*	Bob Curtis	1:00:14	5:23:00	3:38:44	10:01:59
7th*	Thomas Boughey	50:50	5:36:17	3:34:51	10:01:59
9th	Mac Martin	59:50	5:25:22	3:39:14	10:04:27
10th	Kurt Madden	57:58	5:43:56	3:23:27	10:05:21

* Tie

Top 10 Women

Plc	Name	Swim	Bike	Run	Total
1st	Sylviane Puntous	1:00:28	6:20:40	3:22:28	10:43:36
2nd	Patricia Puntous	1:00:31	6:26:12	3:22:33	10:49:17
3rd	Eva Ueltzen	1:02:48	6:05:13	3:53:48	11:01:49
4th	Kathie Rivers	1:05:11	6:12:16	3:52:37	11:10:05
5th	Sally Edwards	1:17:18	6:29:45	3:29:28	11:16:33
6th	Jann Girard	53:35	6:37:32	3:49:50	11:20:57
7th	Annie Dandoy	1:12:55	6:15:45	3:53:26	11:22:07
8th	Elaine Alrutz	1:05:20	6:20:01	4:00:15	11:25:37
9th	Sue Kinsey	1:03:43	6:20:56	4:01:16	11:25:56
10th	Jenny Lamott	55:44	6:19:51	4:13:32	11:29:08
11th	Julie Olson	1:03:23	6:32:06	3:54:50	11:30:20
12th	Shelby Hayden-Clifton	1:28:30	6:14:36	3:47:55	11:31:02
13th	Diane Israel	1:08:44	6:17:46	4:07:16	11:33:46
14th	Anne McDonnell	1:02:41	6:21:45	4:09:39	11:34:05
15th	Kathleen McCartney	1:09:31	6:10:53	4:14:16	11:34:40

1984

Top 10 Men

Plc	Name	Swim	Bike	Run	Total
1st	Dave Scott	50:21	5:10:59	2:53:00	8:54:20
2nd	Scott Tinley	55:54	5:18:52	3:03:57	9:18:45
3rd	Grant Boswell	53:07	5:15:04	3:15:44	9:23:55
4th	Rob Barel	53:03	5:10:22	3:23:45	9:27:11
5th	Mark Allen	50:22	4:59:21	3:45:19	9:35:02
6th	John Howard	1:07:52	4:56:49	3:33:57	9:38:39
7th	David Evans	59:00	5:21:32	3:23:23	9:43:55
8th	Chris Hinshaw	49:07	5:20:26	3:39:15	9:48:49
9th	Steve Sine	1:03:03	5:39:07	3:14:11	9:56:21
10th	Scott Skultety	58:45	5:33:37	3:26:39	9:59:02

Top 10 Women

Plc	Name	Swim	Bike	Run	Total
1st	Sylviane Puntous	1:00:45	5:50:36	3:33:51	10:25:13
2nd	Patricia Puntous	1:00:51	5:50:31	3:36:05	10:27:28
3rd	Julie Olson	1:00:33	5:37:43	3:59:54	10:38:10
4th	Joanne Ernst	1:04:40	5:49:24	3:46:28	10:40:33
5th	Moira Hornby	1:05:32	6:12:49	3:44:58	11:03:20

1985

Top 10 Men

Plc	Name	Swim	Bike	Run	Total
1st	Scott Tinley	55:13	4:54:07	3:01:33	8:50:
2nd	Chris Hinshaw	49:53	4:57:50	3:28:56	9:16:
3rd	Carl Kupferschmid	1:11:47	5:10:35	3:04:09	9:26:
4th	Hannes Blaschke	1:03:24	5:02:13	3:26:36	9:32:
5th	Tom Charles	1:02:23	5:28:09	3:04:41	9:35:
6th	Danny Banks	51:58	5:06:56	3:38:54	9:37:
7th	Mike Pigg	57:52	5:23:12	3:17:06	9:38:
8th	Klaus Barth	55:20	5:19:33	3:28:15	9:43:
9th	Steven Mudgett	1:01:53	5:26:03	3:18:31	9:46:
10th	Michael Kirtley	1:02:27	5:40:23	3:04:31	9:47:

Top 10 Women

Plc	Name	Swim	Bike	Run	Total
1st	Joanne Ernst	1:01:42	5:39:13	3:44:26	10:25:2
2nd	Elizabeth Bulman	1:01:11	6:01:16	3:24:27	10:26:5
3rd	Paula Newby-Fraser	59:38	5:54:26	3:36:59	10:31:0
4th	Nancy Harrison	1:21:04	5:40:38	3:34:54	10:36:3
5th	Sarah Springman	1:06:49	5:45:41	3:55:04	10:47:3
6th	Kathleen McCartney	1:16:54	5:48:35	3:43:11	10:48:4
7th	Bonnie Barton-Hill	1:22:34	6:06:39	3:25:49	10:55:0
8th	Juliana Brening	57:51	5:50:56	4:06:16	10:55:0
9th	Janet Greenleaf	58:19	5:57:50	4:07:16	11:03:2
10th	Elizabeth Nelson	1:21:23	6:00:55	3:41:32	11:03:5

1986

Top 10 Men

Plc	Name	Swim	Bike	Run	Total
1st	Dave Scott	50:53	4:48:32	2:49:11	8:28:3
2nd	Mark Allen	51:00	4:49:29	2:55:34	8:36:0
3rd	Scott Tinley	53:06	4:57:18	3:10:11	9:00:3
4th	Klaus Barth	53:22	4:53:21	3:16:57	9:03:4
5th	Greg Stewart	57:02	4:58:31	3:09:37	9:05:1
6th	Kenny Glah	53:11	5:00:05	3:16:19	9:09:3
7th	Tony Sattler	1:00:45	4:57:33	3:12:06	9:10:2
8th	Marc Surprenant	51:45	5:00:38	3:20:51	9:13:1
9th	Mike Pigg	51:43	5:08:20	3:16:40	9:16:4
10th	Mac Martin	56:54	4:50:27	3:32:38	9:20:0
11th	Jay Larson	55:09	5:18:31	3:08:22	9:22:0
12th	Gerhard Wachter	55:33	5:03:11	3:26:48	9:23:3
13th	Tommy Gallagher	51:44	5:06:45	3:25:40	9:24:1
14th	Mark Blaser	1:03:02	5:11:51	3:11:29	9:26:2
15th	Steven Mudgett	59:46	5:07:09	3:21:23	9:28:1

Top 10 Women

Plc	Name	Swim	Bike	Run	Total
1st	Paula Newby-Fraser	57:03	5:32:05	3:20:05	9:49:14
2nd	Sylviane Puntous	56:24	5:34:57	3:21:51	9:53:13
3rd	Joanne Ernst	57:36	5:26:09	3:36:21	10:00:07
4th	Elizabeth Bulman	56:49	5:40:05	3:30:23	10:07:18
5th	Heidi Christensen	53:31	5:39:57	3:42:51	10:16:20
6th	Juliana Brening	56:40	5:36:36	3:50:52	10:24:09
7th	Beth Mitchell	57:29	5:50:25	3:40:43	10:28:38
8th	Beth Nelson	1:24:01	5:52:18	3:17:49	10:34:09
9th	Nancy Harrison	1:00:56	6:04:36	3:30:40	10:36:13
10th	Louise Mackinlay	1:09:27	5:44:17	3:45:10	10:38:55

1987

Top 10 Men

Plc	Name	Swim	Bike	Run	Total
1st	Dave Scott	50:57	4:53:48	2:49:26	8:34:13

Continued...

Lyn Brooks is an
Ironman legend.
She was the first person
in the history of the event
to complete 20 races in a row.
Photo by Studio 1209

Dave Scott was the first inductee into the Ironman Hall of Fame. Appropriately, his trophy incorporated a six iron to go along with his six Ironman Triathlon World Championship titles. Photo by Rich Cruse

Ironman Triathlon World Championship Hall of Fame Inductees

Dave Scott 1993

Julie Moss 1994

Scott Tinley 1995

Paula Newby-Fraser 1996

Mark Allen 1997

John Collins 1998

Valerie Silk 1999

Tom Warren 2000

Dr. Bob Laird 2001

Bob Babbitt 2002

John MacLean 2003

Gordon Haller   Lyn Lemaire 2004

		Swim	Bike	Run	Total
2nd	Mark Allen	51:00	4:53:47	3:00:31	8:45:19
3rd	Greg Stewart	1:03:16	5:00:00	2:55:36	8:58:53
4th	Mike Pigg	51:01	5:00:54	3:10:38	9:02:34
5th	Kenny Glah	53:22	4:53:30	3:18:24	9:05:17
6th	Scott Tinley	54:35	5:01:25	3:12:36	9:08:37
7th	Nicholaus Martin	1:00:31	5:08:37	3:01:20	9:10:29
8th	Todd Jacobs	58:00	5:09:36	3:05:21	9:12:58
9th	George Hoover	51:22	5:14:43	3:09:46	9:15:53
10th	Pauli Kiuru	56:02	5:20:47	2:59:11	9:16:00

Top 10 Women

Plc	Name	Swim	Bike	Run	Total
1st	Erin Baker	57:42	5:26:34	3:11:08	9:35:25
2nd	Sylviane Puntous	57:50	5:29:43	3:09:23	9:36:57
3rd	Paula Newby-Fraser	58:03	5:22:15	3:20:18	9:40:37
4th	Julie Wilson	58:14	5:35:32	3:28:38	10:02:24
5th	Sarah Springman	1:01:34	5:35:05	3:31:45	10:08:25
6th	Amy Aikman	1:01:10	5:36:29	3:32:57	10:10:37
7th	Nancy Harrison	1:02:48	5:39:56	3:31:15	10:14:00
8th	Luanne Park	1:05:22	5:43:57	3:29:50	10:19:09
9th	Beth Nelson	1:17:01	5:41:15	3:26:01	10:24:19
10th	Terry Schneider	1:02:49	5:40:08	3:42:30	10:25:28

1988
Top 10 Men

Plc	Name	Swim	Bike	Run	Total
1st	Scott Molina	51:28	4:36:50	3:02:42	8:31:00
2nd	Mike Pigg	51:20	4:37:44	3:04:06	8:33:11
3rd	Kenny Glah	51:29	4:40:20	3:06:47	8:38:37
4th	Scott Tinley	56:07	4:44:37	3:02:26	8:43:11
5th	Mark Allen	51:23	4:54:20	2:57:38	8:43:22
6th	Ray Browning	56:11	4:47:30	3:09:57	8:53:38
7th	Dirk Aschmoneit	51:18	4:56:34	3:06:12	8:54:15
8th	Todd Jacobs	56:15	4:55:37	3:04:01	8:55:53
9th	Hideya Miyazuka	59:26	4:54:08	3:04:00	8:57:35
10th	Pauli Kiuru	56:06	4:59:16	3:05:25	9:00:49

Top 10 Women

Plc	Name	Swim	Bike	Run	Total
1st	Paula Newby-Fraser	56:38	4:57:13	3:07:09	9:01:01
2nd	Erin Baker	55:39	5:04:02	3:12:32	9:12:14
3rd	Kirsten Hanssen	1:00:23	5:12:46	3:24:15	9:37:25
4th	Julie Wilson	58:07	5:11:19	3:43:39	9:53:06
5th	Tina Bischoff	55:48	5:35:39	3:22:49	9:54:17
6th	Terry Schneider	1:04:06	5:22:00	3:32:43	9:58:49
7th	Sarah Springman	1:03:20	5:27:50	3:30:51	10:02:02
8th	Luanne Park	1:11:20	5:23:54	3:27:40	10:02:54
9th	Jan Wanklyn	55:49	5:28:12	3:39:24	10:03:25
10th	Laurie Samuelson	55:34	5:35:34	3:36:04	10:07:13

1989
Top 10 Men

Plc	Name	Swim	Bike	Run	Total
1st	Mark Allen	51:17	4:37:52	2:40:04	8:09:15
2nd	Dave Scott	51:16	4:37:53	2:41:03	8:10:13
3rd	Greg Welch	51:39	4:43:43	2:56:53	8:32:16
4th	Kenny Glah	51:24	4:38:57	3:02:10	8:32:32
5th	Pauli Kiuru	53:29	4:43:08	2:56:03	8:32:42
6th	Scott Tinley	54:15	4:38:53	3:03:43	8:36:52
7th	Jürgen Zäck	52:23	4:39:20	3:06:49	8:38:33
8th	Yves Cordier	51:20	4:41:50	3:06:01	8:39:13
9th	Ray Browning	51:33	4:42:04	3:05:57	8:39:35
10th	Wolfgang Dittrich	48:13	4:39:04	3:12:38	8:39:56

Top 10 Women

Plc	Name	Swim	Bike	Run	Total
1st	Paula Newby-Fraser	54:19	5:01:00	3:05:37	9:00:56
2nd	Sylviane Puntous	56:33	5:09:28	3:15:53	9:21:55
3rd	Kirsten Hanssen	53:52	5:05:17	3:25:22	9:24:31
4th	Fernanda Keller	1:02:18	5:20:33	3:15:42	9:38:33
5th	Sue Latshaw	56:36	5:10:31	3:35:52	9:43:00

		Swim	Bike	Run	Total
6th	Jan Wanklyn	52:29	5:27:54	3:22:54	9:43:1
7th	Tina Bischoff	54:31	5:22:23	3:27:41	9:44:3
8th	Julie Wilson	56:38	5:07:31	3:41:26	9:45:3
9th	Leslie Fedon	54:16	5:19:10	3:35:50	9:49:1
10th	Amy Aikman	58:19	5:31:33	3:22:57	9:52:5

1990
Top 10 Men

Plc	Name	Swim	Bike	Run	Total
1st	Mark Allen	51:43	4:43:45	2:52:48	8:28:1
2nd	Scott Tinley	52:36	4:51:33	2:53:30	8:37:4
3rd	Pauli Kiuru	52:48	4:51:32	2:55:04	8:39:2
4th	Rob Barel	52:20	4:50:24	3:03:03	8:45:4
5th	Greg Welch	51:51	4:52:20	3:01:56	8:46:0
6th	Henry Kiens	51:48	4:52:26	3:02:21	8:46:3
7th	N. Paul Huddle	52:47	4:51:30	3:03:19	8:47:3
8th	Jürgen Zäck	53:46	4:49:05	3:07:26	8:50:1
9th	Ray Browning	52:17	4:51:54	3:12:54	8:57:0
10th	Jeff Devlin	57:20	4:55:59	3:04:09	8:57:2

Top 10 Women

Plc	Name	Swim	Bike	Run	Total
1st	Erin Baker	56:37	5:12:52	3:04:13	9:13:42
2nd	Paula Newby-Fraser	57:05	5:14:45	3:08:10	9:20:01
3rd	T. Schneider	1:01:56	5:32:12	3:26:25	10:00:34
4th	Amy Aikman	1:00:00	5:38:04	3:24:49	10:02:54
5th	Jan Wanklyn	55:02	5:46:09	3:23:21	10:04:33
6th	K. Hanssen Ames	55:06	5:31:07	3:31:49	10:08:02
7th	Tina Bischoff	55:17	5:52:05	3:25:46	10:13:10
8th	Krista Whelan	1:02:38	5:39:29	3:33:03	10:15:12
9th	Fernanda Keller	1:01:33	5:41:52	3:33:18	10:16:44
10th	Irma Zwartkruis	1:00:15	5:31:35	3:45:31	10:17:21

1991
Top 10 Men

Plc	Name	Swim	Bike	Run	Total
1st	Mark Allen	50:14	4:46:07	2:42:09	8:18:32
2nd	Greg Welch	51:02	4:45:21	2:48:10	8:24:34
3rd	Jeff Devlin	54:12	4:43:11	2:50:31	8:27:55
4th	Pauli Kiuru	51:08	4:45:20	2:53:38	8:30:07
5th	Wolfgang Dittrich	48:02	4:42:58	2:59:48	8:30:48
6th	Scott Tinley	53:59	4:49:59	2:59:07	8:43:06
7th	Kenny Glah	51:06	4:50:03	3:05:19	8:46:29
8th	Ben Van Zelst	54:02	4:55:08	3:00:39	8:49:51
9th	Cristian Bustos	52:55	4:54:52	3:03:04	8:50:52
10th	Stefan Kolm	51:25	4:52:21	3:09:19	8:53:06

Top 10 Women

Plc	Name	Swim	Bike	Run	Total
1st	Paula Newby-Fraser	54:59	5:05:47	3:07:05	9:07:52
2nd	Erin Baker	56:32	5:08:47	3:18:18	9:23:37
3rd	Sara Coope	1:02:34	5:19:09	3:11:36	9:33:20
4th	Thea Sybesma	1:00:00	5:10:16	3:24:07	9:34:24
5th	Krista Whelan	1:01:36	5:17:28	3:23:54	9:42:59
6th	JulieAnne White	1:02:32	5:29:59	3:14:05	9:46:37
7th	Jan Wanklyn	53:47	5:38:39	3:16:34	9:49:01
8th	Terry Schneider	1:03:11	5:25:00	3:21:38	9:49:49
9th	Louise Bonham	58:54	5:31:32	3:23:02	9:53:29

1992
Top 10 Men

Plc	Name	Swim	Bike	Run	Total
1st	Mark Allen	51:27	4:35:23	2:42:18	8:09:08
2nd	Cristian Bustos	52:35	4:34:16	2:49:38	8:16:29
3rd	Pauli Kiuru	51:18	4:36:26	2:49:45	8:17:29
4th	Wolfgang Dittrich	48:35	4:38:17	2:56:27	8:23:19
5th	Jürgen Zäck	53:34	4:32:28	2:59:02	8:25:04
6th	Greg Welch	49:32	4:37:20	3:00:01	8:26:53
7th	N. Paul Huddle	51:37	4:41:19	2:54:30	8:27:26
8th	Jeff Devlin	54:35	4:39:06	2:56:47	8:30:28

230

| | Teemu Vesala | 57:30 | 4:43:51 | 2:56:08 | 8:37:29 |
| | Ray Browning | 51:26 | 4:41:31 | 3:07:37 | 8:40:34 |

Top 10 Women

Plc	Name	Swim	Bike	Run	Total
1st	Paula Newby-Fraser	53:30	4:56:34	3:05:24	8:55:28
2nd	JulieAnne White	1:02:07	5:02:32	3:17:01	9:21:40
3rd	Thea Sybesma	1:00:40	5:08:14	3:18:03	9:26:57
4th	Terry Schneider	1:00:07	5:04:22	3:24:36	9:29:05
5th	Krista Whelan	1:02:24	5:01:54	3:30:43	9:35:43
6th	Donna Peters	59:59	5:03:46	3:34:18	9:38:03
7th	Fernanda Keller	1:02:34	5:17:07	3:19:21	9:39:02
8th	Katinka Wiltenburg	1:03:07	5:19:24	3:24:15	9:46:46
9th	Sian Williams	56:23	5:00:16	3:53:04	9:49:43
10th	Juliana Nievergelt	54:28	5:11:46	3:46:22	9:52:36

1993
Top 10 Men

Plc	Name	Swim	Bike	Run	Total
1st	Mark Allen	50:40	4:29:00	2:48:05	8:07:45
2nd	Pauli Kiuru	51:05	4:28:06	2:55:16	8:14:27
3rd	Wolfgang Dittrich	48:30	4:30:29	3:01:14	8:20:13
4th	Kenny Glah	50:41	4:33:54	2:59:26	8:24:01
5th	Jürgen Zäck	51:52	4:27:42	3:06:44	8:26:18
6th	Paul Huddle	53:32	4:39:39	2:54:36	8:27:47
7th	Bruce Thomas	50:29	4:38:15	3:00:05	8:28:49
8th	Holger Lorenz	51:47	4:35:29	3:05:35	8:32:51
9th	Jeff Devlin	53:40	4:44:20	2:55:18	8:33:18
10th	Olaf Sabatschus	57:05	4:40:08	2:56:55	8:34:08

Top 10 Women

Plc	Name	Swim	Bike	Run	Total
1st	Paula Newby-Fraser	53:29	4:48:30	3:16:24	8:58:23
2nd	Erin Baker	58:36	4:50:16	3:19:12	9:08:04
3rd	Sue Latshaw	56:05	4:57:49	3:26:46	9:20:40
4th	Karen Smyers	53:34	5:06:25	3:21:13	9:21:12
5th	Wendy Ingraham	51:06	5:00:32	3:31:30	9:23:08
6th	Heather Fuhr	59:20	5:19:09	3:13:17	9:31:46
7th	Fernanda Keller	59:41	5:11:01	3:22:46	9:33:28
8th	Terry Schneider	1:00:05	5:13:39	3:20:31	9:34:15
9th	JulieAnne White	1:02:30	5:10:44	3:23:38	9:36:52
10th	Katinka Wiltenburg	1:04:56	5:03:46	3:29:57	9:38:39

1994
Top 10 Men

Plc	Name	Swim	Bike	Run	Total
1st	Greg Welch	50:22	4:41:07	2:48:58	8:20:27
2nd	Dave Scott	51:48	4:39:16	2:53:28	8:24:32
3rd	Jeff Devlin	58:49	4:34:06	2:59:01	8:31:56
4th	Jürgen Zäck	54:15	4:35:32	3:04:13	8:34:00
5th	Olaf Sabatschus	59:13	4:42:06	2:53:23	8:34:42
6th	Lothar Leder	54:20	4:45:47	2:59:19	8:39:26
7th	Frank Heldoorn	54:13	4:42:53	3:02:53	8:39:59
8th	Jean Moureau	54:12	4:42:23	3:04:19	8:40:54
9th	Kenny Glah	51:48	4:37:42	3:12:13	8:41:43
10th	Hideya Miyazuka	58:32	4:47:23	3:01:32	8:47:27

Top 10 Women

Plc	Name	Swim	Bike	Run	Total
1st	Paula Newby-Fraser	54:19	5:02:25	3:23:30	9:20:14
2nd	Karen Smyers	58:22	5:10:55	3:18:53	9:28:08
3rd	Fernanda Keller	1:05:05	5:15:39	3:22:46	9:43:30
4th	Wendy Ingraham	53:13	5:14:55	3:36:54	9:46:02
5th	Donna Peters	58:40	5:22:33	3:32:26	9:53:39
6th	Ute Mueckel	51:42	5:23:12	3:39:35	9:54:29
7th	JulieAnne White	1:02:59	5:27:39	3:24:03	9:54:41
8th	Sabine Westhoff	54:09	5:21:56	3:40:29	9:56:34
9th	Ines Estedt	1:06:04	5:28:54	3:22:29	9:57:27
10th	Angela M. Milne	1:01:25	5:25:39	3:35:27	10:02:31

1995
Top 10 Men

Plc	Name	Swim	Bike	Run	Total
1st	Mark Allen	51:50	4:46:35	2:42:09	8:20:34
2nd	Thomas Hellriegel	55:17	4:29:37	2:58:05	8:22:59
3rd	Rainer Mueller	52:12	4:45:54	2:47:17	8:25:23
4th	Greg Welch	51:47	4:46:31	2:50:56	8:29:14
5th	Kenny Glah	51:54	4:46:47	2:51:59	8:30:40
6th	Cristian Bustos	56:01	4:49:23	2:48:05	8:33:29
7th	Jürgen Zäck	53:41	4:40:23	2:59:59	8:34:03
8th	Lothar Leder	53:29	4:44:35	2:56:02	8:34:06
9th	Pauli Kiuru	51:59	4:46:55	2:55:14	8:34:08
10th	Timothy DeBoom	51:54	4:47:07	2:59:16	8:38:17

Top 10 Women

Plc	Name	Swim	Bike	Run	Total
1st	Karen Smyers	53:37	5:17:49	3:05:20	9:16:46
2nd	Isabelle Mouthon	55:15	5:17:51	3:12:07	9:25:13
3rd	Fernanda Keller	1:02:08	5:17:53	3:17:47	9:37:48
4th	Paula Newby-Fraser	53:35	5:06:04	3:38:15	9:37:54
5th	Wendy Ingraham	51:44	5:22:22	3:28:30	9:42:36
6th	Susan Latshaw	57:51	5:21:53	3:29:53	9:49:37
7th	Ute Mueckel	51:44	5:31:59	3:27:05	9:50:48
8th	Beatrice Mouthon	56:10	5:32:50	3:24:40	9:53:40
9th	Alison Coote	58:43	5:44:36	3:26:10	10:09:29
10th	Katie Webb	55:19	5:51:32	3:30:09	10:17:00

1996
Top 10 Men

Plc	Name	Swim	Bike	Run	Total
1st	Luc Van Lierde	51:36	4:30:44	2:41:48	8:04:08
2nd	Thomas Hellriegel	54:22	4:24:50	2:46:55	8:06:07
3rd	Greg Welch	51:23	4:35:43	2:51:51	8:18:57
4th	Peter Reid	54:22	4:30:33	2:59:42	8:24:37
5th	Dave Scott	53:16	4:49:55	2:45:20	8:28:31
6th	Alexander Taubert	55:31	4:42:52	2:52:22	8:30:45
7th	Peter Kropko	54:14	4:48:12	2:52:29	8:34:55
8th	Jean Moureau	55:40	4:41:55	2:57:54	8:35:29
9th	Jan Van Der Marel	59:48	4:37:54	2:58:14	8:35:56
10th	Matthias Klumpp	56:57	4:47:12	2:51:59	8:36:08

Top 10 Women

Plc	Name	Swim	Bike	Run	Total
1st	Paula Newby-Fraser	55:30	5:01:34	3:09:45	9:06:49
2nd	Natascha Badmann	1:00:41	4:53:47	3:16:51	9:11:19
3rd	Karen Smyers	54:11	5:02:33	3:22:29	9:19:13
4th	Wendy Ingraham	51:30	5:06:44	3:23:58	9:22:12
5th	Ute Mueckel	51:27	5:16:57	3:18:18	9:26:42
6th	Fernanda Keller	1:02:08	5:09:16	3:16:58	9:28:22
7th	Heather Fuhr	1:01:12	5:16:02	3:14:20	9:31:34
8th	Lori Bowden	1:08:04	5:28:00	3:12:10	9:48:14
9th	Krista Whelan	1:03:47	5:10:23	3:36:24	9:50:34
10th	Juliana Nievergelt	54:09	5:19:54	3:37:12	9:51:15

1997
Top 10 Men

Plc	Name	Swim	Bike	Run	Total
1st	Thomas Hellriegel	53:08	4:47:57	2:51:56	8:33:01
2nd	Jürgen Zäck	52:12	4:45:33	3:01:33	8:39:18
3rd	Lothar Leder	52:22	4:58:53	2:49:15	8:40:30
4th	Peter Reid	52:24	4:56:32	2:54:20	8:43:16
5th	Cristian Bustos	53:17	4:55:43	2:55:02	8:44:02
6th	Cameron Widoff	52:25	4:56:21	2:55:32	8:44:18
7th	Kenny Glah	52:10	4:49:00	3:04:27	8:45:37
8th	Holger Lorenz	52:19	4:59:31	2:54:05	8:45:55
9th	Alex Taubert	53:10	5:03:07	2:51:32	8:47:49
10th	Frank Heldoorn	52:29	4:59:22	2:57:53	8:49:44

Continued...

The Ironman Triathlon World Championship broadcast has garnered 40 nominations and won 14 Emmy Awards since 1991.

She was born on July 24, 1930. When she finished the 2006 Ironman in 16:59:03, 76 year old Sister Madonna Buder became the oldest woman to ever finish the Ironman. Photo by Bakke-Svensson/WTC

He knows when to wage battle
and when to admit defeat.
In 2001, the hellacious headwinds won,
but only for the day.
Bill Bell was 59 when he completed his
first Ironman in Kona in 1982 and 78
when he completed his 18th.

Photo by Robert Oliver

p 10 Women

Name	Swim	Bike	Run	Total
Heather Fuhr	1:01:47	5:23:11	3:06:45	9:31:43
Lori Bowden	1:04:43	5:15:26	3:21:33	9:41:42
Fernanda Keller	57:27	5:26:51	3:25:44	9:50:02
Wendy Ingraham	49:52	5:26:56	3:34:43	9:51:31
Sian Welch	56:16	5:23:55	3:31:30	9:51:41
Lee DiPietro	1:02:29	5:45:51	3:09:31	9:57:51
Martha Sorensen	1:00:18	5:37:18	3:26:53	10:04:29
Isabelle Gagnon	1:00:13	5:36:40	3:38:19	10:15:12
Louise Davoren	1:01:44	5:44:23	3:30:22	10:16:29
Joanna Zeiger	53:03	5:50:17	3:34:38	10:17:58

1998

p 10 Men

Name	Swim	Bike	Run	Total
Peter Reid	52:04	4:42:23	2:47:31	8:24:20
Luc Van Lierde	48:48	4:52:45	2:47:58	8:31:57
Lothar Leder	50:43	4:55:20	2:44:58	8:32:57
Christoph Mauch	51:41	4:50:02	2:53:39	8:38:06
Spencer Smith	49:02	4:53:30	2:53:40	8:39:07
Christopher Legh	55:12	4:46:14	2:56:43	8:40:45
Rene Rovera	55:05	4:55:19	2:48:03	8:41:10
Thomas Hellriegel	52:08	4:41:45	3:08:34	8:45:21
Rainer Muller-Horner	51:47	4:53:55	2:59:03	8:46:52
Timothy DeBoom	49:14	4:52:17	3:04:43	8:48:59

p 10 Women

Name	Swim	Bike	Run	Total
Natascha Badmann	56:02	5:10:00	3:14:50	9:24:16
Lori Bowden	1:01:43	5:15:54	3:07:03	9:27:19
Fernanda Keller	55:43	5:18:14	3:12:17	9:28:29
Melissa Spooner	56:01	5:18:42	3:23:59	9:42:28
Heather Fuhr	1:01:10	5:30:19	3:04:02	9:42:55
Joanna Zeiger	50:46	5:29:50	3:19:05	9:46:30
Isabelle Gagnon	56:13	5:26:12	3:24:33	9:51:38
Sian Welch	53:57	5:16:44	3:38:54	9:52:21
Susanne Nielsen	54:04	5:26:29	3:33:13	9:57:51
Wendy Ingraham	49:11	5:29:14	3:37:04	9:59:43

1999

p 10 Men

Name	Swim	Bike	Run	Total
Luc Van Lierde	50:38	4:41:26	2:42:46	8:17:17
Peter Reid	50:46	4:41:39	2:47:56	8:22:54
Timothy DeBoom	48:51	4:42:58	2:51:23	8:25:42
Christoph Mauch	53:00	4:39:22	2:52:29	8:27:06
Olivier Bernhard	53:38	4:48:44	2:41:57	8:27:12
Thomas Hellriegel	53:07	4:38:38	2:54:03	8:28:49
Frank Heldoorn	53:07	4:49:38	2:51:12	8:36:34
Christopher Legh	50:35	4:48:12	2:55:36	8:37:22
Christophe Buquet	56:45	4:45:43	2:53:07	8:38:21
Peter Sandvang	50:37	4:40:13	3:06:34	8:39:20

Top 10 Women

Plc	Name	Swim	Bike	Run	Total
st	Lori Bowden	1:02:23	5:08:30	2:59:16	9:13:02
2nd	Karen Smyers	53:03	5:15:01	3:09:33	9:20:40
3rd	Fernanda Keller	56:04	5:16:33	3:09:30	9:24:30
4th	Susanne Nielsen	53:02	5:16:08	3:16:36	9:29:23
5th	Beth Zinkand	54:48	5:13:50	3:23:42	9:34:41
6th	Joanna Zeiger	50:33	5:29:52	3:12:34	9:36:39
7th	Louise Davoren	1:00:24	5:14:46	3:19:29	9:38:49
8th	Heather Fuhr	58:31	5:27:52	3:11:02	9:40:39
9th	Joanne King	53:13	5:25:21	3:18:19	9:40:49
10th	Sian Welch	53:17	5:25:46	3:19:43	9:42:09

2000

Top 10 Men

Plc	Name	Swim	Bike	Run	Total
1st	Peter Reid	51:45	4:39:32	2:48:10	8:21:00
2nd	Timothy DeBoom	50:33	4:40:30	2:49:59	8:23:09
3rd	Normann Stadler	52:51	4:35:14	2:56:00	8:26:44
4th	Lothar Leder	51:41	4:43:58	2:50:26	8:28:14
5th	Thomas Hellriegel	51:52	4:38:25	2:59:57	8:33:34
6th	Christoph Mauch	51:39	4:39:05	3:02:40	8:35:37
7th	Peter Kropko	51:38	4:51:03	2:52:28	8:39:17
8th	Spencer Smith	50:47	4:41:33	3:08:31	8:43:05
9th	Cameron Widoff	51:53	4:56:31	2:54:11	8:45:23
10th	Kenny Glah	51:32	4:39:40	3:12:55	8:46:20

Top 10 Women

Plc	Name	Swim	Bike	Run	Total
1st	Natascha Badmann	58:04	5:06:42	3:19:02	9:26:16
2nd	Lori Bowden	1:00:26	5:21:33	3:04:19	9:29:04
3rd	Fernanda Keller	56:37	5:22:11	3:10:43	9:31:28
4th	Beth Zinkand	54:06	5:23:13	3:15:22	9:35:21
5th	Joanna Zeiger	50:52	5:40:20	3:06:24	9:40:23
6th	Lisa Bentley	57:23	5:35:35	3:13:18	9:49:28
7th	Susanne Nielsen	54:33	5:35:07	3:20:39	9:53:38
8th	Wendy Ingraham	50:49	5:28:37	3:30:35	9:54:13
9th	Lena Wahlquist	54:54	5:32:49	3:26:16	9:56:28
10th	Gina Kehr	51:36	5:44:26	3:21:02	10:00:36

2001

Top 10 Men

Plc	Name	Swim	Bike	Run	Total
1st	Timothy DeBoom	52:01	4:48:17	2:45:54	8:31:18
2nd	Cameron Brown	52:16	4:53:29	2:58:05	8:46:10
3rd	Thomas Hellriegel	55:35	4:47:42	3:01:25	8:47:40
4th	Normann Stadler	56:14	4:45:13	3:05:57	8:49:43
5th	Lothar Leder	52:08	4:56:01	2:59:42	8:49:49
6th	Marc Herremans	54:06	4:58:25	2:55:59	8:51:19
7th	Andreas Niedrig	52:13	4:53:26	3:04:44	8:53:00
8th	Cameron Widoff	54:01	5:02:04	2:57:20	8:55:33
9th	Steve Larsen	1:00:45	4:33:32	3:19:09	8:56:28
10th	Christoph Mauch	54:03	5:02:42	2:58:10	8:57:30

Top 10 Women

Plc	Name	Swim	Bike	Run	Total
1st	Natascha Badmann	59:55	5:16:07	3:09:33	9:28:37
2nd	Lori Bowden	1:01:04	5:25:55	3:03:09	9:32:59
3rd	Nina Kraft	54:09	5:29:30	3:14:18	9:41:01
4th	Paula Newby-Fraser	56:31	5:28:42	3:12:55	9:41:35
5th	Karen Smyers	56:56	5:29:19	3:19:31	9:48:34
6th	Fernanda Keller	58:37	5:32:40	3:18:13	9:51:20
7th	Wendy Ingraham	52:15	5:34:10	3:27:34	9:57:33
8th	Gina Kehr	53:15	5:39:14	3:22:57	9:57:36
9th	Heather Fuhr	1:04:48	5:46:06	3:07:19	10:00:58
10th	Jill Savege	52:11	5:51:59	3:15:39	10:03:30

2002

Top 10 Men

Plc	Name	Swim	Bike	Run	Total
1st	Timothy DeBoom	52:02	4:45:21	2:50:22	8:29:56
2nd	Peter Reid	53:20	4:44:15	2:53:48	8:33:06
3rd	Cameron Brown	52:13	4:45:15	2:56:06	8:35:34
4th	Thomas Hellriegel	53:23	4:34:52	3:05:47	8:36:59
5th	Alex Taubert	53:29	4:45:12	2:57:02	8:38:58
6th	Francois Chabaud	52:14	4:39:17	3:05:57	8:40:39
7th	Markus Forster	55:17	4:47:15	2:59:29	8:44:28
8th	Mika Luoto	53:24	4:51:39	2:59:00	8:45:45
9th	Cameron Widoff	52:05	4:44:51	3:06:33	8:45:53
10th	Olaf Sabatschus	55:36	4:44:31	3:00:18	8:46:18

Top 10 Women

Plc	Name	Swim	Bike	Run	Total
1st	Natascha Badmann	59:40	4:52:26	3:12:58	9:07:54
2nd	Nina Kraft	53:27	5:06:15	3:12:03	9:14:24
3rd	Lori Bowden	59:52	5:08:02	3:09:32	9:22:27

Commander John Collins created each of the original hole-in-the-head trophies given out to the 12 finishers of the first-ever Ironman in 1978. The same trophy was used in 1979 as well.
Photo by Robert Oliver

After finishing his 20th Ironman, Scott Tinley decided to hang up his big feet and take some well-deserved time off.
Photo by Lois Schwartz

Continued...

Paula Newby-Fraser, with eight Ironman World Championship titles, is simply the greatest Ironman of them all. Here she is with former Ironman President David Yates when she was inducted into the Ironman Triathlon Hall of Fame. Photo by Robert Oliver

Long time professional cyclist Laurent "Jaja" Jalabert from France made the transition to triathlon and completed the 2007 Ironman. Photo by John Segesta

Joe Bonness is an Ironman legend and a perpetual age group champion. Photo by Rich Cruse

... Continued

Plc	Name	Swim	Bike	Run	Total
4th	Heather Fuhr	1:01:16	5:18:24	3:07:20	9:29:58
5th	Fernanda Keller	58:59	5:09:36	3:18:14	9:31:38
6th	Lisa Bentley	57:53	5:19:44	3:13:56	9:34:19
7th	Kate Allen	57:31	5:13:04	3:20:40	9:38:40
8th	Karin Thuerig	1:13:00	4:55:32	3:29:42	9:42:08
9th	Sibylle Matter	55:24	5:15:07	3:28:03	9:42:51
10th	Joanna Lawn	59:07	5:12:23	3:28:45	9:42:57

2003
Top 10 Men

Plc	Name	Swim	Bike	Run	Total
1st	Peter Reid	00:50:36	4:40:04	2:47:38	8:22:35
2nd	Rutger Beke	00:52:28	4:37:59	2:54:12	8:28:27
3rd	Cameron Brown	00:50:38	4:39:57	2:55:34	8:30:08
4th	Normann Stadler	00:52:44	4:33:40	3:02:50	8:32:47
5th	Luke Bell	00:50:33	4:39:42	3:00:19	8:34:38
6th	Jurgen Zack	00:51:42	4:38:49	3:01:02	8:35:19
7th	Faris Al-Sultan	00:48:57	4:42:01	3:00:29	8:35:51
8th	Cameron Widoff	00:50:39	4:39:43	3:01:40	8:35:59
9th	Michael Lovato	00:52:33	4:44:04	2:56:13	8:36:56
10th	Mika Luoto	00:51:44	4:49:35	2:53:04	8:37:19

Top 10 Women

Plc	Name	Swim	Bike	Run	Total
1st	Lori Bowden	00:56:51	5:09:00	3:02:10	9:11:55
2nd	Natascha Badmann	00:58:43	5:00:02	3:13:45	9:17:08
3rd	Nina Kraft	00:51:45	5:07:34	3:11:18	9:17:16
4th	Heather Fuhr	00:56:16	5:12:13	3:06:03	9:19:02
5th	Lisa Bentley	00:56:04	5:14:30	3:08:13	9:22:41
6th	Karin Thuerig	1:11:59	4:50:41	3:18:56	9:26:28
7th	Gina Kehr	00:50:37	5:19:09	3:22:09	9:36:11
8th	Deirdre Tennant	00:52:36	5:24:02	3:20:07	9:40:54
9th	Kate Major	00:58:38	5:18:45	3:24:27	9:46:03
10th	Belinda Granger	00:54:13	5:15:43	3:31:39	9:46:29

2004
Top 10 Men

Plc	Name	Swim	Bike	Run	Total
1st	Normann Stadler	6:27:00	4:37:58	2:57:53	8:33:29
2nd	Peter Reid	5:12:00	5:01:38	2:46:10	8:43:40
3rd	Faris Al-Sultan	2:39:00	4:55:44	2:54:51	8:45:14
4th	Alex Taubert	5:24:00	4:49:45	3:00:37	8:48:35
5th	Rutger Beke	6:35:00	4:59:57	2:55:55	8:54:26
6th	TorbJorn Sindballe	5:07:00	4:48:51	3:12:32	8:58:45
7th	Cameron Widoff	3:31:00	4:59:36	3:04:07	8:59:25
8th	Timo Bracht	6:54:00	4:58:42	3:05:59	9:03:11
9th	Rene Rovera	8:28:00	5:04:30	2:59:41	9:04:32
10th	Raynard Tissink	5:18:00	5:02:45	3:00:46	9:04:51

Top 10 Women

Plc	Name	Swim	Bike	Run	Total
1st	Natacha Badmann	1:01:36	5:31:37	3:11:45	9:50:04
2nd	Heather Fuhr	1:01:18	5:44:12	3:06:04	9:56:19
3rd	Kate Major	1:01:05	5:38:51	3:17:39	10:01:56
4th	Lisa Bentley	1:01:05	5:50:11	3:06:17	10:04:16
5th	Joanna Lawn	8:37:00	5:46:09	3:17:44	10:05:10
6th	Belinda Granger	11:08:00	5:38:26	3:21:07	10:07:06
7th	Lisbeth Kirstinsen	8:33:00	5:41:25	3:26:29	10:08:55
8th	Fernanda Keller	1:01:15	5:47:40	3:18:05	10:10:49
9th	Tina Walter	1:05:09	5:40:59	3:20:38	10:11:02
10th	Nicole Leder	1:01:06	5:59:56	3:08:21	10:13:46

2005
Top 10 Men

Plc	Name	Swim	Bike	Run	Total
1st	Faris Al-Sultan	49:54	4:25:24	2:54:51	08:14:17
2nd	Cameron Brown	52:23	4:33:08	2:50:13	08:19:36
3rd	Peter Reid	52:23	4:27:51	2:55:59	08:20:04
4th	Rutger Beke	55:01	4:30:30	2:52:41	08:22:30
5th	Cameron Widoff	52:16	4:28:44	2:57:47	08:23:01
6th	Chris McCormack	53:06	4:37:06	2:49:10	08:23:52
7th	Raynard Tissink	54:48	4:31:37	2:55:11	08:25:52
8th	Tom Soderdahl	52:19	4:35:23	2:54:17	08:25:57
9th	Francisco Pontano	49:56	4:35:45	2:58:07	08:27:24
10th	Stephan Vuckovic	52:11	4:36:56	2:56:39	08:29:35

Top 10 Women

Plc	Name	Swim	Bike	Run	Total
1st	Natascha Badmann	1:02:30	4:52:00	3:06:25	09:09:30
2nd	Michellie Jones	54:55	4:54:13	3:18:13	09:11:51
3rd	Kate Major	1:00:07	5:06:13	3:02:19	09:12:39
4th	Joanna Lawn	55:09	5:05:06	3:10:02	09:14:53
5th	Katherine Allen	1:00:15	5:11:57	3:05:00	09:22:08
6th	Katja Schumacher	58:49	5:12:18	3:11:56	09:27:54
7th	Belinda Granger	1:00:05	5:02:01	3:21:25	09:28:16
8th	Kim Loeffler	1:02:28	5:10:48	3:12:06	09:30:18
9th	Karen Smyers	1:00:12	5:02:24	3:22:27	09:30:47
10th	Melissa Ashton	55:35	5:14:49	3:17:22	09:32:20

2006

Plc	Name	Swim	Bike	Run	Total
1st	Normann Stadler	54:05	4:18:23	2:55:03	08:11:56
2nd	Chris McCormack	53:51	4:29:24	2:46:02	08:13:07
3rd	Faris Al-Sultan	53:36	4:29:37	2:50:44	08:19:04
4th	Rutger Beke	54:35	4:33:33	2:48:16	08:21:04
5th	Eneko Llanos	53:45	4:29:26	2:55:00	08:22:28
6th	Marino Vanhoenacker	54:04	4:29:13	2:56:59	08:24:17
7th	Luke Bell	53:57	4:29:34	2:56:55	08:24:26
8th	Cameron Brown	53:55	4:29:26	2:58:05	08:25:22
9th	Chris Lieto	53:48	4:25:35	3:02:47	08:27:37
10th	Patrick Vernay	54:36	4:36:12	2:52:48	08:28:28

Top 10 Women

Plc	Name	Swim	Bike	Run	Total
1st	Michellie Jones	6:29:00	5:06:09	3:13:08	9:18:31
2nd	Desiree Ficker	1:01:46	5:05:06	3:11:50	9:24:02
3rd	Lisa Bentley	1:01:31	5:10:32	3:08:54	9:25:18
4th	Gina Kehr	6:02:00	5:16:11	3:12:29	9:27:24
5th	Katherine Allen	11:48:00	5:10:34	3:14:51	9:30:22
6th	Kate Major	1:01:34	5:08:24	3:17:46	9:31:53
7th	Joanna Lawn	11:48:00	5:10:20	3:18:17	9:32:48
8th	Belinda Granger	11:44:00	5:01:45	3:25:50	9:35:48
9th	Melissa Ashton	11:46:00	5:10:42	3:22:37	9:38:22
10th	Natascha Badmann	1:06:43	4:59:04	3:27:54	9:38:52

2007
Top 10 Men

Plc	Name	Swim	Bike	Run	Total
1st	Chris McCormack	51:48	4:37:32	2:42:02	08:15:34
2nd	Craig Alexander	51:40	4:38:11	2:45:13	08:19:04
3rd	Torbjorn Sindballe	53:25	4:25:26	2:57:25	08:21:30
4th	Timothy DeBoom	51:39	4:38:20	2:48:29	08:22:33
5th	Marino Vanhoenacker	53:21	4:33:06	2:53:00	08:23:31
6th	Chris Lieto	51:37	4:28:18	3:00:16	08:25:49
7th	Eneko Llanos	51:47	4:38:12	2:51:43	08:26:00
8th	Luc Van Lierde	51:42	4:38:18	2:55:28	08:30:01
9th	Michael Lovato	53:27	4:41:32	2:54:03	08:33:33
10th	Patrick Vernay	53:24	4:49:17	2:48:13	08:35:10

Top 10 Women

Plc	Name	Swim	Bike	Run	Total
1st	Chrissie Wellington	58:09	5:06:15	2:59:58	09:08:45
2nd	Samantha McGlone	58:07	5:10:31	3:00:52	09:14:04
3rd	Kate Major	58:08	5:10:16	3:06:35	09:19:13
4th	Joanna Lawn	58:15	5:10:18	3:13:45	09:26:47
5th	Rebecca Preston	58:08	5:17:23	3:07:14	09:26:55
6th	Rebekah Keat	58:13	5:16:03	3:08:17	09:27:19

Dede Griesbauer	53:27	5:13:06	3:22:03	09:33:34
Leanda Cave	53:13	5:13:46	3:24:22	09:36:10
Belinda Granger	58:07	5:10:18	3:24:19	09:37:54
Erika Csomor	1:03:18	5:29:10	3:01:25	09:39:47

978-2007
arters and Fininshers

	Men Start	Men Finish	Women Start	Women Finish	Total Start	Total Finish
7	1304	1232	484	453	1788	1685
6	1243	1198	453	429	1696	1627
5	1278	1243	466	445	1744	1688
4	1297	1192	431	387	1734	1581
3	1251	1200	397	375	1649	1575
2	1227	1116	380	341	1607	1457
1	1124	1056	344	308	1468	1364
0	1203	1128	328	299	1531	1427
9	1180	1141	291	278	1471	1419
8	1183	1100	304	279	1487	1379
7	1189	1101	290	264	1479	1365
6	1133	1038	288	251	1421	1289
5	1163	1068	278	260	1441	1328
4	1131	1047	274	243	1405	1290
3	1179	1109	259	244	1438	1353
2	1091	1037	273	261	1364	1298
1	1115	1063	264	249	1379	1312
0	1130	1013	257	223	1387	1236
9	1024	983	261	248	1285	1231
8	1009	949	266	240	1275	1189
7	1115	1040	266	243	1381	1283
6	829	763	210	188	1039	951
5	829	792	189	173	1018	965
4	878	767	158	136	1036	903
3	836	720	128	115	964	835
82+	758	690	92	85	850	775
82+	531	494	49	47	580	541
81	306	283	20	16	326	299
80	106	93	2	2	108	95
79	14	11	1	1	15	12
78	15	12	0	0	15	12

Two races took place in 1982 (February and October)

Ironman Triathlon World Championship Program Covers, 1981-2007

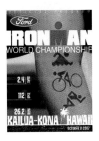

*It's a line you need
to cross to understand.*

Photo by Rich Cruse

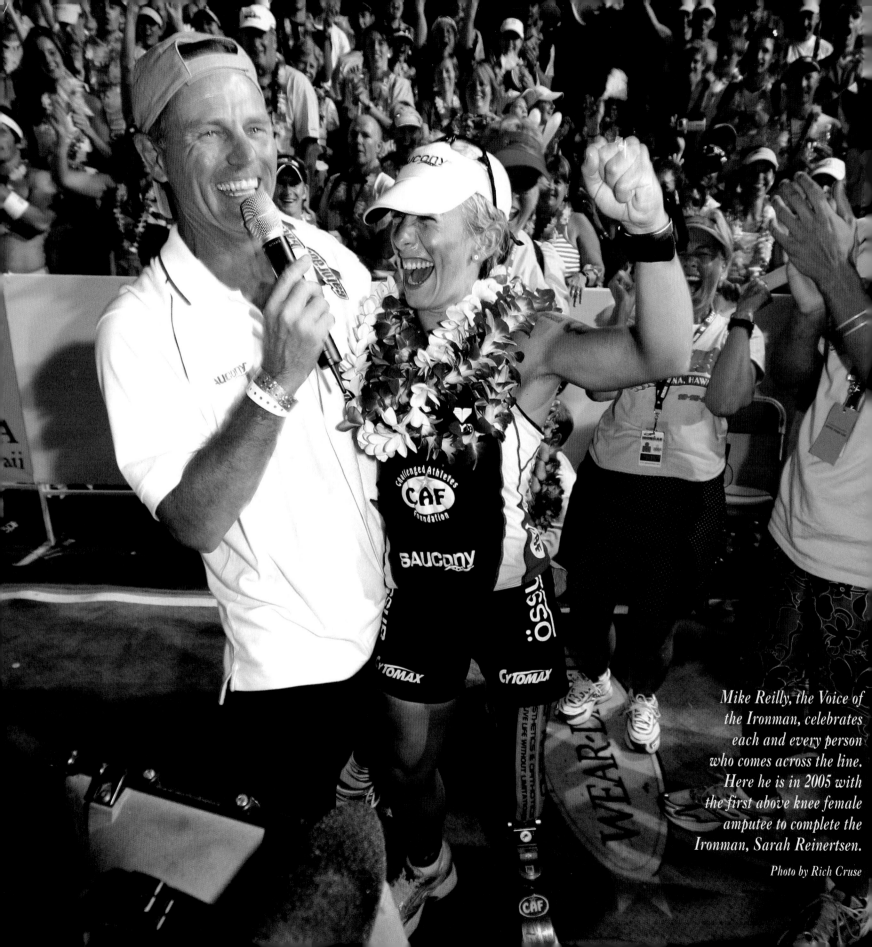

Mike Reilly, the Voice of the Ironman, celebrates each and every person who comes across the line. Here he is in 2005 with the first above knee female amputee to complete the Ironman, Sarah Reinertsen.

Photo by Rich Cruse

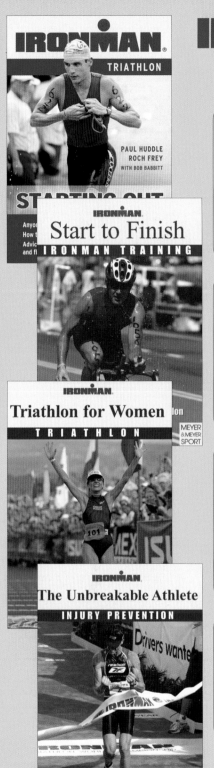

IRONMAN EDITION

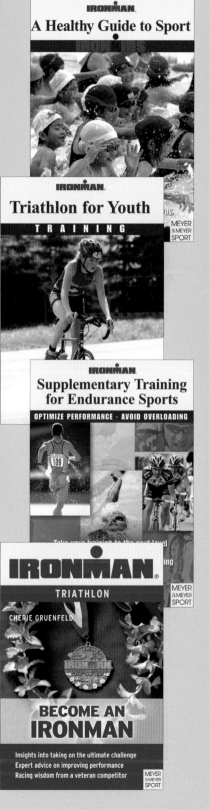

Ironman Edition
Huddle/Frey/Babbitt
Starting out
Training for Your First
Competition

2nd Edition
160 pages, full-color print
81 photos. 16 tables
Paperback, 6^1/$_2$" x 9^1/$_4$"
ISBN: 978-1-84126-101-0
$ 17.95 US
£ 12.95 UK / € 16.95

Ironman Edition
Huddle/Frey/Murphy
Start to Finish
24 Weeks to an Endurance
Triathlon

178 pages, full-color print
52 photos, 5 tables
Paperback, 5^3/$_4$" x 8^1/$_4$"
ISBN: 978-1-84126-102-7
$ 17.95 US
£ 12.95 UK / € 16.90

Ironman Edition
Lisa Lynam
Triathlon for Women
A Mind-Body-Spirit Approach
for Female Athletes

200 pages, full-color print
50 color photos
Paperback, 6^1/$_2$" x 9^1/$_4$"
ISBN: 978-1-84126-108-9
$ 16.95 US
£ 12.95 UK / € 16.95

Ironman Edition
T. J. Murphy
The Unbreakable Athlete
Injury Prevention

152 pages, full-color print
52 photos
Paperback, 5^3/$_4$" x 8^1/$_4$"
ISBN: 978-1-84126-109-6
$ 17.95 US
£ 12.95 UK / € 16.95

Ironman Edition: Ironkids
Kevin Mackinnon
A Healthy Guide to Sport
How to Make Your Kids
Healthy, Happy,
and Ready to Go

128 pages, full-color print
48 photos, 12 illustrations
Paperback, 5^3/$_4$" x 8^1/$_4$"
ISBN: 978-1-84126-106-5
$ 17.95 US
£ 12.95 UK / € 16.95

Ironman Edition
Kevin Mackinnon
Triathlon for Youth
A Healthy Guide to Competition

128 pages, full-color print
50 color photos
Paperback, 6^1/$_2$" x 9^1/$_4$"
ISBN: 978-1-84126-110-2
$ 16.95 US
£ 12.95 UK / € 16.95

Ironman Edition
D. Luechtenberg
**Supplementary Training for
Endurance Sports**
Optimize Performance,
Avoid Overloading

176 pages, full-color print
75 photos, 9 illustrations
Paperback, 6^1/$_2$" x 9^1/$_4$"
ISBN: 978-1-84126-112-6
$ 16.95 US
£ 12.95 UK / € 16.95

Ironman Edition
Cherie Gruenfeld
Become an Ironman

160 pages, full-color print
200 photos & illustrations
Paperback, 6 ^{1}/$_2$" x 9 ^{1}/$_4$"
ISBN: 978-1-84126-113-3
$ 16.95 US
£ 12.95 UK / € 16.95

www.m-m-sports.com

MEYER
& MEYER
SPORT

IRONMAN EDITION

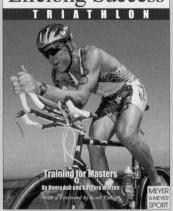

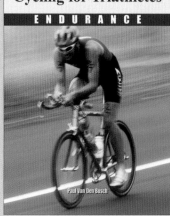

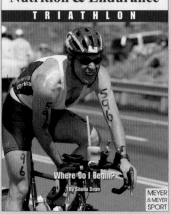

MEYER
& MEYER
SPORT